D0903742

THE POLITICS OF DIVERSITY

MILTON M. KLEIN

THE POLITICS OF DIVERSITY

Essays in the History of Colonial New York

Foreword by Sidney I. Pomerantz

National University Publications
Kennikat Press • 1974
Port Washington, N. Y. • London

Library of Congress Catalog Card No.: 74-77647
ISBN: 0-8046-9081-2

Manufactured in the United States of America

Published by
Kennikat Press Corp.
Port Washington, N.Y./London

for

Edward and Peter

Contents

Foreword by Sidney I. Pomerantz ix

Introduction 3

PART I. THE POLITICS OF ARISTOCRACY AND DEMOCRACY

1. Democracy and Politics in Colonial New York 11

2. Politics and Personalities in Colonial New York 35

PART II. CULTURE AND POLITICS

3. The Independent Reflector 53

4. Church, State, and Education: Testing the Issue in Colonial New York 97

5. The Cultural Tyros of Colonial New York 110

PART III. LAW AND POLITICS

6. The Rise of the New York Bar: The Legal Career of William Livingston 129

7. Prelude to Revolution in New York: Jury Trials and Judicial Tenure 154

PART IV. THE NEW YORK TRADITION

8. New York in the American Colonies: A New Look 183

EPILOGUE

9. New York's Reluctant Road to Independence 209

Index 212

Foreword

This book is no academic exercise in putting together a collection a fugitive pieces of scholarship lest they pass out of sight and out of mind in the ever-mounting output of indefatigable researchers of America's past. Rather it is a bringing forward for critical, careful scrutiny the products of mature study in a meaningful organization and editorial context related to the roots of our nationhood in general and the distinctive experience of colonial New York in particular. In methodology as well as content the work demonstrates an incisiveness of analysis and an originality of approach that adds a new dimension to our grasp of New York provincial politics and all that it implied for independence and union.

Though duly respectful of Carl Becker's theme of social stratification in New York and its elite implications for political change if not revolution, Professor Klein manages to weave into the texture of this cultural tapestry democratic strands of easily discernible hue. While there was a concentration of power in the hands of a landed and merchant aristocracy, small freeholders, independent farmers, militant freemen were heard and heeded. Much had been won before the Revolutionary agitation got under way. This is all adumbrated in incisive studies of men and measures in the evolving role of church-state relations, educational goals, and legal precedents for responsible, limited judicial tenure and trial by a jury of one's peers. The climate of opinion in colonial New York was distinctively American in spirit, and the reputation of a William Livingston, a James Alexander, a Cadwallader Colden transcended provincial boundaries.

As a middle colony, a highway of traffic between the Yankee north and the colonies to the south, the proud possessor of a network of waterways through the wilderness to the Canadian frontier and the western lands, and, best of all, home province of the great and growing port city that bore its name, New York was a prize in imperial calculations whether by the mother country or the fledgling Confederation. Fortunately, the documents are available—thanks to John Romeyn Brodhead, who collected them in the European archives, and to E. B. O'Callaghan and B. Fernow who edited them—for scholarly evaluation and exploitation. Nor must it be forgotten that William Smith, Jr., later Chief Justice of Canada, wrote a history of the province that ranks as a major contribution to colonial historiography.

If the continuing theme in this study is seen in the sharp struggles of provincial politics as revealed long before the Revolutionary crisis in issues of church and state and related matters, the novelty of the research tends at times to minimize what polarization did take place as the colony sought to free itself from the imperial yoke of British mercantilism. But this is set aright by painstaking evaluation of the Becker thesis as it applies to the struggle for home rule. Here Milton Klein brings to bear related research, especially forgotten criticism that Becker was subjected to in 1909 when his *History of Political Parties in the Province of New York, 1760-1776* was first published. Herbert Friedenwald (1904) and especially Henry B. Dawson (1859), previously, had noted the political ferment that set the warring parties of radicals and conservatives at each other as they found common cause in facing an aroused British officialdom. Charles H. Lincoln's dissertation of 1901 on *The Revolutionary Movement in Pennsylvania, 1760-1776* grappled with like elements of interpretation, surprisingly comparable to the simplistic Becker formula.

If the *Independent Reflector* (1752) condemned "superstition, bigotry, priestcraft, tyranny, servitude, mismanagement and dishonesty in office," it mirrored more than Whig-Presbyterian restiveness in a pluralistic society where calls to "Liberty" evoked widespread response among all classes. Provincial New York was a literate society, with all that this implied for popular sovereignty and the complexities and perplexities it generated. Having given Becker more than his due, it would seem, Professor Klein sums it all up by one last look at the evidence. Now the theme is broad and impressive, fixing the colony, along with neighboring New Jersey and Pennsylvania, as persuasive, collective claimant for initiating the American democratic tradition.

Curiously, it fell to Frederick Jackson Turner to do for the Middle Colonies what he had in mind for the West. Before his pathbreaking essay on the frontier, and subsequently, Turner sensed the social and political implications of an emergent urban, commercial and industrial society. In all of this, notes Klein, New York played a unique part, and its heterogeneous city folk faced up to every imaginable crisis, seeking allies up and down the province and in the neighboring colonies. Political gamesmanship was the rule; conflict turned into compromise; rivalry into coalition; and ideology into a national reality of freedom-embracing proportions, defended at last by an appeal to arms.

What J. F. Jameson wrote of the Revolution as a social movement was underscored by Elisha P. Douglass' recognition of the meaning of the struggle for equal political rights and majority rule, goals of special immediacy in the New York area. The road to definitive separation of church and state, abolition of entail and primogeniture, humanitarianism, and freedom of business enterprise was clearly envisioned. It was all to be part of the goodly heritage of a unique colonial experience, rooted in a cosmopolitanism of spirit and action. Out of it came the chance for New York, however reluctantly, to cement the union by ratification of the Constitution. This was a political act, to be sure, as Linda Grant DePauw maintains, but one, nevertheless, of decided socio-economic undertones. It is an aspect of the colonial experience that can well take a volume in itself. The decline of aristocracy had set in, as Dixon Ryan Fox noted, perhaps too affirmatively; but his most perceptive critic, Robert Remini, does not deny that the rise of democracy was in the ascendant, an established fact of statehood and the ultimate triumph of popular rule.

It is a historical truism that every age interprets the past in the light of its own experience, even if it is only an academic experience, at that. This alone would be justification for the publication of these essays. But the time is propitious for a new appraisal in another connection as well. As we approach the Bicentennial of Independence this volume takes on an added relevance in helping us to understand the political and social complexities that transformed a colony into a state, and that state a key pillar in the structure of the young republic.

Sidney I. Pomerantz

THE POLITICS OF DIVERSITY

Introduction

THE PRESENTATION of one's own previously published essays for a second time bears all the marks of conceit. Any volume of historical writing dealing with colonial New York, however, possesses some built-in mitigating justification. Of all the colonies, New York has had perhaps least of its fair share of attention from historians. This somewhat paradoxical neglect in our historical literature of a colony and state as important as New York requires more than casual explanation. In the last essay in this collection, I have described a set of historical and cultural conditions which help to explain this extraordinary inattention of historians to the colony of New York. There is a historiographical basis for the paradox that is more understandable. The most important book on early New York published in this century was Carl Becker's *History of Political Parties in the Province of New York,* which appeared in 1909. Becker's simple paradigm of the coming of the Revolution in the colony as a contest over "who should rule at home," alongside the larger struggle for "home rule" from Britain, proved immensely appealing to his generation of scholars; and the line of argument has been persistently attractive since that time. Becker's proposition that for a large part of New York's colonial history its political and social structure were dominated by its home-grown aristocrats was only an incidental part of his book—no more, really, than its introductory chapter. Yet it came to establish the framework for most subsequent historical writing about the colony and for much of the historiography of the Revolution as a whole.

The appeal of the Becker thesis did not arise solely from the force of its argument in the book in which it first appeared. It stemmed as much from Becker's own enlargement of the dual revolution idea in subsequent works, the alacrity with which it was taken up by other historians, eager to find some framework into which to fit New York's otherwise confused and complex history, and the ease with which Becker's account of New York could be fitted into the larger model of Progressive historiography. Apart from its contribution to our understanding of the role of New York merchants and artisans in the events of 1763-1776—with which Becker dealt largely—the volume sparked a wave of other books and essays designed to test the thesis and to apply it to other colonies and other periods of New York's history.

Becker's signal achievement, then, was to establish the lines along which much of the later historiography of colonial New York was to be pursued. But Becker wrought better than he knew or even intended. His simple, neat, and attractive formula for understanding New York's history left little else for later historians to do than to fill in the details or to expose some dark corners. Few historians deigned to think in other terms. My own debt to Becker and my intellectual bondage to him is illustrated in the first two essays in this collection, in which I sought to demonstrate that Becker erred or exaggerated in reducing New York's pre-Revolutionary history to a simple dichotomy between upper and lower classes. What struck me then, over ten years ago, was the richness and complexity of the political life of pre-Revolutionary New York and the central role already played in its politics by the same multifarious factors that were to characterize its later political history: the force of personality, the clash of religious dogmas, the contest between sections, the tug and pull of the colony's many occupational, ethnic, and cultural groups—all making for a far more subtle and interesting political dynamic than Becker's polarity.

My perception of the weakness of Becker's thesis was not, however, sharp enough to permit the formulation of an alternative interpretation. Even my challenge to the simplicity of Becker's exposition was a more modern and detailed version of an argument posed a half-century earlier by one of the first critics of *Political Parties in the*

Province of New York—although I did not know it at the time I wrote the first of the following essays. The critic was the anonymous reviewer of the volume for the *American Historical Review* (XV [January 1910], 395-397). He expressed his amazement at any history of New York's colonial politics that omitted "the long and bitter contest between Presbyterianism and Episcopacy," the "long struggle" over the establishment of King's College, the controversy between the assembly and the royal executive over judicial tenure, and the "powerful and interesting personalities" of the leaders of the province's politics at the mid-century: "the ambitious William Livingston, . . . the learned William Smith, the courageous Philip Livingston, the shrewd . . . James De Lancey, the stern . . . Cadwallader Colden."

In the peculiar way in which historical scholarship moves in cycles, each generation re-addressing itself to the very same events of a continuous and unending past as its predecessors, I appear to have filled in the outlines of that early observer's perception of the New York political scene. Livingston, Smith, De Lancey, and Colden appear in the foreground of the religious, educational, judicial, literary, and political contests described in the following essays. Considered together, they reveal that well before the start of the Revolutionary Era, New York's political life exhibited a growing maturity and an increasing sophistication, adumbrating the character of its political culture in the post-Revolutionary years, when factions became parties and politics became the legitimate battleground of contending interests in a free but heterogeneous society.

Each of the essays is reprinted here in virtually the same form as it appeared originally, with only minor alterations in the text, largely to correct errors in the original. Footnotes have been consolidated in places and newer references included where appropriate. Never intended as anything but individual essays, they appear nevertheless in retrospect to possess some unity of substance if not of form. After an initial challenge to the oversimplification of the Becker thesis as an explanation of New York's political history, they deal successively with those educational, religious, and judicial issues that comprised more explosive and significant elements in the colony's development than the contest between upper classes and lower classes. In the last essay, I suggest that it is perhaps the very ambiguity and complexity of New York's colonial history that provide the clue to its persistent importance and at the same time its continued neglect by so many American historians. The possible link between New York's colonial history and its decision for independence is suggested in the epilogue.

Recognition should be given to two books which complement the theme developed in this volume: Stanley Katz's *Newcastle's New York: Anglo-American Politics, 1732-1753* (Cambridge, Mass., 1968), and Patricia Bonomi's *A Factious People: Politics and Society in Colonial New York* (New York and London, 1971). All but one of my own essays appeared before either of these books was published, and neither of them was drawn upon in writing any of the essays. Each, however, calls attention to other elements in the New York scene that must be integrated into any future synthesis of the colony's political history: the influence of imperial interests and administration, on the one hand, and the steady development of democratic local government in the midst of provincial-level political factionalism, on the other. The unique combination of all these factors in their distinctive New York setting helped to shape the colony's political culture, determined its response to the crisis of 1763-1776, and then constituted the legacy with which it began its political course in the new nation after independence.

Milton M. Klein

University of Tennessee
Knoxville
1974

I

The Politics of Aristocracy and Democracy

These two essays were intended to suggest some lines of investigation of New York's politics during the colonial period "beyond Becker." The first does not so much dispute Becker's contention that New York's politics were dominated by an aristocratic elite as challenge the proposition that such leadership was based on the primitive political devices of restricted suffrage, open voting, and shadow elections of interest only to the province's landlord-merchant magnates. Conceding that leadership was confined to a rather narrow coterie of prominent families, the second essay proposes that a more interesting line of historical inquiry is not whether Livingstons and De Lanceys dominated the machinery of government but rather how they managed to enlist the interest and energies of so many of New York's diverse citizenry. Perhaps it was the curious interplay of followers and leaders that explains New York's politics rather than the raw domination of the many by the few.

The first essay, written almost fifteen years ago, has sparked a continuing controversy over the question of just how "democratic" New York's politics were. Never intended to be a definitive challenge to the Becker thesis, it has nevertheless been frequently cited as such, often reprinted, and recently dignified by being called "seminal." The intention had not been, however, to close the argument initiated by Becker but to open it. Few historians bothered to pursue new directions for understanding New York's colonial history, as I had hoped. In Chapters 8 and 9 of this volume, I suggest one such direction; Patricia Bonomi in the volume noted in the Introduction offers some others. Hopefully, the "democratic-aristocratic" argument will be allowed to rest in historical peace while more sophisticated and perceptive analyses are developed to illuminate the meaning of New York's colonial past.

1.

Democracy and Politics in Colonial New York

THE CLASSIC description of the political structure of colonial New York was provided by Carl Becker a half-century ago. In his doctoral dissertation and in two articles in the *American Historical Review,* Becker set forth the thesis that throughout most of the colonial period provincial politics were controlled by a few rich and powerful families whose wealth was based on land and commerce. This small coterie, linked among themselves by marriage, exercised a type of leadership that was "essentially medieval in nature—that is, informal and personal"; and political parties were consequently little more than "factions based on personal influence." Party allegiance was thus determined more by personal ties than by differences of political or economic principle, and "personal loyalty, rather than faith in a proposition, was the key to political integrity."[1]

Becker did single out one fundamental source of disagreement between political factions, the continuing dispute between governor and Assembly, but he qualified this. While those supporting the executive at any particular moment might be designated the "court" or "British" party and those opposing him the "popular" or "anti-British" party, men moved into or out of the governor's "interest" not out of conviction or principle but rather as he was able to grant them special

Reprinted from *New York History,* XL (July 1959), 221-246, by permission of the New York State Historical Association, Cooperstown, New York.

favors. When political leaders desired to enlarge their followings, Becker insisted, they did not appeal for popular support by party programs but rather engineered "prudential intermarriages" with other families of the aristocracy. The alliances thus created constituted the real sources of political strength.[2]

The political stage could be monopolized by the aristocracy, according to Becker, because the bulk of the colony's population constituted a passive and inarticulate audience, or, at best, a well-trained and obedient claque. The suffrage was extremely limited, and the undemocratic landholding system of the colony placed most of the population in economic dependence upon a few great proprietors, who insured the political fidelity of their tenants by the coercive surveillance that open voting made possible. Nominations were managed by the aristocracy, tenants were herded to the polls to register their approval of hand-picked candidates, and if revolt should threaten, the leaders could meet it by deferring the election or holding it at odd times and inaccessible places.

The democratization of the political machinery, Becker maintained, took place in the last half of the eighteenth century, and particularly after 1765; and the evidences of the change were the rise of popular nominating devices like the mass meeting, the use of the press to rally popular support, and the disappearance of the "purely personal element" as the cement of political association. A newly articulate electorate took advantage of the democratized machinery to demand a larger share in the political process, and as the Revolution approached, the conflict between mother country and colony was fought alongside the local struggle between the old aristocracy and the new democracy.[3]

Becker's analysis parallels that drawn for most of the other colonies, and his conclusion that the Revolution in New York had a dual character has been generalized into the oft-repeated and felicitous aphorism that the war was fought over the issue of "who should rule at home" as well as over the issue of "home rule."

Both the analysis and the conclusion are still attractive, but recent reappraisals of the political structure of colonial Massachusetts[4] suggest the desirability of a fresh examination of the New York scene. No attempt can be made in a short paper to subject Becker's conclusions to exhaustive reexamination, but three questions arising from his analysis will be reconsidered here: (1) Were New York's political parties largely medieval-type personal factions? (2) Was the electoral machinery controlled by the aristocracy through the landlord-tenant relationship? and (3) Was the franchise severely restricted?

As Becker saw it, the political divisions of the first half of the eighteenth century were personal in character, and the so-called parties that developed during this period were no better than "factions based on personal influence." As evidence, Becker offered the well-known contest between the Livingston and De Lancey families, which appears to run like an unbroken thread through the colony's political history. Becker did not suggest the origin or the basis of the contest, but he saw these two families emerging, after fifty years of feuding among the various factions, as "the leaders in the struggle which was, though political in some degree, after all very largely personal in its nature . . . and that the struggle was personal rather than political is indicated by the fact that the parties were known by the names of their respective leaders."[5]

The rivalry between the Livingstons and the De Lanceys was indeed long and bitter, but their disagreement was neither private nor personal in its origination, and the political parties that formed around them were rooted in substantial differences of a political and economic character. The contest began during the administration of Governor William Burnet (1720-1728), and it was inspired not by simple attachment or opposition to the governor's interest but rather by large differences between two rival economic groups over Indian policy and the fur trade.

Robert Livingston, the founder of that family's American fortunes and the first lord of the Livingston Manor, was also the colony's Secretary for Indian Affairs. A fur trader in addition, he conceived an ambitious and far-sighted program of imperial-Indian relations designed to promote the interests of the Empire and of his own trade at the same time.

The heart of the Livingston program was a discontinuance of the traffic in furs that had developed between some traders in Albany and certain Montreal fur dealers. The latter got their skins from the Indians and from the French trappers (*coureurs de bois*) who lived among the western tribes. They then exchanged the pelts on a wholesale basis with the Albanians, who paid in English "stroud" and wares, which the natives preferred to the inferior French manufactures. In conducting this trade, both the Canadians and the Albanians ignored the interests of their home governments. French policy made the export of beaver from New France a legal monopoly and required all skins to be shipped to France; English policy demanded that the western Indians be diverted from their French allegiance, a policy that could hardly succeed as long as the natives depended upon Montreal for their supply of cloth, guns, and hardware.[6]

Livingston was disturbed at the continuing business relationship between Albany and Montreal for economic as well as political reasons. As a "direct" or "retail" trader who sent his agents into the Indian country to secure skins directly from the native source, Livingston came into competition with those Albanians who conducted their trade "wholesale" through the Montreal merchants. He became convinced that unless the Indians could be induced to redirect the flow of furs to the English, France would ultimately dominate not only the fur trade but the Indians and the Continent as well. To prevent this, he suggested that a chain of fortified posts be built in the Indian country to impress the natives with British power and to serve as centers of the fur trade, that young New Yorkers be trained as scouts and "bushlopers" to compete with the *coureurs de bois,* and that Protestant missionaries be sent among the natives to counteract the work of the Jesuits. To make the program effective, a ban on trade between Albany and Montreal must be imposed.[7]

Around Livingston rallied the other retail traders, the imperialists, and the land speculators with holdings in the Mohawk Valley. The success of the Livingston scheme would pacify the natives, encourage settlement in the back country, and boost land values. Men like Robert Livingston, Jr., Lewis Morris, and Cadwallader Colden joined to promote the new policy. They organized a "Livingston-Morris Party," secured the support of Governor Burnet, and launched the program with a law prohibiting trade with Canada and the establishment of a trading post and fort at Oswego, on Lake Ontario.[8]

An opposition party was quickly organized by the wholesale traders and their allies, and its leadership was provided by Stephen De Lancey, Peter Schuyler, and Adolph Philipse. Schuyler was the spokesman of the Albanians who monopolized the traffic with Montreal; De Lancey and Philipse represented the New York merchants who supplied the traders with their English wares.[9] The Livingston program threatened their interests in two ways. The prohibitory legislation would undermine the source of their prosperity, and the money for the new trading posts would be secured by fresh import levies that would fall most heavily on merchants like De Lancey who were so deeply involved in the Canada trade.[10]

The immediate victory of the Livingstons was shortly nullified as the De Lanceys managed to win control of the Assembly, to oust Livingston as speaker in favor of Adolph Philipse, and to secure a royal disallowance of the law barring trade with Canada; but the significance of the contest, in terms of the Becker thesis, is the politico-economic character of the party division and the superficial part that personal relationships played in the contest. Family ties, indeed, served less to clarify the lines of political divergence than to obscure them. Thus, Stephen De Lancey and Peter Schuyler, leaders of the anti-Livingston forces, were both related to Robert Livingston by marriage, the one as nephew, the other as brother-in-law; and De Lancey's son, Peter, married the daughter of Cadwallader Colden, a leader of the Livingston faction![11]

Kinship was equally inconspicuous in dictating the political loyalty of the second generation of the Livingston family. Philip Livingston inherited his father's wealth, but not his political principles. Himself a Canada trader, he was unenthusiastic about the Livingston-Burnet trade program.[12] While he remained nominally allied with his father's former supporters, thus gaining a seat on the Governor's Council under Burnet, he also maintained good relations with the De Lanceys, not quite certain which of the Indian policies would become permanent. This happy faculty of keeping a discreet foot in both camps served Livingston especially well during the hectic days of the Zenger trial. Personal relationship should have placed him in the camp of the Zengerite "popular" party, since its leaders were his father's old friends, Lewis Morris, James Alexander, Cadwallader Colden, and William Smith, Sr.; but as a member of the Executive Council, he found himself, perforce, one of the De Lancey "court" party.[13] Publicly, Livingston professed his attachment to the De Lanceys, unwilling to jeopardize his place on the Council; privately, he lent his aid to the Zengerites in their efforts to thwart Governor William Cosby. But Livingston's defection from the De Lanceys was not the result of his personal affection for or his family ties with the Alexander-Morris group. Cosby's high-handed tactics in challenging existing land titles simply threatened Livingston's own fortune.

Superficially, the dispute between Cosby and his critics revolved about the governor's attempt to collect the salary paid to Rip Van Dam, who had served as acting governor during the interval between

Cosby's appointment and his arrival in New York. To collect, and to keep the case away from a jury, Cosby established a Court of Exchequer in which the proceedings could be conducted. Livingston, along with the Zengerite leaders, feared that the new juryless court might also be used to achieve Cosby's personal ambition to carve out a landed estate for himself. When Cosby began to resurrect old land titles and to demand quitrents long in arrears, Livingston took alarm.[14] Some of his own land acquisitions from the Indians were so tainted that they could hardly stand the light of scrupulous examination. Land titles, he conceded, were "not drawn in right form" and "flaws may be found in Severall of them."[15] To James Alexander, the mouthpiece of the Zengerites, he wrote that "If Mr. Van Dam had suffered himself to be devoured, certainly another Morcell would have followed, [and] no Person could have expected to escape."[16] In extending his secret support to the Zenger leadership, Livingston confessed frankly that "we Change Sides as Serves our Interest best."[17]

For the next two decades, the Livingstons pursued the same calculating political course, now allying with the De Lanceys, now opposing them, and at times preserving a cautious neutrality. When Governor George Clinton (1743-1753) turned upon Philip Livingston and attacked him for defrauding the Indians and trading with the enemy during King George's War, the family renewed their alliance with the De Lanceys.[18] With the death of Philip Livingston, the second manor lord, in 1749, the personal ties between the Livingstons and the Alexander-Morris group became even stronger,[19] but the family remained in the De Lancey fold while the old Zengerites moved into the circle of "the court." Not until 1754 did the descendants of Robert Livingston and his earliest political allies rejoin forces, and again it was "interest" not friendship that determined the Livingston choice. The De Lancey-controlled Assembly refused to assist the family in its dispute with Massachusetts over the manor's boundary and was slow in soliciting Parliament to defer the new Iron Act long enough to allow the manor's iron works to be expanded.[20] In deserting the De Lanceys once again, the Livingstons demonstrated how well they had learned the hard lesson that in politics there was "no such thing as friendship, abstracted from political Views."[21]

In the light of the above evidence, it is difficult to accept Becker's assertion that "strictly speaking, . . . there were no political parties" but rather "two centers of influence," or that family connections provided the solid underpinnings of the colony's political structure.[22]

Contemporary observers were well aware of the tenuous character of family loyalty as the cohesive element in political organization. James Alexander himself confessed with a wisdom born out of long experience that "Interest often connects people who are entire strangers and sometimes separates those who have the strongest natural ties." William Smith, Jr., conceded that the Livingston party "did not always proceed from motives approved of by that family." And Cadwallader Colden, a veteran of New York's political battles, summed up his own extensive acquaintance with the colony's history in the observation that although parties "at different times have taken their denominations from some distinguished Person or Family who have appeared at their head," their roots lay in the "different political and religious Principles of the Inhabitants."[23]

The Revolution may well have hastened the transformation of New York's political parties from "personal factions" to modern-type associations on "a basis of principle," as Becker suggested, but the process had been initiated early in the eighteenth century. The political rivalry between the Livingstons and the De Lanceys bears a closer resemblance to the later contests between Federalists and Democratic-Republicans than it does to the medieval feud between the Guelphs and the Ghibellines. And if Becker was right in insisting that the "essence of the aristocratic method" in politics is "that men are governed by personality rather than by principle," then colonial New York's early political parties were less aristocratic than democratic.[24]

Next to the marriage relationship, the principal instrument of aristocratic political control, according to Becker, was "the economic relation of tenant to proprietor." New York's undemocratic system of landholding, perhaps the most undemocratic of all the colonies, appears at first glance to substantiate Becker's thesis. A few individuals engrossed vast estates, manorial and non-manorial; most small farmers held their lands as tenants rather than as owners; and the terms of many leases were irritating and onerous, involving personal services of a medieval nature and restrictions on the sale and use of the property. From these conditions, Becker drew the inference that tenant voters were politically dependent upon the will of their economic overlords. The inference was never specifically documented, Becker being content with the statement: "That tenant voters would be largely influenced by lords of manors is perhaps sufficiently obvious."[25]

Economic power certainly endowed the great proprietors with a large share of political influence, but landlord control was neither automatic nor absolute, nor were lessees universally at the mercy of the owners because of stringent conditions of tenure. The leases on the Livingston Manor were generally considered among the most burdensome,[26] but even here some tenants held their lands on generous terms. In 1737, for example, Philip Livingston granted land to some German families rent-free for the first nine years and supplied each of them with three horses, two cows, and provisions for a year besides. Three years later he offered leases "gratis" and others rent-free for the first ten years in order to attract "good people." On the James Duane estate, such liberal terms were not unusual.[27]

Tenants on all the estates were usually permitted to begin farming without any down payment, rents were often nominal, and non-payment was not always followed by eviction. In 1757, William Smith, Jr., reported that on the Van Rensselaer and Livingston Manors, rents had "as yet been neither exacted nor paid" even though they amounted to only a tenth of the produce of the leaseholds. The total rent on a 160-acre farm was seldom more than twenty-five dollars, and some lands rented for as little as two or four pounds per 100 acres.[28]

Tenant status did not render the small farmers politically impotent, nor did it preclude their political independence. On the Westchester County manors there was a considerable amount of self-government, the "inhabitants" of Philipsburgh, for example, meeting regularly to "mak[e] town laws" and to choose constables, collectors, assessors, poundmasters, clerks, and highway overseers.[29] Even where political "bossism" prevailed, it was not impossible for the small farmers to revolt against the "organization" nominee and threaten to set up a candidate of their own. In 1748 such an incipient revolt occurred among the farmers of Canajoharie against the Albany County machine, and two years later a similar protest movement originated among the tenants of Henry Beekman, Jr., in Ulster and Dutchess Counties. Beekman's machine was a well-disciplined one, but not even his political control was foolproof. In 1751 he expressed fears that unless his friends united around his nominee for the assembly seat, the place would go to "one w[hi]ch we will Like worse."[30]

According to Becker, once the political "bosses" of the counties selected the candidates for provincial office, the tenant voters followed "their lead as a matter of course."[31] But if the landlords were so sure of the votes of their tenantry, one wonders why they went to such a considerable extent to buy votes. Not even the most powerful of the political machines or the greatest proprietor could guarantee success in an election campaign without a large war chest. By 1753, the business of "election jobbing" and political bribery was so widespread that it became the subject of public protest from one anguished citizen who was outraged that so many voters should be willing to barter away their prized and traditional franchise for no more than "Beer and Brandy," "a Pound of Beef," or "a Treat" and "a Frolick."[32]

The practice was common in Beekman territory, Henry Beekman providing his tenants with free beef, bacon, cider, and rum a day or two before the polls opened. In Albany, votes were bought at prices that ranged from a mere bottle of wine to as much as forty pounds![33] Perhaps the most revealing evidence to dispute Becker's contention that tenants merely registered the wishes of the great proprietors is the experience of Robert Livingston in 1761. Despite his economic power as lord of the manor, Livingston could not guarantee the political adherence of his tenants unless they were paid for their votes. "The Camps will not move to an Election without being payed for their time," he advised his friend, Abraham Yates, Jr., who was running for the assembly seat in Albany County. At forty shillings a man, however, Livingston had no doubts that "they may be had." He warned Yates quite plainly that unless sufficient funds could be raised, the election would be lost, "for money are the Senues of War, in this as well as in other affairs."[34]

Just as Becker appears to have overestimated the extent of political control that stemmed from proprietorship, so did he exaggerate the role that open voting played in insuring landlord control. Becker's statement that "Every voter was watched, we may be sure, and his record was known,"[35] is another of those irritating generalizations based largely on assumption rather than proof. As a matter of fact, there is little evidence to suggest that tenants considered *viva voce* voting either oppressive or undemocratic, or that the great proprietors regarded it as essential to their political control.

There were many small farmer uprisings in the eighteenth century, culminating in the "Great Rebellion" of 1766, but the complaints of the tenantry always revolved around land titles, rents, security of tenure, and their personal obligations to the manor lords.[36] The secret ballot was never one of the demands of the dissidents. How lightly the aristocracy considered the practice as an instrument of political control is revealed by the attempt, in 1769, to pass a secret ballot bill in the Assembly. The bill was given its strongest endorsement in the house by the Livingston party, the traditional spokesmen of the landed interest, and was attacked by the De Lanceys on the grounds that it would enable "crafty and subtle" lawyers to *influence* the voters![37] The question was argued most heatedly in New York City, where landlord control was not a significant issue; and among the most ardent supporters of the measure, in addition to the Livingstons, were the Sons of Liberty, a group that was entirely out of sympathy with the tenants during their "rebellion" a few years earlier.[38]

When the written ballot was ultimately incorporated into the New York State Constitution of 1777, it was done at the suggestion not of a representative of the tenantry but of John Jay, whose conservatism is epitomized in his comment that "those who own the country ought to govern it."[39] The innovation did not work any great change in tenant voting habits or in landlord control. Van Rensselaer tenants continued to elect the patroon or a member of his family to the state legislature, and for twenty-one years they chose a Van Rensselaer to represent them in Congress.[40]

If *viva voce* voting was an essential ingredient of the undemocratic political structure of New York, then there is patent incongruity in the failure of both the aristocracy and tenantry to recognize it as such. Undoubtedly the landed aristocrats exercised great influence in the colony's politics, but their influence is better ascribed to voter illiteracy and indifference than to open balloting or the landlord-tenant relationship. It is not without significance that when in 1788 a tenant in Albany County recalled publicly that he had often in the past given his "assent" to the will of his landlord "in supporting his political importance," he added: "I was ignorant of my own rights."[41]

Becker's contention that suffrage restrictions left over half the adult white male population without any political privileges[42] is difficult to corroborate because of the few census returns and the even fewer election statistics available for the colonial period. The figure is open to considerable question, however, based upon Becker's own reckoning. The unfranchised, he claimed, included the smaller freeholders, the leasehold tenants, and the "mechanics," and this resulted in an electorate so narrow that in 1790 it comprised only 12 percent of the total population. The latter figure is, in the first place, deceptive, since the "total" population included women, children, and Negroes. A recent calculation of the electorate in New York City in 1790 discloses that virtually 100 percent of the *adult white males* qualified under the suffrage requirements of the state constitution of 1777.[43] Moreover, Becker was absolutely wrong in excluding the mechanics of New York City and Albany on the ground that they were neither freeholders nor freemen, and in casually dismissing the number of freemen in these cities as "insignificant."[44]

The freemen of Albany and New York City were those merchants and handicraftsmen who had been admitted to the freedom of the town by the municipal corporation. The practice was a European one, intended originally to reserve the benefits of town industry to its inhabitants, but in New York freemanship quickly lost its original character. Wholesale traders were early exempt from its limitations, the city never enforced the monopoly, and by the eighteenth century an increasing number of tradespeople were carrying on business in open violation of the law.[45] New Yorkers continued to seek the privilege, however, for the political rather than the economic benefits it bestowed: freemen along with freeholders could vote in municipal and provincial elections and hold municipal office.[46]

In New York City, freemanship was conferred liberally, and the number of freemen who participated in the city's elections was scarcely "insignificant." Indeed, freemen played a decisive role at the polls. The privilege was not restricted to skilled laborers, the term "handicraftsman" being interpreted so loosely that among those admitted under this category were carmen, porters, painters, fishermen, boatmen, gardeners, yeomen, and mariners, along with others classified simply as "laborers."[47] The cost of purchasing the freedom of the town might well have served to bar mass admissions. In Albany it ranged from thirty-six shillings to three pounds twelve shillings for merchants, and from eighteen to thirty-six shillings for handicraftsmen. In New York City, rates fluctuated similarly, merchants paying from twenty shillings to five pounds and handicraftsmen from six shillings to one pound four shillings, with three pounds and twenty shillings being the respective averages. However, skilled laborers did not find the sum excessive during a period when they earned an average of more than seven shillings a day, and natives of the city and those completing an apprenticeship in the city were even less concerned with the cost, since they could secure their freedom by simply paying the clerical fee of about two shillings. Finally, in New York City, those citizens "that are poor and not able to purchase their Freedoms" were admitted "gratis," by a decree of the Common Council in 1703.[48]

These liberal regulations permitted an increasing number of mechanics and laborers to secure the freedom of the city. By the middle of the eighteenth century, they comprised two-thirds of all the admissions; in 1765, they made up almost half the new freemen. Still another index of the increasing accessibility of freemanship is the rising number of persons admitted as "Registrants" rather than "Purchasers," the former being those who because of their birth or apprenticeship in New York merely had to have their names recorded on the rolls and pay the nominal clerical fees. From 1735 to 1740, three times as many new freemen were registered as purchased their freedom, and in 1765 twice as many were admitted by registration as by purchase.[49]

Albany's regulations paralleled those of New York City, freemanship here too proving more important as a political than as an economic institution. The town fathers were less interested in barring non-freemen from the economic life of the city than in encouraging them to purchase their freedom. Here also the privilege was extended liberally, natives of the city paying only a few shillings to be registered and others being admitted free. In 1702, for example, the right was conferred by action of the Common Council on the entire military company stationed at the fort![50] About the only persons disfranchised in Albany as a result were bound servants and foreigners not naturalized.[51]

Freemanship played a vital role in the political life of the two largest cities of the colony of New York. In New York City itself, admissions to freemanship serve as a kind of barometer of political activity, rising in periods of political excitement and falling during the calms between political storms.[52] Freemen were not "an insignificant portion of the electorate," as Becker believed, nor was the institution of freemanship a handmaiden of the aristocracy's system of political control. In the elections of 1768 and 1769 in New York City, no less than two-thirds of the voting electorate were freemen.[53] Freemanship was not an obstacle to popular participation in politics but rather a democratic device which opened the polls to all classes of citizens and gave virtually all the adult white males the opportunity of exercising the franchise.

Outside of Albany and New York City, the franchise was probably more restricted, but perhaps not nearly as much as Becker indicated. The large number of tenant farmers who made up the bulk of the rural population were not necessarily barred from voting by the colony's suffrage restrictions. In 1699 the legislature limited the right to vote in provincial elections (apart from the freemen of New York City and Albany) to freeholders over twenty-one years of age who possessed lands or tenements to the value of forty pounds, free of all encumbrances; but two years later it defined as "freeholder" any person who held land for his own life or that of his wife, mortgages notwithstanding. The modification amounted to a liberalization since it qualified all those tenants whose leases ran for a term of lives or for at least twenty-one years.[54]

The number of persons thus enfranchised is difficult to determine in the absence of sufficient tax rolls. However, all the tenants on the Livingston and Van Rensselaer Manors undoubtedly qualified as freeholders, leases on the former being for at least one life and those on the latter being freehold estates. The status of the tenants on the Van Cortlandt and Philipse Manors is less clear, but whatever the terms of their leases, the tenants of the Westchester County manors were regarded as politically powerful.[55] In any case contemporaries were unable to draw clear distinctions in tenant status, Lieutenant Governor Cadwallader Colden reporting to the Board of Trade in 1765 that all the farmers in the province were regarded as holding their lands in "fee simple."[56] This would presumably have made all of them eligible to vote providing their lands were of sufficient value.

Just how many estates were valued at forty pounds or more is not known, but contemporaries like the historian, William Smith, Jr., complained that the great proprietors had a tendency to rate their lands "exorbitantly high."[57] On the manors, where the assessors were selected locally, it would not be difficult for the manor lords to secure courtesy valuations of forty pounds for as many of their leaseholds as they desired. Certainly tenants played an important and at times a decisive role in elections in Albany, Westchester, and Dutchess Counties, but in the absence of fuller statistical data, their precise numerical significance is unknown.[58] A few figures are available, but they are disappointingly inconclusive. In Westchester County in 1763, for example, less than 25 percent of the adult white male population was able to meet the *sixty-pound* freehold qualification for service on juries.[59] In Albany County in 1720, however, about 44 percent of the adult white males were listed as freeholders in a census of that year,[60] and in New York City at least 48 percent were freeholders in 1768.[61]

If disfranchisement under the existing suffrage requirements was a source of tenant discontent, it was singularly missing, along with *viva voce* voting, among the grievances loudly voiced by rural leaseholders during the agrarian disturbances of the 1750s and 1760s.

One other basis of disfranchisement is worth noting. Catholics and Jews were both barred from the polls by actions of the Assembly in 1701 and 1737, respectively, but the effect of these restrictions was minimal.[62] The number of Catholics in the colony was insignificant, and the law seems not to have been applied to Jews with any regularity. In the city of New York, where virtually all of the Jews of the province resided, the poll lists of 1761, 1768, and 1769 carry such Jewish names as Moses Benjamin Franks, Baruch Hays, Judah Hays, Solomon Hays, Benjamin Laziere, Hayman Levy, Isaac Moses, Aaron Myer, and Isaac Myer.[63]

Somewhat more information exists for those who *did* vote than for those who *could* vote. In New York City, voting returns for four years disclose the following degrees of participation:

	Adult White Males[64]	Number of Voters[65]	Percent of Adult White Males
1735	1465	812	55.4
1761	2581	1447	56.1
1768	3589	1924	53.6
1769	3733	1515	40.6

In Westchester County, figures are available for the famous poll of 1733 on the green of St. Paul's Church, Eastchester, in which Lewis Morris, recently deposed from the chief justiceship by Governor Cosby because of his role in the Van Dam affair, ran for the assembly seat. In that election, which became a *cause célèbre* in the Zenger trial, participation was smaller than in the New York City polls already noted:

Adult White Males[66]	Number of Votes[67]	Percent of Adult White Males
1276	420	32.9

If participation in elections during the colonial period was only as extensive as it was in 1788, when about half of those eligible in New York City voted,[68] then the electorate of the colony was still an extremely broadly based one, amounting to virtually all the adult white males in New York City (and probably in Albany), and to about 65 percent in the rural counties. The latter figure, moreover, may well be an underestimate in view of the fact that transportation difficulties, political indifference, and illiteracy kept rural participation in elections below the level of New York City's. The *qualified* electorate in the rural areas may quite possibly, then, have been as large as that of New York City and Albany.

While there is no intention of suggesting that the reappraisal offered in this paper is conclusive, there appears to be enough evidence to warrant redrawing the conventional picture of colonial New York's politics. Surely Becker's relegation of early political parties to quasi-feudal factions of a personal nature requires reconsideration in view of the continuing economic self-interest, rather than the ties of blood and marriage, which explains the political tergiversations of great families like the Livingstons and De Lanceys. Their political somersaults placed them alternately within or outside the circle of "the court," but this was purely incidental. The De Lanceys could shift from the gubernatorial to the popular side without disturbing the essential bases of their party organization, and the Livingstons could similarly pose as champions of prerogative or flaming representatives of the people depending upon their own political or economic principles. That such political gyrations disturbed family ties or personal relationships was also quite incidental. Coldens married De Lanceys and Livingstons married Alexanders without reconciling existing political enmities between the respective families.

One of the Livingstons diagnosed the fundamental bases of the colony's political alignments with acute perception when he noted of the Morrises that they "sett their witts to work to gain a party" only when their personal interests were "touched."[69] Kinship took but second place to "interest."

There appears considerable exaggeration, too, in Becker's impression of early parties as highly informal in character and undisciplined in organization. Party machinery seems to have been well developed long before 1765, with party "bosses," campaign chests, vote-getting devices, and patronage rewards all in existence. Appeals for popular support on the grounds of "principle" and through the medium of the press were common in the late 1740s and early 1750s. "Paper war" accompanied almost every election. That of 1750 in Westchester County produced a particularly heavy barrage of pamphlets and broadsides.[70] Two years later, the election campaign in New York City was so violent that the printer of one of the local newspapers, the *Gazette,* made public apology for the many vituperative essays that appeared in its columns.[71] During 1754-1755, the controversy over the founding of King's College generated so much literary heat in the *New-York Mercury* that its printer was frequently compelled to publish supplements to carry the non-controversial news and regular advertisements.[72]

The frequency with which political leaders resorted to the press and the regularity with which they lured voters to the polls with financial blandishments suggest a far greater degree of political independence among the small-farmer electorate than Becker assumed. The economic bond between landlord and tenant was never so strong that shrewd party leaders could afford to take the latter's allegiance for granted. Even so firmly entrenched a political leader as Henry Beekman was careful to solicit the wishes of his constituents and to introduce legislation in the Assembly that would prove "Beneficiall for the country."[73] Other party leaders were equally aware of the strength of the independent voter. When the triumvirate of young lawyers, William Livingston, William Smith, Jr., and John Morin Scott, undertook to thwart the Anglican scheme to establish King's College on terms favorable to the Church of England, their political strategy was to arouse the country voters to deluge the Assembly with petitions against the plan and thus to maintain such "an unremitting pressure from their constituents" as to keep "irresolute" assemblymen "warm in their attachment to the anti-Episcopal cause."[74] And while they sought support from the wealthy landlords who controlled political machines in the rural counties, their major appeal was addressed to the small farmers themselves, with local lawyers, public officials, and Presbyterian clergymen acting as their agents and campaign managers.[75]

The electorate was not only more articulate and more active than Becker believed, but it was also more extensive. Even the incomplete figures offered in this paper indicate a franchise that was surprisingly broadly based, particularly in New York City and Albany where about one-third of the adult white male population of the colony resided,[76] and an electorate that took advantage of its suffrage in at least as great a measure as did the qualified voters under the new state constitution after the Revolution.

The Revolution in New York was not "the open door through which the common freeholder and the unfranchised mechanic and artisan pushed their way into the political arena," to use Becker's language, simply because the door had never really been closed throughout most of the colonial period. The local aristocracy did occupy a commanding position in the colony's politics, and they continued to do so after independence; but the explanation for their political leadership must be sought in factors other than the strength of family ties, their economic power as landlords, or an excessively restricted franchise.[77]

Notes

1. Carl Becker, "Nominations in Colonial New York," *American Historical Review,* VI (1901), 260-275; "Growth of Revolutionary Parties and Methods in New York Province, 1765-1774," *ibid.,* VII (1901), 56-76; and *History of Political Parties in the Province of New York, 1760-1776* (Madison, Wis., 1909).

2. *Political Parties,* 8, 11-14; "Nominations in Colonial New York," *Am. Hist. Rev.,* VI (1901), 262-263; "Growth of Revolutionary Parties," *ibid.,* VII (1901), 57.

3. *Political Parties,* 21-22; "Nominations in Colonial New York," *Am. Hist. Rev.,* VI (1901), 271-274; "Growth of Revolutionary Parties," *ibid.,* VII (1901), 59-60.

4. Robert E. Brown, "Democracy in Colonial Massachusetts," *New England Quarterly,* XXV (1952), 291-313, *Middle-Class Democracy and the Revolution in Massachusetts, 1691-1780* (Ithaca, N.Y., 1955), "Reinterpretation of the Revolution and Constitution," *Social Education,* XXI (1957), 102 ff.; B. Katherine Brown, "Freemanship in Puritan Massachusetts," *Am. Hist. Rev.,* LIX (1954), 865-883, "Puritan Democracy: A Case Study," *Mississippi Valley Historical Review,* L (1963), 377-396, "Puritan Democracy in Dedham, Massachusetts: Another Case Study," *William and Mary Quarterly,* XXIV (1967), 378-396.

5. "Nominations in Colonial New York," *Am. Hist. Rev.,* VI (1901), 263.

6. On the French side of the fur trade problem, see Jean Lunn, "The Illegal Fur Trade out of New France, 1713-1760," Canadian Historical Association *Reports,* 1939 (Toronto, 1939), 61-76. The intermediaries in the trade between Albany and Montreal were the converted Iroquois of the Jesuit mission at Caughnawa. During Queen Anne's War, the Albany traders managed to negotiate a private neutrality with the French at Montreal which permitted the traffic in furs to continue uninterrupted, despite the conflict between the respective mother countries and the bloody warfare that was carried on between the New England colonies and the Canadians. For this, Peter Wraxall, New York's Indian Secretary after 1749, condemned the Albanians as a "worthless Crew" who made "an immediate temporary interest their only rule." See Wraxall, *An Abridgment of the Indian Affairs,* ed. Charles H. McIlwain (Cambridge, Mass., 1915), 66 note, 132 note, 152 note. For British Indian policy in New York, see Arthur Buffinton, "The Policy of Albany and English Westward Expansion," *Miss. Valley Hist. Rev.,* VIII (1922), 327-366; Wraxall,

Abridgment, introd., especially xlvi-1; Allen W. Trelease, *Indian Affairs in Colonial New York: The Seventeenth Century* (Ithaca, N.Y., 1960); and Douglas E. Leach, *The Northern Colonial Frontier* (New York, 1966).

7. Livingston had been pressing his program on the governors of New York since 1691, but the ablest presentation of his views was contained in his Memorial to the Board of Trade, May 13, 1701. See E. B. O'Callaghan, ed., *Documents Relative to the Colonial History of the State of New York,* 15 vols. (Albany, 1853-1887), III, 783, IV, 500-501, 648-652, 656-661, 870-879 (hereafter cited as *N.Y. Col. Docs.*).

8. William Smith, Jr., *History of the Late Province of New-York from its Discovery, to the Appointment of Governor Colden in 1762,* 2 vols. (New York, 1829), I, 214-216; Alexander C. Flick, ed., *History of the State of New York,* 10 vols. (New York, 1933-1937), II, 224-225; *N.Y. Col. Docs.,* V, 726 ff.; Buffinton, "Albany and Westward Expansion," *Miss. Valley Hist. Rev.,* VIII (1922), 352-353; Ruth L. Higgins, *Expansion in New York with Especial Reference to the Eighteenth Century* (Columbus, Ohio, 1931), 61, 62-64, 66-67; Alice M. Keys, *Cadwallader Colden: A Representative Eighteenth Century Official* (New York, 1906), 112 ff. Colden's famous *History of the Five Indian Nations* was an extended *apologia* for the Livingston-Burnet trade program. On Robert Livingston's political career, see Lawrence H. Leder, *Robert Livingston, 1654-1728, and the Politics of Colonial New York* (Chapel Hill, 1961).

9. The investment of the Canada traders was considerable, the trade being estimated at between £10,000 and £20,000 annually. De Lancey was commonly believed to "almost entirely" engross it, and his fortune was reputed to be the largest in the colony. See *N.Y. Col. Docs.,* V, 552; Wraxall, *Abridgment,* lxvii note; New York Historical Society *Collections,* 1868, 221.

10. Smith, *History,* I, 214; Keys, *Colden,* 112. Governor Burnet exacerbated De Lancey's enmity by engaging him in two personal quarrels during 1724 and 1725, both of which were aired publicly. On one occasion, the governor intervened in an internal dispute within the French Reformed Church to support the group opposed by De Lancey, a leader of the congregation. On another, Burnet challenged De Lancey's right to his Assembly seat on the ground that he was not a citizen. Even the Livingstons recognized the latter as a blunder, since it appeared as an executive encroachment on the legislature's traditional right to judge the qualifications of its own members. See Smith, *History,* I, 230-233; N.Y. Hist. Soc. *Collections,* 1868, 210-211; Philip to Robert Livingston, Sep. 23, 1725, Livingston-Redmond Papers, Franklin D. Roosevelt Library, Hyde Park, N.Y.

11. Stephen De Lancey was married to Anne Van Cortlandt, who was Mrs. Robert Livingston's niece, and Schuyler was Mrs. Livingston's brother.

12. Philip Livingston was heavily engaged in the Montreal trade before 1720, observed the ban initiated by his father's program, but decided by 1736 that he could not compete with the Oswego traders except by doing business with Canada. See William I. Roberts, "Samuel Storke: An Eighteenth-Century London Merchant Trading to the American Colonies," *Business History Review,* XXXIX (1965), 147-170, especially 166-167.

13. Livingston Rutherfurd, *John Peter Zenger* (New York, 1904), 22-23; James Alexander, *A Brief Narrative of the Case and Trial of John Peter Zenger,* ed. Stanley N. Katz (Cambridge, Mass., 1963), 5.

14. Smith, *History,* II, 23; Beverly W. Bond, *The Quit-Rent System in the American Colonies* (New Haven, 1919), 269. In his efforts to create a landed estate, Cosby reached out for property already claimed by Livingston and some of the Zengerites. See Edith M. Fox, *Land Speculation in the Mohawk Country* (Ithaca, N.Y., 1949), 16-24. On the Cosby controversy, the following are

illuminating: Alexander, *Zenger Trial,* ed. Katz, 2-22; Katz, *Newcastle's New York: Anglo-American Politics, 1732–1753* (Cambridge, Mass., 1968), chaps. 4-5; and Joseph H. Smith and Leo Hershkowitz, "Courts of Equity in the Province of New York: The Cosby Controversy, 1732-1736," *American Journal of Legal History,* XVI (1972), 1-50.

15. Philip Livingston to Samuel Storke, Sep. 2, 1734, Misc. MSS, 5:23, New York State Library, Albany, N.Y.; to [Gilbert?] Livingston, Aug. 11, 1735, Livingston MSS, New York Historical Society.

16. Philip Livingston to James Alexander, Jan. 7, 1735, in Livingston Rutherfurd, *Family Records and Events* (New York, 1894), 17-18.

17. Philip Livingston to Jacob Wendell, Oct. 23, 1737, Livingston Papers, Museum of the City of New York. On Livingston's support of the Zengerites, see also Livingston to Storke and Gainsborough, Dec. 5, 1734, Misc. MSS, 5:33, New York State Library; and Beverly McAnear, "An American in London, 1735-1736, [The Diary of Robert Hunter Morris]," *Pennsylvania Magazine of History and Biography,* LXIV (1940), 164-217.

18. Clinton denounced the Livingstons as a "vile family," and Philip Livingston responded that the governor had "used me so Ill nay abuzd me that I have no Concern with him." Clinton to Newcastle, Nov. 18, 1745, *N.Y. Col. Docs.,* VI, 286; Livingston to Jacob Wendell, Feb. 13, 1747, Livingston Papers, Museum of the City of New York.

19. Peter Van Brugh Livingston married Mary Alexander, and William Alexander married Sarah Livingston. William Livingston studied law under James Alexander and William Smith, Sr., and the younger Smith and Livingston became close legal, literary, and personal associates. Smith married Janet Livingston and moved directly into the Livingston family circle.

20. Smith, *History,* II, 133, 136-137; *N.Y. Col. Docs.,* VII, 335-336. On the manor's boundary controversy with Massachusetts, see Oscar Handlin, "The Eastern Frontier of New York," in *New York History,* XVIII (1937), 50-75. It has also been suggested that the defection of the Livingstons from the De Lanceys reflected a disagreement over taxation, the former representing the landed interest that preferred excises and tariffs to property taxes as sources of provincial revenue, while the latter were spokesmen of the mercantile interests that sought to shift the burden of taxes to property. Since four of Philip Livingston's sons were prominent merchants in New York City, it is not clear how this difference could have been decisive. On this issue, see Beverly McAnear, "Mr. Robert R. Livingston's Reasons against a Land Tax," *Journal of Political Economy,* XLVIII (1940), 63-90.

21. William Livingston to Robert Livingston, Feb. 4, 1754, Livingston-Redmond Papers, Hyde Park, N.Y.

22. Becker, *Political Parties,* 7-8, 12, "Nominations in Colonial New York," *Am. Hist. Rev.,* VI (1901), 263. Bernard Bailyn has observed similarly of New York parties that "groups form, dissolve, and re-form, leaders appear first on one side then on another, issues precipitate formations without apparent relationship to previous or succeeding groupings. Those leading politicians, the Morrises, . . . are simply all over the map, leaders of the 'popular' faction on one page and conniving plunderers of executive patronage on the next." *Wm. and Mary Qtly.,* XIV (1957), 601.

23. James Alexander to Peter Van Brugh Livingston, Feb. 11, 1756, quoted in Martha Lamb, *History of the City of New York,* 2 vols. (New York and Chicago, 1877, 1880), I, 658 note; Smith, *History,* II, 273; Cadwallader Colden to the Earl of Hillsborough, July 7, 1770, *The Colden Letter Books,* 2 vols. (N.Y. Hist. Soc. *Collections,* 1876-1877), II, 223-224.

24. "Nominations in Colonial New York," *Am. Hist. Rev.,* VI (1901), 265.

25. *Ibid.*, 264; *Political Parties,* 12. For the general terms of leasehold tenure, see Irving Mark, *Agrarian Conflicts in Colonial New York* (New York, 1940), 62-73.

26. See, for example, the complaint of Livingston tenants in 1795 that the terms of their leases were "oppressive and burthensome" and degraded them to the status of "SLAVES AND VASSALS." E. B. O'Callaghan, ed., *Documentary History of the State of New York,* 4 vols. (Albany, 1849-1851), III, 834-841 (hereafter cited as *N.Y. Doc. Hist.*).

27. Philip Livingston to Jacob Wendell, Oct. 23, 1737, Feb. 27, March 4, 1740, Livingston Papers, Museum of the City of New York; Mark, *Agrarian Conflicts,* 72-73. A recent examination of New York's landlord-tenant relations confirms the view expressed here that estate owners tended to be liberal rather than harsh in their leases, in an effort to secure settlers. See Sung Bok Kim, "A New Look at the Great Landlords of Eighteenth-Century New York," *Wm. and Mary Qtly.*, XXVII (1970), 581-614.

28. Smith, *History,* I, 266; E. P. Alexander in *N.Y. Hist.*, XXVI (1945), 381-382; E. Wilder Spaulding, *New York in the Critical Period, 1783-1789* (New York, 1932), 54-55; Mark, *Agrarian Conflicts,* 70. Richard Smith, a Jerseyite who toured New York in 1769, reported that some tenants on the Philipse estate paid only £7 for 200 acres, others in Orange County paid the same for 100 acres, and one on the Beekman estate paid only 20 bushels of wheat for a 97-acre farm. In 1776, the Maryland delegate to the Continental Congress, Charles Carroll, visiting the Hudson Valley estates, commented similarly on the liberal terms of the leases held by tenants. See Francis W. Halsey, ed., *A Tour of Four Great Rivers . . . in 1769, Being the Journal of Richard Smith* (New York, 1906), 5, 6, 10; Brantz Mayer, ed., *Journal of Charles Carroll of Carrollton during His Visit to Canada in 1776* (Baltimore, 1845), 45.

29. "The Town Book of the Manor of Philipsburgh [1742-1779]," *New York Genealogical and Biographical Record,* LIX (1928), 203-213.

30. Philip L. White, *The Beekmans of New York in Politics and Commerce, 1647-1877* (New York, 1956), 161, 169-170, 206; Becker, "Nominations in Colonial New York," *Am. Hist. Rev.*, VI (1901), 266; Henry Beekman to Henry Livingston, Dec. 19, 1751, "A Packet of Old Letters," Dutchess County Historical Society *Yearbook,* 1921, 34-35.

31. *Political Parties,* 14; "Nominations in Colonial New York," *Am. Hist. Rev.*, VI (1901), 265.

32. "Of ELECTIONS, and ELECTION-JOBBERS," in William Livingston et al., *The Independent Reflector,* ed. Milton M. Klein (Cambridge, Mass., 1963), 278-284 (July 5, 1753).

33. Henry Beekman to Henry Livingston, Jan. 23, 1752, "A Packet of Old Letters," Dutchess County Hist. Soc. *Yearbook,* 1921, 35-36; Joel Munsell, ed., *Collections on the History of Albany,* 4 vols. (Albany, 1865-1871), I, 250.

34. Robert Livingston to Abraham Yates, Jr., Feb. 8, 1761, Yates Papers, New York Public Library. Mindful of the general disapproval of election jobbing, Livingston cautioned that although he would assist Yates "all in my Power, and Even Spend fifty pounds out of my pocket on the Election to gitt you in," the contribution must be kept secret "lest it might be determental to me on other occasions." Livingston to Yates, Feb. 4, 1761, *ibid.*

35. "Nominations in Colonial New York," *Am. Hist. Rev.*, VI (1901), 265; also *Political Parties,* 15. The same view of open voting as an influential factor in landlord control is repeated in Elisha P. Douglass, *Rebels and Democrats: The Struggle for Equal Political Rights and Majority Rule during the American Revolution* (Chapel Hill, 1955), 63.

36. Mark, *Agrarian Conflicts,* chaps. 4, 5.

37. *Journal of the Votes and Proceedings of the General Assembly of the Colony of New-York, From 1766 to 1776, Inclusive,* 9 vols. in one (Albany, 1820), Dec. 22, 1769, Jan. 9, 1770; *New-York Journal,* Jan. 11, 1770; *New-York Mercury,* Jan. 15, 1770.

38. William Smith, Jr., praised the secret ballot proposal as a "highly reasonable" measure. See "Hand Bill in Favor of Elections by Ballot . . . ," Dec., 1769, William Smith Papers, New York Public Library; *New-York Journal,* Dec. 7, 1769; also "The Mode of Elections Considered," Dec. 29, 1769, "To the Freeholders, and Freemen of the City and County of New-York," Jan. 4, 1770, and "The Times . . . ," [March 2, 1770], in New York Public Library Broadsides; *New-York Journal,* Jan. 4, 1770; *New-York Mercury,* Jan. 8, 22, 1770; *New-York Gazette,* Feb. 5, 1770.

39. Daniel Pellew, *John Jay* (Boston and New York, 1894), 79, 84-85; Frank Monaghan, *John Jay: Defender of Liberty* (New York and Indianapolis, 1935), 95. Jay was married to Sarah Van Brugh Livingston, a niece of the third lord of the Livingston Manor.

40. Dixon Ryan Fox, *The Decline of Aristocracy in the Politics of New York* (New York, 1919), 142.

41. *New-York Journal,* April 29, 1788, quoted in Spaulding, *Critical Period,* 81.

42. *Political Parties,* 11.

43. Robert Brown, *Charles Beard and the Constitution* (Princeton, 1956), 63-64. See also Henry P. Johnston, "New York after the Revolution, 1783-1789," *Magazine of American History,* XXIX (1893), 311. Alfred F. Young has offered new figures for New York City's electorate in 1790, intended to dispute Brown's claim that virtually all adult white males were enfranchised. The calculation seems dubious, showing only 12 freeholders in the city worth £100. In any case, by indicating that over two-thirds of the city's adult white males *did* vote in 1790, it surely suggests that a far larger number *could* vote. See *The Democratic-Republicans of New York: The Origins, 1763-1797* (Chapel Hill, 1967), 585-587.

44. *Political Parties,* 10.

45. The failure of freemanship as an effort to monopolize the economic life of the city is clearly demonstrated by Beverly McAnear in "The Freeman in Old New York," *N.Y. Hist.,* XXI (1940), 418-430. Illustrative of the failure is the petition of ninety-three freemen to Governor Clinton in 1747 demanding forceful measures against the large number of artisans, particularly bricklayers and carpenters, who were working in the city as non-freemen. The only punitive action that appears to have been taken, however, was the application of pressure on the offenders to become freemen, some sixty-two persons being admitted to freemanship that year following the date of the petition. See *The Burghers of New Amsterdam and the Freemen of New York, 1675-1866* (N.Y. Hist. Soc. *Collections,* 1885), 158-160, 507-510.

46. Albert E. McKinley, *The Suffrage Franchise in the Thirteen English Colonies in America* (Philadelphia, 1905), 211-212.

47. *The Burghers of New Amsterdam . . . , passim.*

48. Munsell, *Albany Collections,* I, 127; Munsell, *Annals of Albany,* 10 vols. (Albany, 1850-1859), II, 143, VIII, 297; Samuel McKee, Jr., *Labor in Colonial New York, 1664–1776* (New York, 1935), 34–39; McAnear, "The Freeman in Old New York," *N.Y. Hist.,* XXI (1940), 429. Freemanship was conferred so liberally that when the Common Council was called upon to respond to Governor Clinton in 1747 regarding a complaint that the trade monopoly was not being enforced, it conceded that "the Bulk" of the freemen-

petitioners were "obscure people altogether unknown to us." *The Burghers of New Amsterdam . . .*, 510.

49. McKee, *Labor in Colonial New York,* 30-32, 39-41.

50. Munsell, *Albany Collections,* I, 144, 172; *Albany Annals,* II, 143, 158, 175, 177, VII, 11.

51. In this connection, see the extended hearings on the disputed aldermanic elections of 1773 in *Albany Collections,* I, 250-257.

52. From 1751 to 1760, when no election contests for the provincial Assembly took place in New York City, admissions to freemanship averaged only about 62 a year; but in 1765, 1769, and 1770, when the issues of British taxes, the right of trial by jury, non-importation, the support of the British military establishment in the city, the McDougall Affair, and the proposed American episcopate were all being hotly debated. admissions increased to 313, 298, and 190, respectively. See McAnear, "The Freeman in Old New York," *N.Y. Hist.,* XXI (1940), 426-427; *The Burghers of New Amsterdam . . .*, 201-213, 216-235.

53. Half of these, it should be noted, qualified as both freemen and freeholders. The exact figures are:

	1768		1769	
	Number	Percent of total	Number	Percent of total
Freeholders	687	35.6	507	33.6
Freemen	812	42.2	599	39.5
Both	421	22.0	409	26.9
Neither	4	.2		
Total	1924	100	1515	100

See *A Copy of the Poll List of the Election for Representatives for the City and County of New-York . . . MDCCLXVIII . . .* (New York, 1880), and *A Copy of the Poll List of the Election for Representatives for the City and County of New-York . . . MDCCLXIX . . .* (New York, 1880).

54. McKinley, *Suffrage Franchise,* 210-213; Spaulding, *Critical Period,* 60-61, 92.

55. Mark, *Agrarian Conflicts,* 67-72; John Bigelow, ed., *The Writings and Speeches of Samuel J. Tilden,* 2 vols. (New York, 1885), I, 190-191. Mark believes that leases on the Van Cortlandt Manor were all for long terms of years, or for lives, and that those on the Philipse Manor were all life estates. A contrary view is expressed by John T. Scharf, *History of Westchester County,* 2 vols. (Philadelphia, 1886), I, 91, and by E. Marie Becker, "The 801 Westchester County Freeholders of 1763," *New York Historical Society Quarterly,* XXXV (1951), 283-321, and particularly 300-301. Richard Smith, who visited the Philipse Manor in 1769, found that at least some of the tenants held life tenure; and Charles Carroll, during his tour of the Hudson Valley in 1776, was told that leases were generally for three lives. See *A Tour of Four Great Rivers,* 5; and *Journal of Charles Carroll,* 45.

56. Colden to the Secretary of State and Board of Trade, Dec. 6, 1765, *Colden Letter Books,* II, 68-69. Tenants themselves were not always certain whether their leases were for a "very long Term," one life, or several lives. See Richard Smith's *Tour of Four Great Rivers,* 10. The most recent study of the colonial franchise concludes that more leaseholds qualified as freeholds for suffrage purposes in New York than in any other colony except Virginia. Chilton Williamson, *American Suffrage from Property to Democracy, 1760-1860* (Princeton, 1960), 27-28.

57. Smith, *History,* I, 276.

58. *Colden Letter Books,* II, 394; Scharf, *Westchester County,* I, 92; Becker, *Political Parties,* 14.

59. E. Marie Becker, "Westchester County Freeholders," *N.Y. Hist. Soc. Qtly.*, XXXV (1951), 296.

60. The list is in *N.Y. Doc. Hist.*, I, 370-373. It shows 503 freeholders. The adult white male population over 16 years of age in 1723 was 1,515 (*ibid.*, I, 693). Twenty-five percent of this figure was deducted as a rough estimate of the number of men above 16 but under 21, leaving a total of 1,134 potential electors.

61. In the poll list cited in note 53 above, there were 687 who voted as freeholders alone and 421 who voted as both freeholders and freemen, for a total of 1,108. Estimating the adult white male population in 1768 at 3,589 (see note 64 below), the percentage of those holding freehold estates who voted in 1768 is computed as 48.4 percent.

62. McKinley, *Suffrage Franchise,* 214-215; Smith, *History,* II, 37-40.

63. In addition to the poll lists for 1768 and 1769 previously cited, see *A Copy of the Poll List of the Election for Representatives for the City and County of New-York . . . MDCCLXI . . .* (New York, 1880).

64. For the 1735 figure, the census returns of 1737 were used. They show a total of 4,341 white males. An examination of more detailed returns for 1746, 1749, and 1756 discloses that about 45 percent of the white males in those years were under 16 years of age. Accordingly this proportion was deducted from the 1737 figure. The resulting total of 1,953 was then further reduced by 25 percent to account for those over 16 but under 21 years of age.

The figures for 1761, 1768, and 1769 are estimates based upon the census returns of 1756 and 1771. White males between 16 and 60 for these two years are given as 2,308 and 5,083, or an increase of about 185 a year during the fifteen-year interval. For the age group 60 and above, the census figures were 174 and 280, or an increase of about 7 a year. Based on this projection, the adult white male population has been computed at 3,442 for 1761, 4,786 for 1768, and 4,978 for 1769. Twenty-five percent was then deducted from these totals to exclude those above 16 but under 21.

All census returns used are in *N.Y. Doc. Hist.*, I, 694-697.

65. The figures for 1761, 1768, and 1769 have been obtained by actual count from the poll lists of those years. The 1735 figure is from Valentine's *Manual* for 1869 as cited in George W. Edwards, *New York as an Eighteenth Century Municipality, 1731-1776* (New York, 1917), 46.

66. This estimate is obtained from the census returns of 1731 (*N.Y. Doc. Hist.*, I, 694), which show a total white male population of 2,933. Since this was broken down only into under and over 10-year age groups, an examination of the more detailed 1756 and 1771 returns for Westchester County (*Ibid.*, I, 696, 697) was made. This disclosed that in those years 44 percent and 40 percent, respectively, of the population was under 16. An average of 42 percent was used to determine the number of males above 16 in 1731. This number was 1,701. It was further reduced by 25 percent to account for those over 16 but under 21.

67. The figure was reported in the *New-York Weekly Journal,* Dec. 24, 1733, cited in Scharf, *Westchester County,* I, 166 and note.

68. Spaulding, *Critical Period,* 91.

69. John Livingston to Robert Livingston, Aug. 28, 1750, Livingston-Redmond Papers, Hyde Park, N.Y.

70. See particularly [Lewis Morris], "Queries Humbly offered to the Freeholders in the County of Westchester . . . ," [1750], New York Public Library Broadsides, and [William Livingston], *A Letter to the Freemen and Freeholders of the Province of New-York, Relating to The Approaching Election of their Representatives* (New-York, Aug. 22, 1750).

71. James Parker, the printer, explained that while he regarded these "Party Dissentions with Grief," he believed that "all Englishmen have a Right to speak their Sentiments." *New-York Gazette,* Feb. 24, 1752.

72. This particular paper warfare was carried on in the *Mercury* from November 1754 to November 1755. On this subject, see Chaps. 4 and 5 below.

73. White, *The Beekmans,* 204 note.

74. William Livingston to Chauncey Whittelsey, Aug. 22, 1754, Letter Book A, 1754-1770, Livingston Papers, Massachusetts Historical Society.

75. See especially William Smith, Jr., "Dr[aft] Acco[unt] of the College," n.d., Smith to Rev. Silas Leonard, July 5, 1754, Jan. 20, 1755, Smith to Rev. Chauncey Graham, Sep. 11, 1754, Smith to Messrs. Miller and Cornell, May 29, 1754, Smith to Benjamin Hinchman, July 8, 1754, Hinchman to Smith, July 12, 1754, Peter Van Brugh Livingston to Smith, [June, 1754?], all in William Smith Papers, New York Public Library; William Livingston to Henry Livingston, [June-July, 1755?], Dutchess County Historical Society *Yearbook,* 1921, 52–53.

76. Based on the distribution of population in 1749 and 1756. See *N.Y. Doc. Hist.,* I, 695, 696.

77. For a more extended critique of Becker's "dual revolution" thesis, see Robert E. Brown, *Carl Becker on History and the American Revolution* (East Lansing, Mich., 1970), and the present writer's essay, "Detachment and the Writing of American History: The Dilemma of Carl Becker," in Alden T. Vaughan and George A. Billias, eds., *Perspectives on Early American History: Essays in Honor of Richard B. Morris* (New York, 1973), 120-166. A more favorable estimate of the Becker thesis is Bernard Mason's "The Heritage of Carl Becker: The Historiography of the Revolution in New York," *N.Y. Hist. Soc. Qtly.,* LIII (1969), 127-147.

2.

Politics and Personalities in Colonial New York

NEW YORK was perhaps the most aristocratic of all of Britain's North American colonies in the eighteenth century. There were none north of the Mason-Dixon Line and few south of it where both social and political life were so singularly dominated by a privileged class of landlord-merchants organized into a number of great families. Intermarriage strengthened the bonds between families but did not widen the circle of influence measurably. Outsiders who wed into the circle did not extend its perimeters so much as they brought new talent to the core. Men like James Duane, John Jay, and William Smith, Jr., all married Livingstons, but the enlarged family grouping remained The Livingstons and did not become the Livingston-Jays or the Livingston-Duanes. A Watts, a Walton, a Colden could enter into the De Lancey family by marriage without attenuating the influence of the De Lanceys themselves in the family group. Unkind critics complained to the Crown that royal influence could never be made secure in New York unless the power of the ruling families was broken, but the attempts of numerous royal governors to curb their influence by reducing or restricting their

Reprinted from *New York History*, XLVII (January 1966), 3-16, by permission of the New York State Historical Association.

landholdings all failed. When Abraham De Peyster died in 1767, the twenty-five different family names represented among the one hundred mourners at the funeral attested the continuing strength of the ruling families within the colony.[1]

What kind of political life could a colony so aristocratic in tone and social organization be expected to produce? One answer was provided some sixty-five years ago by a distinguished historian, Carl Becker. To him, New York's politics resembled the feudal rivalries of the Middle Ages, families clashing over personal rather than political issues and enlisting their relatives much as the chief assembled his clansmen in medieval Scotland to meet the onslaught of a rival clan. What passed for political parties, according to this view, were simply personal machines, and the issues over which political contests were waged were merely the family's interests.[2]

Credence appeared to be given to this conception of early New York politics by the lack of ideological content to election campaigns; the identification of political factions by the names of the great families which led them—the Morrises, the Livingstons, the De Lanceys; the virtual monopoly of high political office held by the prominent merchants, landlords, and lawyers; a system of landholding which vested vast estates in the hands of a few men—three such holdings amounting to 1,000,000 acres or more each; and the control over elections which such extensive economic power seemed to confer. From this appraisal of the New York political scene stemmed the conclusion that "New York was controlled by an aristocracy of wealth and ability, and this control was essentially medieval in nature—that is, informal and personal."[3]

A political system founded upon such a substructure certainly bears little resemblance to that of our own day. It suggests that political parties of the modern type owe little to their colonial progenitors. And if one looks through the New York newspapers of the early eighteenth century, the evidence for this position seems to mount even further. When political parties are mentioned, the tenor of the references is one of deprecation and distaste. Party was equated with "faction," "self-interest," and "private gain" and contrasted unfavorably with "disinterested Patriotism." Party divisions were condemned for having subverted whole nations and destroyed public spirit. "Party is the Madness of many for the Gain of a few," wrote one newspaper commentator. The eighteenth-century ideal of the press was political unity and the public welfare.[4]

But this conventional picture of colonial New York's political life is both superficial and deceptive. To dig deeper than a few newspaper references and to dissect the province's social structure with a finer scalpel is to disclose a political system of surprising sophistication and considerable modernity. Such a reconsideration also reveals the significant contribution of New York's eighteenth-century patrician leaders to the political heritage of the nation. New York, in fact, better than any of the other American colonies, provided the paradigm which the nation was to follow in constructing its political edifice.

The political temper of the colony of New York can better be judged by the way men *acted* rather than by the way they *spoke* of parties and factions and patriotism; and what distinguished New Yorkers above all the other colonists was that they not only accepted political divisions but reveled in the excitement generated by political contests. The newspaper references to the desirability of political peace and harmony are no more than pious bows to a theoretical ideal. They are about as meaningful as the plague on both Republican and Democratic houses which a modern-day voter might call down during the midst of some particularly rancorous election campaign. The very same editorialists who deplored factionalism in the New York newspapers conceded that too "long and uninterrupted [a] Calm" in any government might be a dangerous thing. An excess of harmony could well conceal political villainy. To infer that popular liberties were "safe and unendanger'd" merely because there were no political contests was both "illogical and fallacious." Parties were considered necessary, however regretfully, as a "check upon one another" and as guardians of the "public Liberty." The man who was willing to surrender the calm of his private retreat to "intermix with *Faction*" whenever an important enough issue was at stake assumed the character of a hero and patriot.[5]

But it is not necessary to seek circumstantial evidence of the existence of political parties from guarded references in newspapers. The political history of colonial New York *is* the story of party rivalries. The Glorious Revolution in England precipitated the rise of New York's first parties, the Leislerians and the anti-Leislerians. Jacob Leisler assumed control of the province in 1689 upon receipt of the news of James II's downfall, but his authority was not recognized by the men of property and position in the colony. They would not admit to the rule of one so "mean in his abilities, and inferior in his degree."[6] They portrayed Leisler as a rabble-rouser and the leader of the unlettered Dutch mobocracy. The portrait was overdrawn. Leisler did have the support of most of the Dutch farmers and artisans, but he was no proletarian. He represented rather the men of moderate wealth who aspired to a share in the colony's political leadership. Leisler's opponents were those already entrenched in the positions of prestige and power.[7] The repressed ambitions of Leisler and his lieutenants, however, do not explain the Leisler movement fully, nor did Leisler's demise extinguish the movement he had sired. The political divisions that emerged from Leisler's short-lived administration secured sufficient popular support to throw the colony into "convulsions" and to sow "the seeds of mutual hatred and animosity" for three decades.[8]

By 1720 political rivalries had not abated, but they had changed their complexion. No longer were defeated political leaders executed, as were Leisler and his son-in-law, Jacob Milburne. Neither were they jailed and stripped of their property, as happened to the anti-Leislerians Nicholas Bayard and Robert Livingston. Thereafter, political power was used not as an instrument of personal vengeance but as a vehicle for achieving a political purpose.[9] In the 1720s Robert Livingston and Lewis Morris organized a party which proposed a political program of aggressive military action against the French, an interdiction of the fur trade with Albany, and the development of direct trade with the Indians in western New York. Against them was formed an opposition headed by those whose fortunes were dependent upon a continuation of the fur trade with Montreal through Albany.[10] The rancor and personal malice of an earlier decade were absent from these political contests, but the intensity of the conflict was no less real. In the 1730s, the famous trial of Peter Zenger climaxed a bitter rivalry between the followers of Governor William Cosby and the supporters of Chief Justice Lewis Morris. The issues were different from the decade past, but the leadership of the parties was surprisingly unchanged. Aligned with Cosby were a De Lancey and a Philipse, and in the camp of Lewis Morris were those who had opposed the De Lancey-Philipse coalition on the fur trade question a decade earlier—James Alexander, William Smith, Sr., and Cadwallader Colden. During the 1740s and 1750s, the De Lanceys led the party in opposition to Governor George Clinton, while Clinton's allies were De Lancey's former opponents—Alexander, Morris, Smith. By 1760, the contending forces had solidified around the Livingston and De Lancey families, and it was their political rivalry which underlined the history of New York until the Revolution.

To a casual observer, the shifting loyalties of Morrises, Livingstons, and De Lanceys—now in the camp of a governor and then again stalwart supporters of the people against a governor—might well appear as capricious; but there was calculated method to such political madness. "We Change Sides as Serves our Interest best," was the explanation of one of the landed magnates of his own political somersaults.[11] But do not the appearance and disappearance of these same names confirm the charge that colonial New York's political contests were not really party disputes but merely family rivalries? Since the Morrises are at one time supporters of the governor or "the Court" and at another time flaming patriots in opposition to the executive, are they not without principle? And can there be any continuity of political tradition when a party changes its colors so readily? I am not sure these questions are very relevant. No one would challenge the authenticity of the modern Democratic and Republican parties simply because no direct line of continuity can be established between them and the Republicans and Federalists of 1800. Colonial parties did not always have a continuous history. The Leislerians of the 1690s did not become the Livingstons of the 1760s, but at any one point in the colony's history, two parties are observable, contending vigorously over issues and employing much of the paraphernalia of the modern political process: slates of candidates, pamphleteering, speech-making, blandishments to the electorate, slogans and catchphrases, appeals to minority groups, and rounding up the voters. If the party's principles changed from time to time along with the party leadership, this is to say no more than that colonial parties were much like those of a later day. Even in the twentieth century, parties out of power, whether Republicans or Democrats, have cried out loudly against federal spending and the destruction of states' rights, but when in office, the tune has changed for both. Eighteenth-century politicians played the game by the same rules.

Certainly there was little question among colonial New Yorkers themselves that parties existed and that they represented more than personal rivalries between great families. An anonymous newspaper writer of the mid-eighteenth century conceded that the history of the province was characterized by "divided Opinions in politick Matters" and that the divisions were the result of differing opinions of "Interest, of Power, [and] of Management."[12] William Smith, Jr., the eighteenth-century historian of New York and himself an active participant in its politics, confided to his diary in 1770 that the province of New York was "divided into two great Parties," the Livingstons and the De Lanceys; and he attributed the ascendancy of the Livingstons after 1758 to their "Property Reputation and extensive Connections." As for the personal character of the Livingston party, Smith acknowledged that the party did not always follow policies approved of by the family even though it continued to carry the Livingston name.[13] Cadwallader Colden, the colony's lieutenant governor from 1760 to the Revolution and a veteran of its political wars, was even more emphatic about the existence of parties. They had existed, he assured British officials in 1770, and they always would exist as long as the colony's inhabitants professed "different political and religious Principles."[14] And Robert Livingston, the first manor lord, shrewdly perceived that it was the division of the colony into parties that made it possible for clever governors to entrench themselves. They simply allied themselves with one of the parties in order to defeat the other.[15]

But what of the allegation that one cannot really discern clear-cut economic, political, or religious issues dividing the contending parties? To concede that these issues were not the determinants of party divisions in the eighteenth century is to say at worst that such issues have never determined party alignments in this country. Our parties, one contemporary political scientist has observed, are "big and clumsy and loosely hung together"; and the reason is that our country is big and clumsy and loosely hung together. The observation is somewhat applicable to colonial New York. The student of its politics must work his way through a tangled morass of related elements involving the interplay of family alliances and rivalries; conflicting economic interests—land and trade, monopolists and free traders, wholesalers and retailers; ethnic and national differences; religious tensions; and sectional divisions—the Hudson Valley, New York City, Long Island. As early as the seventeenth century New York began to reflect the cosmopolitanism which characterizes it so preeminently today. Governor Thomas Dongan was astounded to observe in 1684 that there were thirteen different denominations in the province, which led him to conclude somewhat facetiously: "in short of all sorts of opinions there are some, and the most part of none at all."[16] Two decades later, Robert Livingston attributed the colony's political confusion to its heterogeneous population—"a mixture of English, Dutch, and French."[17] And as late as 1758, an

English traveler confessed his inability to give New Yorkers any precise character because of their many national, religious, and linguistic variations.[18]

The complexion of New York's political parties, then, merely followed the social configuration of the colony itself. Parties, then as now, represented broad alliances of different interest groups, grand coalitions with programs broad enough to appeal to the colony's cosmopolitan population. If their platforms contained no single unifying political adhesive, they were no worse than the ambivalent, fence-straddling platforms which issue from our national political conventions every four years. Then as now, parties used their platforms like train platforms—something to get in on, not to stand on.

Were there, then, no issues on which the parties took opposing stands? There is no doubt that there were such issues, and while they changed from decade to decade, they were concerned with matters of substantive importance and popular interest. In the economic realm, the New York City monopoly of bolting and the export trade had much to do with the division between Leislerians and anti-Leislerians, and Indian policy and the fur trade were fundamental in the rivalry of the first Livingston and De Lancey parties.[19] The security of their estates was always an issue on which the great proprietors joined the anti-gubernatorial party if the governor threatened those estates. In the political sphere, the burning issues during the time of the Zenger trial were the constitutional principles of impartial justice, the independence of the Council, and the administration of local government.[20] The "popular party" invariably took its stand in opposition to royal governors who sought to enlarge the executive or prerogative power at the expense of the Assembly, to tamper with the courts, to curb the Assembly's control over the revenue, or to limit the freedom of the press. Perhaps the most heated issue to split parties was that of religion. The dissenting sects challenged Anglican governors who tried to enlarge the authority or extend the influence of the Church of England. In 1753-1755, Dissenters and Anglicans fought a furious political battle over the chartering of King's College; and in 1768 and 1769, Presbyterians and Churchmen were again in the political arena waging war over the proposal to establish an Anglican bishopric in America. Political leaders like Robert Livingston, the third manor lord, viewed the Assembly elections in 1769 as a clear case of "whether the Church or Meeting shall rule," and Episcopal clergymen were in no doubt that a victory for the Livingston party would be a disaster for the established church.[21]

Few of these issues remained constant sources of political disputation, but they were always real issues, neither superficial nor artificial. The leadership of the parties which contended for them changed, too, as men looked to their own interests, but the parties remained constant. And what made New York's politics more than aristocratic factionalism was the cosmopolitanism of its population and its broadly based electorate. A single family's interest never constituted a popular enough platform on which to appeal to New York's extraordinarily heterogeneous voters. Nor could the power of personality alone, however dynamic, enlist the participation of the many New Yorkers who were eligible to take part in election contests; for contrary to a long-held misconception of the nature of the colonial political process, the right to vote was liberally granted and widely exercised. Probably 90 percent of the adult white males in New York City and Albany could vote, and well over half of those eligible did so; and in the rural areas, the qualified electorate comprised about two-thirds of the adult white males.[22] It was this combination of aristocratic leadership and popular followership functioning in a heterogeneous and articulate society that gave colonial New York its unique political character.

The earlier historians who misinterpreted the role of the provincial aristocracy in the colony's political life distracted us from the more challenging question raised by New York's extraordinary political development. It is simply to explain how these native aristocrats succeeded in influencing the political life of the colony so effectively while operating within a relatively democratic framework. Why did they enter the political arena in the first place? Why did the political process engage their energies so actively? What charismatic qualities enabled them to secure the support of ethnic, religious, and economic groups outside of their own family circle? And, finally, did this patrician class contribute anything more than a primitive elitism to the future American political dynamic?

Before these questions can be answered, we need to know a great deal more about the personalities involved than we now do. For some unaccountable reason, we do not have adequate biographies of most of these fascinating figures who move so dramatically across the political stage of colonial New York. In the 1920s, colonial historians were warned away from the study of biography for the period from 1660 to 1763 on the ground that those years produced no "heroes" who contributed anything of importance to the events of this era![23] We are no longer so naive, and we have since been called to task for our neglect, but the net result is still insignificant.[24]

We know little about the colonial governors of New York—perhaps the only true aristocrats in the colony since they brought their English titles with them—neither the conscientious and competent ones like Robert Hunter, William Burnet, and George Clinton, nor the avaricious and unqualified ones like William Cosby. Within the various strata of the native aristocracy, we are without biographies of most of the manor lords, the merchant princes, the lawyers, or the upper officialdom. The most politically active and influential of the manor lords were the Livingstons, Van Cortlandts, Morrises, Philipses, and Van Rensselaers, but except for a recent biography of Robert Livingston, the founder of that dynasty, we must search the documentary records and local histories for flesh and blood portraits of the others.[25] The history of New York without James De Lancey—merchant, land magnate, chief justice, lieutenant governor, and party leader extraordinary—would be a *Hamlet* without the Prince; and yet no biography of this remarkable colonial politician has yet been written. For three decades, from the time of the Zenger trial to the French and Indian War, he dominated the political stage, either from the wings or up front. His contemporaries denounced him as a man who "knows no such thing as friendship abstracted from political Views, and the purpose of Trimming and popularity." And a more recent historian has described him as a combination of schemer and demagogue who seems to have stepped onto the New York scene directly "out of the supple politics and exaggerated postures of [the] Italian Renaissance."[26] But these harsh characterizations are simply the greater tributes to his political acumen; and they merely whet our appetites for a full-length literary portrait.

Neither contemporaries nor modern researchers have minimized the striking influence which the legal profession exerted on New York's politics. Thomas Jones, an eighteenth-century New Yorker, began a two-volume history of the province with a long lament for the political peace which prevailed before the lawyers began spreading seditious ideas of republicanism in government and independency in religion.[27] Lieutenant Governor Colden attributed all of his problems during the Stamp Act troubles to the domination of the lawyers. Their power was such, he assured British officials in London, that every man was afraid of offending them and none dared oppose them publicly.[28] Despite these and many other acknowledgments of the prestige and influence of the gentlemen of the bar, there are no published biographies of the most important of them—James Alexander and William Smith, Sr., who were Zenger's attorneys in the famous trial, or William Livingston, William Smith, Jr., and John Morin Scott, the "Presbyterian triumvirate" which was the bane of the De Lanceys, Episcopal clergymen, and royal governors for two decades.[29]

Finally we are without biographies of the chief appointed officials of the colony—the members of the Council, the surveyors general, the attorneys general, the receivers general—who as dispensers as well as recipients of patronage played key roles in provincial politics. Standing among them as a giant by reason of his virtuosity is Cadwallader Colden—historian, philosopher, scientist, physician, engineer, and savant, as well as surveyor general, member of the Executive Council, and lieutenant governor. The most loyal, conscientious, tireless, and ageless of New York's public servants, Colden is memorialized only by a half-century-old life which has been aptly characterized as a classic example of how not to write a biography.[30]

Without the raw material which such biographical research must provide, we can only speculate as to why these men of social position and affluence entered with such vigor into the contentious world of politics. Had the estates of the great proprietors been organized like the southern plantations, their management might have consumed the energies and the time of the New York magnates fully. But many of these estates were speculative holdings only and remained largely unpopulated up to the Revolution. Others were organized on the leasehold basis, with the active work of farming left to the largely independent tenantry. In either case, the landed proprietors had time and energy enough to devote to the game of politics. Perhaps, too, New York's proprietors were never so sure of the legality of their estates—many having been obtained by chicanery if not outright fraud—that they could hardly afford *not* to be at or near the centers of political power as a measure of simple self-defense. Merchants and lawyers were under no such compulsion, but since they were so often allied with the landed gentry by ties of family and economic interest, their political participation may have followed as a matter of course, as tails to the proprietors' kites. In any case, the concentration of merchants and lawyers in New York City provided them with a perfect arena for politicking—the city, with its many enfranchised freemen and the opportunity for electioneering provided by its taverns, clubs, and outdoor meeting places. Perhaps these native aristocrats entered politics simply to fill the vacuum created by Britain's failure to organize an efficient corps of English-trained civil servants to administer the government of colonial New York. The New Yorkers were not so much pushed into the void as they were sucked into it, their social and economic position making them the logical legatees of the political power waiting to be seized.

What emerges, then, from the foregoing survey is a description not only of a remarkably sophisticated political system—for its day—but also a group of remarkable political leaders. Out of the earlier chaos of narrowly self-centered family factions, these native aristocrats brought order into the conduct of government and purpose to the party structure. They early grasped the fact of New York's unique cosmopolitanism and adjusted the political machinery to it. They introduced New Yorkers with remarkable prescience to the role which parties were destined to play in the later life of the nation. But even more, these early political leaders demonstrated that there need be no inconsistency between a democratic society and patrician leadership. In the new republic which emerged from the Revolution, as in the government of colonial New York, the artisans and small farmers committed their political fortunes to the leadership not of croppers, cartmen, and coopers but of "gentlemen." If, as some historians have suggested, the central fact of early American history is the continuing contest between the forces of democracy and those of aristocracy, then there is some paradox in the fact that the democrats had to call so often upon the aristocrats to lead them.

In 1768, Governor Francis Bernard of Massachusetts commented that while in that colony politics engaged chiefly "Men of Middling or low Rank," in New York they attracted "Men of Rank and Ability."[31] It was the New York model which the nation subsequently followed more often than that of Massachusetts. And if American history has been colored by a continuing dialogue between Demos and Aristos, then perhaps Emerson's thoughtful observation about parties in his day provides the best epitaph for the aristocrats of colonial New York. The democrats may have had the best cause, Emerson remarked, but the aristocrats had the best men.

Notes

1. Becker, *Political Parties,* 13; Flick, ed., *History of New York,* III, 148.

2. Becker, *Political Parties,* chap. 1.

3. Becker, "Nominations in Colonial New York," *Am. Hist. Rev.,* VI (1901), particularly 260.

4. *New-York Gazette and Weekly Post-Boy,* Jan. 9, 1749; Livingston et al., *Independent Reflector,* ed. Klein, 143-148, 215-220 (Feb. 22, May 3, 1753).

5. *Ibid.,* 147-148 (Feb. 22, 1753); *New-York Gazette,* March 18, 1733; *New-York Gazette and Weekly Post-Boy,* Jan. 9, 1749; *A Letter to the Freemen and Freeholders of the Province of New-York, Relating to the Approaching Election of their Representatives* (New York, Aug. 22, 1750), 12; *New-York Weekly Journal,* Jan. 26, 1736.

6. Smith, *History,* I, 86.

7. Michael Hall, Lawrence H. Leder, and Michael G. Kammen, eds., *The Glorious Revolution in America* (Chapel Hill, 1964), 84-85.

8. Smith, *History,* I, 85-86.

9. Lawrence H. Leder, "Robert Livingston: A New View of New York Politics," *N. Y. Hist.,* XL (1959), 358-367.

10. Chap. 1, above, especially pp. 13-15.

11. Philip Livingston to Jacob Wendell, Oct. 23, 1737, Livingston Papers, Museum of the City of New York.

12. *New-York Evening Post,* Sep. 16, 1751.

13. Smith, *History,* II, 273; William H. W. Sabine, ed., *Historical Memoirs from 16 March 1763 to 9 July 1776 of William Smith* (New York, 1956), 95.

14. Colden to the Earl of Hillsborough, July 7, 1770, *Colden Letter Books,* II, 223-224.

15. Livingston to William Lowndes, June 2, 1707, quoted in Lawrence H. Leder, "The Politics of Upheaval in New York, 1689-1709," *N. Y. Hist. Soc. Qtly.,* XLIV (1960), 426.

16. E. T. Corwin, ed., *Ecclesiastical Records of the State of New York,* 7 vols. (Albany, 1901-1916), II, 879-880.

17. Livingston to Lowndes, June 2, 1707, quoted in Leder, "The Politics of Upheaval," *N. Y. Hist. Soc. Qtly.,* XLIV (1960).

18. Rev. Andrew Burnaby, *Travels through the Middle Settlements in North America, in the Years 1759 and 1760,* ed. Rufus R. Wilson (3rd ed., London, 1798; reprinted, New York, 1904), 117.

19. Hall, Leder, and Kammen, eds., *The Glorious Revolution,* 85; Chap. 1, pp. 13-15 above.

20. James Alexander, *Brief Narrative of the Zenger Trial,* ed. Katz, 6-7.

21. Peter R. Livingston to Robert Livingston, Jr., June 14, 1769, Livingston-Redmond Papers, Hyde Park, N.Y.; Carl Bridenbaugh, *Mitre and Sceptre: Transatlantic Faiths, Ideas, Personalities, and Politics, 1689-1775* (New York, 1962), 262.

22. Chap. 1 pp. 20-25 above; Williamson, *American Suffrage,* 27-29.

23. Charles M. Andrews, *The Colonial Background of the American Revolution,* rev. ed. (New Haven, 1931, reprinted, 1961), 180-181.

24. See, in this connection, Lawrence H. Leder's plea for further biographical studies of the early eighteenth century in his "A Neglected Aspect of New York's Forgotten Century," *N. Y. Hist.,* XXXVII (1956), 259-265; and

Edward N. Saveth's suggestive article, "The American Patrician Class: A Field for Further Research," *American Quarterly,* XV (1963), 235-252.

25. The Livingston biography is Lawrence Leder's *Robert Livingston.*

26. William Livingston to Robert Livingston, Feb. 4, 1754, Livingston-Redmond Papers, Hyde Park, N.Y.; Arthur Pound, *Johnson of the Mohawks* (New York, 1930), 30.

27. Thomas Jones, *History of New York during the Revolutionary War,* ed. Edwin F. De Lancey, 2 vols. (New York, 1879), Vol. I, chap. 1.

28. Colden to the Secretary of State and Board of Trade, Dec. 6, 1765, *Colden Letter Books,* II, 70-71.

29. A recent work on Alexander by Henry Noble MacCracken, *Prologue to Independence: The Trials of James Alexander, American, 1715-1756* (New York, 1964), is neither biography nor legal history. Since the original appearance of this essay, a creditable biography of the younger Smith has appeared—L. F. S. Upton's *The Loyal Whig: William Smith of New York & Quebec* (Toronto, 1969).

30. The book is Alice M. Keys, *Cadwallader Colden,* and the trenchant comment is by Lawrence Leder in his "A Neglected Aspect of New York's Forgotten Century," *N. Y. Hist.,* XXXVII (1956), 262.

31. Bernard to Lord Barrington, Feb. 7, 1768, in E. Channing and A. C. Coolidge, eds., *The Barrington-Bernard Correspondence* (Cambridge, Mass., 1912), 142.

II

Culture and Politics

That New Yorkers lack an intellectual culture is a charge leveled as often in the modern era as in the colonial period. The charge is misleading by virtue of its formulation. There are various forms of culture other than the aesthetic, and the following three essays attempt to delineate some aspects of New York's distinctive contribution to the culture of the American colonies. THE INDEPENDENT REFLECTOR *was the province's first essay-magazine and the only periodical published serially in the colony other than newspapers. It was in many respects the most interesting magazine published in all the colonies. Instead of a miscellany of material republished from other sources, the* REFLECTOR *offered originally composed observations on manners, morals, and, above all, government, politics, and religion. Patterned originally after* THE SPECTATOR *and* THE TATLER, *it soon abandoned mere literary essayism and mirrored the vigorous radicalism of the English "commonwealthmen," particularly John Trenchard and Thomas Gordon. Often borrowing wholesale from these authors, the trio who edited and wrote the* REFLECTOR *applied Whig radicalism to the New York scene and communicated English principles in an American idiom. If the American Revolution, as Bernard Bailyn has so forcibly observed, was essentially an ideological movement, few publications present in so comprehensive form the evolution of that ideology and at so early a date as does the* REFLECTOR. *Long available only in scarce copies of the original 1752-1753 publication, the* REFLECTOR *was republished in its entirety by the Harvard Press, in its John Harvard Library, in 1963. The introduction to that edition is reprinted here.*

One issue that came to dominate the year's existence of the REFLECTOR *was the contest between Anglicans and Presbyterians over the founding of King's College. In challenging the Anglican effort to establish a "seminary of the Church," in traditional colonial pattern, the editors of the* REFLECTOR *set forth strikingly novel propositions regarding the civic purpose of education and the need for state rather than church control. In making the college issue a religious and political question, the editors of the* REFLECTOR *converted what might have been a mere parochial and local matter into one of high principle and governmental import. The transformation of the contest along these lines also demonstrates the rapidity with which small affairs could become large ones in the volatile context of New York's cultural, ethnic, and religious diversity. The second essay discusses the nature of this transformation. In the third essay, attention is called to the remarkably talented politicians who led both sides in these literary struggles, and it is suggested that their energies, thus monopolized by the powerful attraction of politics and religion, were necessarily diverted from the pursuit of more aesthetic interests. Whether the distraction served any better purpose, and whether New York and the colonies might have profited more by purely intellectual products from the pens of these men, is a nice question. My own feeling is that the New Yorkers paid more than enough dividends in demonstrating how religious and ethnic passions could be diffused by political expression and how the irrationality of sectarian contention could be transformed into a more legitimate competition of creedal beliefs in an open society.*

3.

The Independent Reflector

THE APPEARANCE of the *Independent Reflector* on November 30, 1752, should have created a stir in colonial New York. Until then, the province had never had a periodical publication other than its regular newspapers; it would not have another until 1787.[1] The *Reflector* gave New York City a kind of literary parity with Philadelphia and Boston, which had entered the magazine-publishing field about ten years earlier. Since the Pennsylvania and Massachusetts experiments had failed, New York, with the *Reflector* (and the other journals it sired), was for the time the center of periodical-publishing in the English colonies of North America. The preeminence was to endure for five years: in 1757 Philadelphia made a second attempt to produce a literary periodical.[2] The distinction of the *Independent Reflector,* however, lay not merely in its priority of publication but in its style, its content, and its impact on the political, religious, and educational history of New York.

Strictly speaking, the *Reflector* was not a magazine in the eighteenth-century sense. To its English originators and its American imitators, a magazine was literally a "storehouse" or "miscellany" of

---

Reprinted by permission of the publishers from *The Independent Reflector: or, Weekly Essays on Sundry Important Subjects More Particularly Adapted to the Province of New-York,* by William Livingston and others, edited by Milton M. Klein (Cambridge, Mass.: The Belknap Press of Harvard University Press, Copyright 1963 by the President and Fellows of Harvard College), pp. 1-48.

writings sometimes original but more often excerpted from other publications. It was a "Repository of Ancient and Modern Fugitive Pieces, Prose and Poetical"—the self-characterization of the Philadelphia *American Museum;* or a collection of "curious and entertaining pieces in Prose and Verses, . . . the most recent Occurrences, . . . and several Advertisements," as the *New-Jersey Magazine* described itself. Appearing monthly, the magazine usually included instructive or moral essays; entertainment in the form of poetry, fiction, riddles, etc.; feature articles on scientific discoveries or experiments; public notices; summaries of foreign and domestic news; climatological information; and lists of books recently published. The pattern was set in England in 1731 by the *Gentleman's Magazine,* and American periodicals strove to imitate this model. They succeeded so well that the historian of American magazines can say of the Boston *American Magazine and Historical Chronicle* that "except for the imprint it might have been printed in London."[3]

Like their English exemplars, the early American magazines were largely eclectic. About ninety percent of Benjamin Franklin's Philadelphia *General Magazine, and Historical Chronicle* (1741) consisted of material copied from other publications. Authors were less disturbed at pirating than at distortions, which were often so egregious that the "natural Parent" could not recognize the pilfered compositions in their new dress. Editors and publishers made no apologies for their imitative proclivities. The *New-England Magazine* confessed that it was less interested in presenting essays on *new* subjects than in "giving Things that *are known* an applicable or agreeable Turn." "A *new* Author's *Expression* and *Application,*" it added, "is what we are chiefly to admire," not his originality.[4]

The editorial ideal was an article of timeless rather than timely quality. The aim of the publisher was to offer a collection of "entertaining" and "useful" compositions that would comprise "a Piece of valuable Furniture in the Library of a Gentleman." The publication should also give persons "at a distance a just idea of the public state of these *American* colonies," and "enable Posterity to form an Idea of the Learning, Wisdom, . . . abilities, . . . Temper, Taste, . . . Customs, Manners, Morals, Religion and Politics of their Forefathers."[5] The earliest magazines sought to be comprehensive, not selective; English, not American; entertaining, not didactic.

Before 1752 there had been five attempts at magazine publishing in the American colonies. None had proved either a literary or a financial success. Philadelphia gave birth to two periodicals in 1741, the *American Magazine* and the *General Magazine,* but the first lasted only three issues and the other, six.[6] Two years later Boston erupted with three journals: *The Christian History,* the *Boston Weekly Magazine,* and *The American Magazine and Historical Chronicle.* The first was less a magazine than an extended chronicle of the Great Awakening; the second did not survive beyond three numbers; the last was most successful, running for three years, but it was so deliberately imitative of English periodicals as scarcely to be called American. Neither its inception nor its demise created any ferment in Boston, and it made little impress on the literary history of America.[7]

The *Independent Reflector* differed singularly from its predecessors. Its model was the single-essay journal of original composition which Joseph Addison and Richard Steele had elevated to literary art in the *Tatler* and the *Spectator.* Where earlier magazines sought to amuse and please, the *Reflector* purposed to expose, attack, and reform. The journal's excursions into politics were not intended to explain New York public affairs to its neighbors but to enlighten New Yorkers about their own. Its didactic essays were not directed at posterity but at readers in its own day; the topics it discussed were not those of universal interest but those "More particularly adapted to the Province of New-York."[8] The *Reflector* lacked neither wit nor caustic humor, but these were employed to satirize and burlesque rather than to please and amuse. The frivolous discourses on female fashions, love, courtship, marriage, the weather, and human frailties which entertained readers of the *Tatler* were missing from the *Reflector.* Its tone was serious rather than sportive, its contents reflective rather than diverting; and while other periodicals were circumspect in their observations on controversial matters like religion and politics, the *Reflector* aimed boldly, as its first number declared, at exposing "the Abuses and Encroachments" of both priests and politicians and at vindicating the "*civil and religious* RIGHTS" of countrymen from enemies of "whatever dignified Shape."

The expectation of most editors and publishers of early American magazines was first to make money and second to improve and promote culture. The editor of the *Reflector* earned nothing by his literary efforts. Indeed, his law practice suffered because he devoted so much energy to his journalistic interests. His was a labor of love, not of advantage. The printer, although paid for his efforts, undertook the project at the solicitation of the editor and as an accommodation. Both editor and publisher undoubtedly hoped that the *Reflector* would enhance the reputation of New York for culture and learning; but when the paper, in its second issue, assailed the inequitable excise system of the province and, in the third, lashed out at municipal road repair and police protection, it became obvious that culture yielded to civic improvement among its objectives.

Other magazines steered clear of controversy for fear of losing subscribers. The ironic price paid for attention to popularity was historic oblivion. Expecting to interpret their age for posterity, they succeeded only in obscuring it. The *Reflector,* by contrast, reveled in controversy. Its most forceful essays were born of contention. Its pungent and passionate language and its timely observations on New York problems provide grist for the historian's mill; its appearance excited the attention of contemporary readers and excites that of latter-day chroniclers. Literary historians have praised the *Reflector* for raising American essay-writing to a new height in exposition and argument and for infusing into eighteenth-century English periodical literature needed vigor and trenchancy.[9] Political scientists searching for roots of American political thought have found in the *Reflector's* essays on religion and government clues to the colonial mind of the mid-eighteenth century; and historians concerned with the more prosaic task of describing the pattern of municipal life in colonial New York have mined the columns of the *Reflector* for their material.

Contemporaries paid the journal the compliment of denouncing its boldness before the third issue had appeared. An essay on the excise system was assailed by a number of "wrathful Gentlemen" who accused the editor of writing "contemptuously" about government. Rather than deterring the editor, the charge spurred him to enter other forbidden pastures. In the sixth issue he shocked the orthodox by a defense of the Moravian Brethren, a heterodox sect, and by an attack on the dogmas of all denominations. In the seventeenth number he launched a full-scale assault on the proposal for a college in New York under Church of England auspices. The "clamour" that erupted after the college essays relegated the excitement over the Moravians to a mere flurry; and, as the Loyalist historian of New York recalled some years later, these essays

> produced answers, a paper war was the consequence, and persons of all degrees, of all denominations, of all religions, and almost of all ages, joining either the one side or the other, the Colony, in a short time, . . . became a scene of confusion, of uproar, and disorder, thanks to the triumvirate Livingston, Scott, and Smith, and to them only.[10]

The triumvirate to whom Jones paid his unintended compliment were William Livingston, William Smith, Jr., and John Morin Scott, and the *Independent Reflector* was their handiwork. All three shared in planning the journal; all three contributed essays to it; and when it came under attack, each defended it. Yet when defenders and detractors rendered their differing respects to *the* editor of the *Reflector,* they directed them always to the senior member of the trio, the principal author of its essays, William Livingston.

In 1752 Livingston was twenty-nine years old. By accident or design, the first issue of the periodical came off the press on his birthday, November 30.[11] The youngest of the six sons of Philip Livingston, second lord of the Livingston Manor, William was already a more prominent public figure than his older brothers. His youth had been spent in Albany, where his father maintained his business and one of his many residences. Here William was reared in circumstances which he later recalled as those of "ease and affluence."[12] After the customary "grammatical education," he was sent to Yale, which three of his brothers—Peter, John, and Philip—had already attended; but at this point his career diverged sharply from theirs. The three Livingston sons who were graduated from Yale, together with brothers Robert and Henry, entered the mercantile field; but commerce was neither to William's liking nor in the interest of the family. The Livingston Manor was more than a system of agricultural landholding; it was a vast complex of ships, stores, warehouses, mills, mines, forges, and farmlands, with centers in Albany, New York City, and the manor on the Hudson, and appendages in New England, old England, and the West Indies. The first two manor lords, Robert and Philip, had directed these extensive enterprises each almost alone, as landlord, merchant, storekeeper, manufacturer, ironmaster, and lawyer; but by 1741, when William left Yale, the family's economic interests had become too varied for such unsystematic management.[13] Philip Livingston educated each of his six sons for his specialized role in the family's economic empire; and William's destiny lay in the law. The decision was not his, but his father's; and before he completed the required apprenticeship Livingston demonstrated his disapproval in a variety of ways, some of which shocked his family and all of which evidenced the strain of quixoticism and intemperance characteristic of his career.

Three-quarters of the way through his clerkship in the office of James Alexander, dean of the New York bar and a friend of the family, Livingston impetuously dispatched to the press a scathing indictment of the system of legal apprenticeship, including some harsh words for masters who made a "young Fellow trifle away the Bloom of his Age" in the endless drudgery of copying forms, cases, statutes, and precedents. Only the use of a pseudonym saved him from the irate Alexander's reprimand. Less than a year later Livingston touched his master in a rawer spot, by publicly attacking Mrs. Alexander, the dowager of New York society, for excessive vanity and social pretentiousness. The penalty was quick: Livingston was dismissed from Alexander's law office.[14]

Livingston completed his apprenticeship in the office of another distinguished New York attorney, William Smith, Sr. He devoted himself seriously to the practice of law for the next twenty-five years, but he never developed any genuine affection for it.[15] His first love remained belles lettres, of which he had become a devotee at Yale. His greatest pleasure came not from pleading or even winning law suits, but from writing. He was a facile and an inveterate penman. His youthful literary forays were merely exordiums to his long successful career as essay-writer, versifier, and political pamphleteer-extraordinary. "Never . . . expect from me what they call fine letters," he cautioned Noah Welles, his Yale classmate, at the commencement of their long correspondence, "for we will not dispute the field with weapons of witt and Eloquence." "Witt," he added, "is not my Talent, nor Eloquence my Property."[16] The modesty was feigned—both wit and eloquence flowed from his pen, and he cultivated each talent deliberately.

Livingston's fondness for writing is at least partly explained by his limitations as a speaker. Though forthright to the point of imprudence as a writer, he was reserved, almost shy, as a public speaker, and uncomfortable in large gatherings. Tall, lean, awkward, and unhandsome, he shunned balls and theaters, preferring the company of a few close friends to the crowded assemblies of New York high society or the press of political meetings. He once ruefully described himself as one of those "ordinary fellows . . . whose noses hang parallel with their chins." On another occasion he called himself "spindle Shanks." He early became accustomed to the rebuffs of young ladies "who are tickled with an handsome appearance"; and while the experience did not distort his personality, it encouraged him to cultivate his literary skills.[17] He compensated for taciturnity in conversation by "being the more garrulous . . . with the quill," and the consequence was the extravagant ornamentation and the diffusiveness which marred his literary style.[18]

The *Independent Reflector* was Livingston's most important early publishing venture, but he did not emerge into literary maturity full-blown in 1752. He had served his literary apprenticeship simultaneously with his law clerkship. In addition to the two intemperate essays he sent to the press while he was in Alexander's office, Livingston managed to complete two short poems, attempt a play, write a treatise on the history of the drama, and publish a long pastoral. Neither of the two bits of verse appeared in print at the time. One was a poetic paraphrase of the Lord's Prayer. The other was a conventional panegyric to "Eliza." The dissertation on the drama was sent to Noah Welles, who was so impressed that he proposed submitting it to the *American Magazine and Historical Chronicle* in Boston, but Livingston demurred—the piece was "too incorrect and superficial to obtrude on the Publick."[19] He did not often display such modesty.

The young law clerk-turned-versifier demonstrated less reluctance in sanctioning, in 1747, the publication of a longer poem, *Philosophic Solitude, or The Choice of a Rural Life*. Unoriginal in form and content, this extended eclogue is patterned after an English work by the Reverend John Pomfret, *The Choice,* which had a wide vogue in England among those pretending to taste and knowledge. In 684 lines of rhymed couplets imitative of Pope, *Philosophic Solitude* rhapsodizes the life of rural retirement, moderate elegance, and intelligent idleness —the aristocratic ideal of the age.[20] Twentieth-century critics have seen in it nothing but a "faint echo" of Pomfret, but Livingston's contemporaries were more impressed. Fellow Yalensians hailed it as the first contribution to "polite" literature by a graduate of the New Haven college, and Noah Welles introduced it with a prefatory eulogy:

> Yalensis smiles the finished piece to view,
> And fondly glories in a Son like you.[21]

Dr. Benjamin Colman, the prominent Boston clergyman, was sufficiently interested to ask New Jersey friends about the author. Jonathan Belcher, governor of the colony, read the poem and sent copies to England in order to "disabuse" the authorities at home "in the wrong Opinion they entertain of our Ignorance and barbarism, and to shew them that America produces some Geniusses little inferior to the most Eminent Europeans."[22]

Whatever its shortcomings, *Philosophic Solitude* achieved an uncommon popularity during the author's lifetime; and its repute survived his death. If by 1833 it rested in oblivion—in the words of a critic of that day—it had endured remarkably up to that time.[23] As a separate publication it went through thirteen editions, the last in 1790. It was a favorite of magazine editors and anthologists during the Revolution and the early years of the Republic,[24] and it made its author colonial New York's first and principal poet.

Despite his fondness for versifying, Livingston's most effective literary medium was prose; and by 1752 he had already received his baptism as an essayist and political pamphleteer. In 1749, only a year after his entrance to the bar, he published an appeal for speedier legislative action on the college then under public discussion, *Some Serious Thoughts on the Design of erecting a College in the Province of New-York,* under the enigmatic pseudonym, "Hippocrates Mithridate. Apoth."[25] It was prompted by his concern over lagging popular interest in a project which had been initiated by a public lottery under the Assembly's sponsorship three years earlier.[26] King George's War and the "perplexity" of public affairs threatened to relegate the college project to a legislative side-show. Livingston was determined to keep the issue alive; and in the pamphlet he expounded, with a judicious mixture of humor and earnestness, the "numberless Advantages" of a "publick Seminary of Learning." This nine-page publication was one of the rare Livingston fabrications that did not provoke controversy, principally because it was non-political in tone.

A year earlier, Livingston had demonstrated that he could wield a sharper quill when he concentrated his efforts on a political target. Neither the circumstances nor the publications themselves are known precisely, but two pamphlets appear to have been written by him late in 1748 burlesquing the political aspirations of one of Governor Clinton's closest aides. A brief literary skirmish ensued. The maligned politico was publicly defended by one of his associates; Livingston prepared a rejoinder; literary honors appear to have been about even.[27]

Such political pamphleteering was exceptional during Livingston's clerkship period. New York politics were too confused and Livingston's political loyalties as yet too imprecise to permit him to embark on the sea of political journalism with any sense of direction. His friends and future coadjutors on the *Reflector* and his law tutors were all in the camp of Governor Clinton. The governor considered the Livingstons a "vile family." William's father returned the compliment by declining to have any "Concern" with Clinton and by denouncing him for having "abuzd" all those who would not do his bidding.[28] New York politics were a weird mixture of economic rivalries, ethnic-religious factionalism, family feuds, personal enmities, and sectional differences; and the reason for the shifting allegiance of families like the Smiths, Alexanders, Livingstons, De Lanceys, and Morrises is not always clear. What is evident in 1750, however, is the continued hostility between the Livingstons and Governor Clinton, despite the demise in 1749 of the second manor lord, Philip Livingston. In the provincial elections of that year the Livingstons fought to defeat the Clinton candidates for the Assembly; and in New York City William contributed a small pamphlet to the effort.

This was a twelve-page *Letter to the Freemen and Freeholders of the Province of New-York,* which appeared over a characteristic pseudonym, "Tribunus Populi."[29] The content of the publication is of less interest than its style. Abounding in abusive satire, sparked by pungent witticisms, replete with classical allusions, and written in language both florid and eloquent, it foreshadowed the manner of the *Independent Reflector.*

Livingston's pen was not idle during the next two years. He wrote another political tract satirizing Governor Clinton and Chief Justice James De Lancey for engaging in an absurd jurisdictional feud over the right to try one of His Majesty's sailors for an alleged homicide committed in New York harbor;[30] he celebrated the defeat of the Clintonites at the polls in 1750 in a brief valedictory for the newspapers; he penned another *Letter to the Freemen and Freeholders* in the election of 1752;[31] and he engaged in a heated pamphlet exchange with some Jersey landowners over the disputed boundary between that province and New York. When politics did not engage him, he joined with his colleague William Smith, Jr., to press for higher standards of admission to the bar and to prepare a much-needed codification of the laws of the colony.[32]

It was therefore no literary novice who commenced the editorship of the *Independent Reflector* late in 1752. The planning of the new journal was a collaborative effort representing over three years of cerebration among its founders. The scheme was conceived early in 1749, and Livingston wrote of the project to Noah Welles in Connecticut on February 18:

> I Begg leave to inform you that the two Mr. Smiths, Scot[t] and myself have form'd a Design of publishing weekly Essays as soon as possible upon the plan of The Spectator, for correcting the taste and improving the Minds of our Fellow Citizens. We propose to write a paper a month re-

spectively till we have about 150 and then publish our Scheme, and when the printer has a sufficient number of Subscr[ibers?], print 1 or 2 a week according to the Encouragement we meet with. But we are apprehensive that we shall stagger under the Burden unless we engage you in the Design, and we doubt not but so generous, and (if well managed) useful an Undertaking will meet with your approbation and assistance. Essays on Religion and Molarity [Morality] are your peculiar province. Nor are you a Stranger to the fashionable vices and foibles of the age, and your pen is able to rally them. One paper a Month can scarcely interfere with the Duties of your function. Part of a Sermon thrown into a somewhat different form, may often make a beautiful Speculation.

The quadrumvirate named in Livingston's letter represented a combination of talents formidable enough to realize the ambitious project even without Welles's assistance. Of the four, William Peartree Smith proved ultimately to be the least active contributor. Like the others, a graduate of Yale, Peartree Smith studied law but never practiced it. A bountiful inheritance from his father and a profitable marriage freed Smith from putting his law studies to use. Apart from his collaboration with the triumvirate on the *Reflector* and its successor, "The Watch-Tower," little is known of his New York career. He was active in the city's Presbyterian Church, helped to found the College of New Jersey (Princeton), and served on its board of trustees. He moved to Elizabethtown, New Jersey, in 1757, where he served as mayor for many years.[33]

William Smith, Jr., and John Morin Scott were Livingston's closest collaborators not only on the *Reflector* but also on the many other projects which engrossed his attention for over twenty years. In fact, in few New York projects of any significance from 1750 to the eve of the Revolution did the triumvirate fail to play a major and often a decisive role. Did New York need a public library? The trio would found one—the New York Society Library. Was the city lacking a serious discussion group? The three sons of Eli would organize a Society for the Promotion of Useful Knowledge. Did the law require reform? The three young attorneys would organize a primitive bar association, The Moot, at which legal problems could be discussed and the law professionalized. Were the tenure of judges and the jury system endangered by the highhandedness of a provincial governor? The triumvirate would lead the attack on Lieutenant Governor Cadwallader Colden and come to the court's defense. Was New York lukewarm in supporting the war against France? The trio would rush into print to arouse the war spirit. Had the mother country gone mad after 1763 and begun to load New Yorkers with intolerable taxes? The

Assembly would call on Livingston, Smith, and Scott to pen the colony's remonstrance. Was America about to receive the dreaded Episcopal establishment? The three Presbyterian lawyers would found a new paper to sound the alarm.[34]

By 1765 their steady espousal of "independent principles" in politics and religion had earned for them the suspicion of Episcopal churchmen and the enmity of arch-royalists. Tories who saw in the three "popular lawyers" the harbingers of republicanism and free-thinking were consistently astigmatic. The triumvirate's bold assertions of civil and religious liberty were not much more than sound English Whiggism; but to British officialdom their opposition to "encroaching" prerogative and religious authoritarianism appeared as pure radicalism. The trio enjoyed the compliment. They relished shocking the sensibilities of traditionalists, delighted in controversies which would permit them to use their collective pen, and excelled in literary warfare. "The Press is to them what the Pulpit was in times of Popery," was the bitter plaint of their most persistent foe, Cadwallader Colden. Reverend Samuel Johnson, another of the trio's opponents, conceded grudgingly that it was "indeed fencing against a flail to hold any dispute with them," so artful had they become in press warfare.[35]

The *Independent Reflector* was born of the same motivations that impelled the trio to embark on their other civic enterprises; but the links that bound them in such intimate association were forged before 1752. Like Livingston, Smith and Scott were educated at Yale. All three young men served all or part of their apprenticeship in the law office of Smith's father, William Smith, Sr. Livingston was admitted to the bar in 1748; Smith, two years later. The two legal tyros quickly formed a partnership; Scott joined them upon his own entrance into the profession in 1752.

Livingston shared not only the professional interests of his fellow Yalensians but also their aspirations to intellectual sophistication. Livingston had not been long out of Yale before he complained of the sterility of learning in New York City and the necessity of associating with sturdy "bumper men" unless he chose to live in "hermitage."[36] The arrival of Smith and Scott from New Haven obviated the necessity of retirement; and the three Yale graduates, together with Peartree Smith and William Alexander, the son of Livingston's former law teacher, made up a company of youthful "philosophers" who regarded themselves as above the level of the majority of the younger set.

William Smith, Jr., shared Livingston's fondness for scribbling. He had begun writing at the precocious age of sixteen, and before the appearance of the *Reflector* he had published a full-length work of literary criticism. Five years younger than Livingston, Smith did not always pay his older colleague the deference that his years commanded. He sharply criticized the first draft of *Philosophic Solitude* and reproached Livingston for intemperate drinking when at Yale. Livingston heatedly denied the charge as a "malevolent aspersion"—"Drunkenness I really think is the last Vice that ever I shall fall into"—and alluded unflatteringly to "Billy Smith's ministerial Severity" and his priggish "Compunction of Conscience" in joining his friends around the punch bowl.[37]

Smith bore a reputation for piety and seriousness throughout his life. A devout Presbyterian, "rigid" in his orthodoxy, and regular in church attendance, he shunned drinking and card playing. His enemies saw in his "steady, demure, puritanical countenance" only the disguise of "a most profound dissembler . . . a noted flatterer, [and] a great sycophant," but more sympathetic observers were impressed with his charm, grace, and urbanity.[38]

In contrast to the earnest, subtle, and cool Smith, John Morin Scott was bluff, hearty, and jovial; as fluent in conversation as Smith but less smooth; always at ease in company and warm in his personal relationships. His humor, candor, and generosity earned him the admiration even of political foes, who thought his only error of judgment was his naiveté in joining the crafty Smith-Livingston combination and allowing himself to be "duped" by them. Less adroit with the pen than his friends, Scott could yet write with vigor and clarity; and he lacked neither intelligence nor learning. His inclusion in the trio completed the assortment of talents the group required to achieve its ends. Smith's aristocratic bearing permitted him to move easily in New York high officialdom; Scott's rough, ingenuous manner made him an ideal manager of popular meetings held in the taverns and in "the fields"; Livingston, always uncomfortable in the salons and on the streets, and lacking both Smith's suavity and Scott's geniality, provided the intellectual leadership and the literary energy.

Either his age—he was five years older than both Smith or Scott—or his talent earned Livingston the sobriquet of "boss" early in their association, and the title remained throughout their joint career. The heart of their association was their shared affection for belles lettres and their common concern for "popular" rights against the infringements of governors at home or Crown and Parliament abroad; but kinship and religion added new links to their friendship.

Scott's forebears came from Ancrum, Scotland, the ancestral home of the Livingstons; and a sister of the first Livingston in America had married the Reverend John Scott. Smith's sister was the wife of one Livingston, and he himself married another.[39] All three men were Presbyterians. Smith's attachment to the denomination was more earnest and more doctrinaire than Livingston's and Scott's, who were newcomers to the fold, having shifted from the Dutch and French Reformed Churches about the time of the founding of the *Independent Reflector*. More casual in observance than the "rigid" Smith, they were no less suspicious of the Church of England nor less zealous in opposing Anglican encroachments on the religious liberties of dissenting sects in New York.[40]

Their common conviction that New York was an intellectual wasteland led the three to organize an informal literary club which by 1748 bore the title "Society for the Promotion of Useful Knowledge" but was dubbed by its critics the "Society of Sage Philosophers."[41] It was probably at one of its meetings that the idea of launching the *Independent Reflector* was born. Despite contemporary charges that the society was a "Whig Club" or a hotbed of atheism and that the *Reflector's* objective was the formation of a new Livingston Party, there appears to have been no political or religious motivation behind either. The club was divided in political loyalty and religious affiliation in 1748. James Alexander and William Smith, Sr., the society's senior members, were confidantes of Governor Clinton; the Livingstons in its ranks were anti-Clinton. Alexander and his son were Anglicans; the Smiths, Presbyterians; others among the members, Quakers and Dutch Reformed. The three future editors of the *Reflector* were themselves in different political camps in 1749 when the journal was conceived. It seems clear from their letter to Welles of that year that the aim of the periodical—as of the Philosophic Society—was simply "improving the Minds of our Fellow Citizens."[42]

Moreover, it is highly unlikely that James Parker, the *Reflector's* printer, would have chosen to become associated with a partisan journal. As the colony's official printer, he could not afford to offend either the civil or the religious authorities. A few years earlier, he had irritated the Assembly by declining to publish one of its "Remonstrances" against the governor; and only a few months before the *Reflector's* appearance, he had been indicted for a "blasphemous libel" against Christianity in his newspaper, the *Gazette*. Only Benjamin Franklin's intercession and a promise to be more "circumspect" in the future kept him from jail. The *Reflector's* bland announcement in its first two numbers that it would eschew political controversy and decline contributions with too strong a "Tincture of Party-Spirit" must have been reassuring to Parker. There seems little reason for questioning his explanation, made some years later, that he undertook to publish the *Reflector* because "all the Printing done here was very poor, and in some Measure a Disgrace to the Country."[43]

Neither the printer nor the editors could have foreseen how quickly the *Reflector* would change its tone and character, how soon it would become embroiled in heated controversies of both a religious and a political nature, and how out of these contests a new political combination of Livingstons and former Clintonites would be formed. It was only after the *Reflector* itself was dead that some color would be given to the frenetic accusation of the Loyalist, Thomas Jones, that its three editors,

> presbyterians by profession, and republicans in principle; being all of the law, nearly of an age, and linked together in friendship, in principles, in politics, and religion, . . . formed themselves into a triumvirate, and determined . . . to pull down Church and State, to raise their own Government and religion upon its ruins, or to throw the whole province into anarchy and confusion.[44]

Three years elapsed between the germination of the idea and the appearance of the *Reflector*. During the interval it underwent a change in character. When the paper emerged it was not merely a pale imitation of the English *Tatler* and *Spectator,* nor were its editors content to fill its pages with literary and philosophic speculations. By the time of its publication the *Reflector* had been refashioned into a crusading as well as a speculative journal, a change that reflected the growing concern of the editors with the extension of Anglican clerical power in the American colonies. The three-year delay was unintentional. Livingston's interest had remained undiminished, but his colleagues had become too absorbed in their legal and business affairs to render him much assistance. Since the original plan contemplated deferring publication until at least 150 essays were ready, the founders obviously anticipated a long life for their brain child; and, confined to the literary essays of the *Tatler* and *Spectator* variety, the journal might have run on for years. The title first selected, "The New-York Guardian," suggests the degree to which the New Yorkers intended to emulate Addison and Steele: *The Guardian* was the successor to the *Tatler* and *Spectator*.[45] By the time the *Reflector* appeared, however, Livingston had developed an even warmer admiration for two other English essayists, Thomas Gordon and John Trenchard.

Trenchard was a wealthy lawyer and country squire; Gordon, an obscure and poor Scotsman who became Trenchard's companion and amanuensis. Both were staunch Whigs who shared a common suspicion of standing armies, Tory politicians, divine right theorists, and High Churchmen. In 1720 they began writing two series of essays for the press which became known, collectively, as *The Independent Whig* and *Cato's Letters*. The Cato series was launched as an attack on the political malefactors who engineered the infamous South Sea Bubble speculation, but it soon took a wider range. The *Whig* was narrower in focus, concentrating on the dangers of a Catholic revival and the threat of Popery to English civil and religious liberties.[46]

These two essay-series achieved a phenomenal popularity in the American colonies. Fifty-three of the *Whig* papers were collected in a single volume and published in 1721. By 1750 the book had gone through seven editions in England, two in America, and one in France.[47] In collected form the essays bore the subtitle: "A Defence of Primitive Christianity . . . against the exorbitant claims of fanatical and disaffected clergymen." *Cato's Letters,* somewhat less mordant in their anticlericalism, also discussed freedom of speech, the importance of education, the right of resistance, and limited versus unlimited sovereignty. They were republished in book form but never in an American edition. American newspapers simply pirated the work by extensive and frequent republication of the essays. The Philadelphia *American Weekly Mercury* began reprinting the *Cato* letters in 1722, while they were still running serially in the British press, and the New York, Boston, and South Carolina papers quickly followed suit. By the middle of the eighteenth century American newspapers were referring to Gordon and Trenchard in adulatory terms as "that incomperable [*sic*] Lay Author" and "the Divine English Cato." Only Anglican clergymen were disturbed by the extensive popularity of such "pernicious" writers.[48]

Livingston and his colleagues joined in the general acclaim accorded to the *Whig* authors, who were "invincible Writers," "Geniusses sublime and inimitable," and those "Great and . . . Good" essayists;

and when early issues of the *Reflector* were dismissed by Anglican critics as mere imitations, William Smith, Jr., responded:

> You could not, Sir, have done greater Honour to the Abilities of the *Independent Reflector,* than by allowing him a Capacity to imitate the *Independent Whigg,* who had one of the finest Pens in Europe, and is justly esteem'd, a signal Ornament to the Republic of Letters.[49]

The anticlericalism of the *Independent Whig* coincided almost perfectly with Livingston's own religious views. Reared in the easy, liberal religious atmosphere of Dutch Albany, Livingston had known neither the zealotry of the enthusiast nor the rigid conformity of the doctrinaire. He had experienced both at Yale and recoiled from each. He was shocked by the narrow formalism of Connecticut Congregationalism, to which he was subjected as a student. When he wrote caustically in the *Reflector* of sermons that were "so replete with abstruse *Erudition*" as to be "unintelligible to forty-nine in fifty" of the congregation and more calculated to make one a "Critic or Pedagogue than a good Man or a Christian," he was undoubtedly thinking of the dry oratory of New Haven preachers.[50]

Searching for a religious philosophy that avoided the evils both of enthusiasm and of rigid conformity, Livingston early arrived at the spiritual position he held for the rest of his life. Rejecting all orthodoxy as irrational—"every Man is *orthodox* to himself, and *heretical* to all the World besides"—Livingston adopted a "pure and simple" Christianity, shorn of doctrinal rigidity and ritualistic complexity. If this placed him outside the bounds of denominational religion, he would be content, "with a set of sound principles and a good heart, to pass almost for any thing." Publicly and privately he insisted that since "true piety" had never been agreed upon by mankind, he would not permit "any human tribunal" to "settle its definition" for him.[51]

In such a latitudinarian mood Livingston became increasingly receptive to the anticlericalism of Gordon and Trenchard; but these authors merely reinforced the prejudices toward the clergy that Livingston already had developed. The Great Awakening, with the fratricidal strife it engendered among New England Congregationalists and Middle Colony Presbyterians, shocked Livingston into a recognition of the dangers of hard doctrinal positions. In his view not only were disputations on matters of organization, ritual, and doctrine irrational, they weakened all the dissenting churches in their larger struggle against the common foe, Episcopacy. He was particularly disturbed at the large number of Dissenters who, disillusioned with the excesses of the revivalists, turned to the stability of the Anglican Church. The process was occurring in Livingston's own Dutch Church, where he could observe its baneful effects at first hand. Although the dispute in the Reformed Church was not entirely the product of the Great Awakening, it was related to the revival. The issues that split conservatives and liberals among the Dutch were the proposals for introducing English as the language of the service and the organization of a separate American "Classis" or church council. The inflexibility of the traditionalists in retaining both the Dutch language and the organizational connection with the Amsterdam Classis drove many younger, more liberal members out of the Reformed Church directly into the Anglican.[52]

While Livingston's own rational theology made him suspicious of every "little Flutterer in a Gown and Cassock" and hostile to the "Popes and Persecutors of all Churches, whether . . . of Rome, England, Holland or Geneva," in practice the brunt of his biting attacks on "priestcraft" was borne by the Church of England. Its "ridiculous Ceremonies Idolatrics and Superstitions" were of a piece with Roman Catholicism; it had

> too many popish relicks, not to say, gross Superstitions, to approve itself to the Judgment of any person who knows that true Religion consists in the internal purity of the heart, and the soul's being as it were moulded into the image of God, . . . and not in a multitude of ridiculous fantastical rites, that seem to make religion more cumbersom[e], and often betray a Man into many Sins of Omission by neglecting what (tho indifferent in itself) he has been taught to look upon as a matter of Duty.[53]

This sentiment Livingston expressed when still a law clerk. By 1752 he had added to his suspicion of "ecclesiastical trumpery" a compelling fear of "ecclesiastical tyranny" in the form of an official establishment of the Church of England in the colonies. His letters to Noah Welles were increasingly filled with aspersions upon the Anglican Church and its clergymen. When, in 1747, New England Dissenters and Episcopal churchmen became embroiled in a brief, hot paper war over the relative merits of episcopal as against presbyterian ordination, Livingston gladly lent a hand, sponsoring a republication in New York of one of the anti-Anglican pamphlets. Its virtue, Livingston decided, was that it perfectly confuted all the "glib Nonsense" Anglicans had invented "to palliate superstition and bigotry." [54]

As additional polemics poured from the press, Livingston purchased or borrowed them all, read them, and rejoiced at every Dissenter literary victory. Absorbed in the controversy, he began to study the question of Episcopal claims to jurisdiction in the colonies and prepared a lengthy paper on the extent of the Crown's prerogative in ecclesiastical matters. He noted with alarm every sign of Anglican "bigotry" in New York City. One such was church pressure to compel strict observance of Good Friday; and while he did not want to exaggerate isolated incidents of clerical power, he was fearful that "Great Things rise from small Beginnings." Unless the "monster Tyranny" were nipped in the bud, it might proliferate beyond the capacity of Dissenters to curb it. Then New York's highly prized liberty of conscience would be irretrievably lost.[55]

Livingston's transfer of religious allegiance from the Dutch to the Presbyterian Church sometime in 1752 provided him with another vantage point for his view of the Church of England. The Anglican Trinity Church in New York City not only possessed a royal charter but also received financial support from the taxpayers under a law passed in 1693. The aim of the law had been to provide public support of "a good sufficient Protestant Minister" in the four southern counties of the colony, but interpretation by royal governors had resulted in Trinity's drawing to itself the exclusive benefits of the act.[56] The Presbyterians were disturbed because, while Trinity enjoyed both financial and legal privileges, their own church in New York City had repeatedly failed to secure a royal charter of incorporation. They attributed their precarious position to the opposition of Trinity Church. To acquire some legal status it had become necessary for the Presbyterian Church to vest title to its property in the Church of Scotland.[57]

Livingston shared the resentment of his coreligionists against Trinity Church, but both he and William Smith, Jr., had still another basis for their mistrust of the Anglicans: indignation over the labors of the missionary arm of the Church in America, the Society for the Propagation of the Gospel in Foreign Parts. The missionaries, Livingston and Smith charged, were more bent on the advancement of "Prelacy" than of Christianity and spent more energy seducing Dissenters into the Anglican fold than in bringing the Gospel to the Indians, which was the work the Society was formed to do.[58]

The *Reflector* thus mirrored the new orientation Livingston acquired as a result of his preoccupation with Anglican power; its contents revealed the heavy debt of its editor to the English anticlericals, Gordon and Trenchard. Of the fifty-two numbers of the *Reflector*, only five dealt with "the fashionable vices and foibles" of the day. Twelve were on religion and related topics, most of them heavily tinged with Livingston's anticlericalism. And the first issue of the *Reflector* was strikingly patterned after the *Independent Whig*.

The first two numbers of the *Independent Whig* were "The Introduction" and "The Design of this Paper." Livingston labeled his own first issue: "The Introduction, or Design of this Paper." Gordon and Trenchard had stated that "Whoever goes about to reform the world, undertakes an Office obnoxious to Malice, and beset with Difficulties." Livingston parroted the sentiment: "Whoever sets up as a Reformer of public Abuses, must expect to encounter innumerable Difficulties." The *Whig* announced that "neither these, nor any other Difficulties or Discouragements, shall hinder me from the generous Attempt of endeavouring to reform Mankind. I have the Magnanimity to face them all." The *Reflector* duplicated this warning: "None of these Discouragements shall, however, deter me from vindicating the *civil and religious Rights* of my Fellow-Creatures. . . . I have the Magnanimity to attack the Enemies of [the] human Race, in whatever . . . Shape they appear." The *Whig* disavowed political partisanship: "For my self, who have no manner of Attachment to any Party, I shall not be afraid to speak my Mind of All." The *Reflector* reiterated the same sentiment: "The Author, being under no Attachment to any Party, thinks himself the better qualified to make impartial Remarks on the Conduct of every Party." The *Whig* modestly disclaimed any particular talent for its authors: "I . . . have long wished some abler Genius would have undertaken it." The *Reflector* echoed the humility: ". . . 'tis to be hoped a Design so generous and humane . . . might be carried on by an abler Genius."

Despite these similarities, the *Independent Reflector* was no more a carbon copy of the *Whig* than of the *Tatler* and *Spectator*. Gordon and Trenchard were too narrowly religious in their interest to suit Livingston's mood in 1752; and while anticlericalism weighed heavily on his mind, he desired the freedom to discuss "sundry" other subjects relating to the province of New York.

The choice of a title for his journal reflected Livingston's enlarged outlook. Borrowing from the *Reflector*, an English literary magazine of 1750 modeled on the *Tatler* and *Spectator*, as well as the *Whig*, Livingston arrived at the happy compromise, the *Independent Reflector*. The new periodical would adopt the politico-religious liberalism of the *Independent Whig* and employ the didactic style of the

Addisonian *Reflector*. The name was thus a felicitous representation of the paper's dual character.[59]

The *Reflector's* one-year existence proved to be stormy, but its demise was more spectacular than its birth. Parker advertised its appearance by reproducing the entire first number in his weekly newspaper, but surplus copies continued to pile up in his office during the first month of publication. By the fifth week, however, New Yorkers began to warm to the new periodical. New subscriptions came in so rapidly that back copies of the first six issues were exhausted, and such subscribers were informed that they would have to wait until the following spring before a new printing would permit them to complete their sets. Critics disparaged these claims as the fabrications of the editors, insisting that the subscribers constituted only a "scanty Number" and the paper lay "by Fifty's" in Parker's office.[60] It is unlikely that the business-minded printer would have been a party to such deception; and there is typographical evidence that in March, 1753, Parker did reprint the first six issues as promised.[61] In any case, within a few years after its demise, the *Reflector* was a scarce item in the New York literary market, prospective American purchasers being unable to secure copies to satisfy the curiosity of English readers.[62]

The precise circulation of the *Reflector* is unknown. Weekly newspapers of the time averaged about 600 copies, which was the minimum required by a publisher to achieve even a modest profit. Monthly magazines, much fuller in content and more expensive to print, required only a circulation of 400 to remain self-supporting.[63] The *Reflector's* circulation probably approximated that of the weekly newspaper. If the journal had 500 subscribers, it provided about one copy for every ten potential adult readers in New York City. This would make it an influential organ of public opinion in the city.[64] Besides, the influence of both newspapers and magazines in mid-century America was far out of proportion to the actual number of copies printed. Reading matter was not a common article of the daily mail, and every page of every newspaper and periodical was actually read with care by many persons other than the subscriber.

The subscription price of ten shillings a year was somewhat less than that of earlier magazines and was fixed largely to cover the cost of publication. The *Reflector* was not intended as an addition to Livingston's income; "his Circumstances," he informed his readers in the first issue, "put him above the Aids of this Paper for Subsistence."

The ringing statement of purpose with which Livingston introduced the paper should have warned New Yorkers that a new element had been added to its seething political and religious situation. The equanimity of local politicians was shaken when Livingston indicted the tax-farming system in the second issue and followed in the third with a slashing indictment of the local police and road-repair apparatus. The city fathers took alarm. If the *Reflector's* crusade against inefficient fire-fighting, medical quackery, and extravagant funerals left them undisturbed, the paper's criticism of tax-farming, the sale of public offices, and electoral corruption stung them sharply. They began denouncing the publication, hinting that the authors were political "levellers." Undaunted, in the third number Livingston promised these "Wretches" he would make them "the marks of the public Resentment," and in the tenth issue he printed a sensational exposé of a shady land deal by which some local businessmen, in collusion with the City Council, planned to get valuable shoreline property for a song.

The anguished cries of politicians were shortly augmented by the agonized protestations of clergymen. In his defense of the Moravians in the sixth issue, Livingston denounced the "little Popes" of all denominations. The pulpits were now employed to impugn him as an atheist; clergymen demanded that the *Reflector* be recommended to the grand jury as libelous; and Anglican priests began marshaling a corps of penmen to mount a counterattack. The *Reflector's* indiscriminate disparagement of clergymen and churches offended not only Anglicans but also Congregationalists and Dutch Reformed churchmen; and the latter were Livingston's prospective supporters and allies in any full-scale assault launched against the Church of England. Livingston himself preferred to believe that the "prodigious Noise" provoked by the Moravian essay was confined to "High Church of all kinds." Nevertheless, he was given pause by a suggestion from his friend Welles that he moderate his anticlericalism or at least differentiate between worthy and unworthy clerics; and the warning was reinforced by a public admonition to the *Reflector* from a Dutch divine. Since the author of the public rebuke was a member of the liberal wing of the Dutch Reformed Church, with which Livingston was most closely allied, the advice could not be ignored.[65] For the next month Livingston checked his natural inclination to lock horns with his ministerial critics, but in the eleventh issue he returned to the attack.

Anglicans responded, Smith defended Livingston, and "paper war" commenced in earnest.[66]

In the press warfare that now reached its zenith, the Anglicans had a powerful advantage. The *Gazette,* Parker's paper, was effectively closed to the triumvirate; the *Mercury,* the city's other regular newspaper, was the Anglicans' exclusive preserve. Livingston could either utilize the *Reflector* itself or remain silent. He was not, however, without other weapons to continue the contest with the Episcopal clergy. One technique was the use of pamphlets. The Anglicans initiated this mode of warfare during the summer of 1753 with two satirical commentaries on Livingston's notions of pristine religion.[67] Livingston and his friends responded by republishing an old anticlerical tract of Gordon, *The Craftsmen,* to which they added a new preface reminding the public of the revival of "Priestianity" in New York with all its "violent Thirst for Persecution and Dominion."[68]

The *Reflector,* however, was still Livingston's big gun, and while he engaged in scattered fire with Anglican clergymen on theological matters, he prepared to destroy them with a more powerful salvo. The opportunity was provided by an Anglican proposal for a college in New York to be chartered by the Crown and placed under the supervision of an Episcopal clergyman. Livingston gleefully planned his new barrage. "The Town," he wrote Welles in jubilant anticipation, "is not yet ripe for loosing plainer Truth. The Veil must be removed from their eyes by slow degrees."[69] The unveiling process commenced on March 22, 1753, when Livingston published the first of six essays on the subject of the projected college.

The controversy between Livingston and his clerical critics reached its climax in their irreconcilable differences over the constitution of the proposed New York college. Anglican sponsors of the project contended for a royally chartered, private institution in which the Episcopal Church should have "a preference." Livingston countered with a vigorous plea for a legislatively incorporated and publicly controlled school under the management of no particular religious denomination but with an "equality" of privilege accorded to all Protestants. Despite its theological and political repercussions, the college controversy was not simply a clash between contending religious sects nor a contest between rival political factions. It was largely Livingston's one-man crusade for a more liberal system of higher education; and despite the political and religious overtones of the affair,

Livingston's own role remained peculiarly and often quixotically personal. There was no cant in his public defense, early in 1754, of the anti-Anglican stand he took in the *Reflector* on the college issue:

> The affair of the College, I considered as one of the most important matters, that ever fell under the consideration of our Legislature. It will either prove one of the greatest blessings, or an execrable source of the keenest and most complicated disasters. If it is constituted upon a foundation generous and catholic, there is nothing we can fall upon, that will spread more real felicity thro' the Province. But should it on the other hand, be made the tool of a faction, and an instrument in the hand of one sect, for the advancement of itself, and the oppression of the rest, what can we expect . . . but either the deprivation or the abridgment of our civil and religious liberties?[70]

The idea of a college in New York was not Livingston's, but few could deny the persistence or the sincerity of his interest. As early as 1749 he had complained:

> The want of a liberal Education has long been our Reproach and Misfortune. Our Neighbours have told us in an insulting Tone, that the Art of getting Money, is the highest Improvement we can pretend to: That the wisest Man among us, without a Fortune, is neglected and despised; and the greatest Blockhead with one, caress'd and honour'd: That, for this Reason, a poor Man of the most shining Accomplishments, can never emerge out of his Obscurity; while every wealthy Dunce is loaded with Honours. . . .[71]

From this intellectual discontent arose his activity on behalf of a New York college and his *Reflector* essays on the subject—not from political motivations.

The movement for a college in New York was part of the "college enthusiasm" which stirred all the northern colonies in the decade after 1740. To some degree, the revived interest in higher education was an outgrowth of the Great Awakening, old and new churches vying with each other in founding seminaries for the training of ministers. To a larger degree, however, the college movement represented a stage in the maturation of the colonies as prosperity, leisure, and stability led men to divert some of their energies from mere physical existence to building an American culture.[72]

The efforts at college building bore first fruit in New Jersey and Pennsylvania, with the founding of the College of New Jersey (later Princeton) in 1746 and the Philadelphia Academy (later the University of Pennsylvania) in 1749. "A jealousy of our neighbors," Livingston observed later, "at length gave a spring to our ambition."[73] The result was a series of public lotteries, beginning in 1746, authorized by the New York legislature for "the Advancement of Learning." By 1751, £3,443 had been raised, the money vested in a board of ten trustees, empowered to lend the funds at interest and receive proposals for the site of the college.[74] Of the ten trustees, seven were members *ex officio;* of the three appointed by name, Livingston was one. The religious composition of the members of the board was similarly uneven: seven Episcopalians, two Dutch Reformed, and Livingston, Presbyterian.

The disproportionate strength of the Episcopalians on the board did not reflect their numbers in the colony's population; only about ten percent of New York's inhabitants were Anglicans. It did, however, reflect the intense interest of Episcopal churchmen who had long complained of Harvard and Yale as "nurseries of sedition." The success of the Presbyterians in founding the New Jersey College irritated them even more. There was all the more reason, then, in the Anglican view, that the proposed New York school should be "an Episcopal College" established "upon a Foundation, that may give a Prospect of promoting religion in the way of the National Ch[urch]."[75]

The Anglican proposal represented the fulfillment of a scheme that had been at least a half-century in the making. The idea had first been broached when Trinity Church received a grant of valuable Crown property in New York City in 1705—some thirty-two acres west of Broadway and south of Warren Street and known as the "Queen's Farm." In petitioning for the land, Anglicans had noted that it would be "a Proper Place for a Colledge."[76] They never changed their opinion; and their support of the lottery legislation of the 1740s was conditioned by their understanding that the prospective college would be the Episcopal seminary of their studied contemplation. They had already settled upon the Reverend Samuel Johnson, Episcopal pastor at Stratford, Connecticut, as the president. Their control of the lottery trustees seemed to ensure success.

On March 5, 1752, the Vestry of Trinity Church officially tendered part of the Queen's (now the King's) Farm to the trustees as a site for the proposed college.[77] No conditions were attached to Trinity's offer. None were necessary. "We always expected," Trinity's vestrymen said some years later, " that a Gift so valuable in itself . . . would be a Means of obtaining some Priviledges to the Church."[78]

Livingston was not taken into Trinity's confidence, and as a member of the trustees of the lottery funds, he offered no objections to receiving the church's offer or to viewing the proffered property. The composition of the trustees he regarded as "so partial as could not but excite the Jealousy of every unbiased mind";[79] but this observation was made two years later, with the benefit of hindsight. In 1752 he was less disturbed about the possibility of Anglican control than by the prospect of the college's stillbirth because of public apathy. Six months later, however, he found more substantial cause for alarm, as the Anglicans made public their intentions. William Smith, later Provost of the Philadelphia Academy, in November, 1752, wrote a letter to both city newspapers proposing that the intended college be established by royal charter, that Dr. Samuel Johnson of Stratford become its president, and that Johnson be named as a rector of Trinity Church simultaneously in order to permit him to "subsist honourably upon a less Salary from the College."[80]

The arrangement, a most "convenient" economy to the Anglicans, horrified Livingston; and he turned to the *Independent Reflector* to air his suspicions. The arguments he expounded in detail in six issues of the *Reflector* were foreshadowed almost perfectly in a letter to Noah Welles a month in advance. In mid-February he wrote his classmate:

> There is a thing . . . which has long been the Subject of my thoughts and which I should be glad to transmit to the Reflector in a course of Letters. . . . The case is this—Our future College will undoubtedly be of great Importance to this Province, and is like to fall without a vigorous opposition, under the sole management of Churchmen. The Consequence of which will be universal Priestcraft and Bigotry in less than half a Century. The Trustees lately proposed were every one Churchmen, and many of them the most implicit Bigots. The Church can assign no colour of Reason to have the Direction of the Affair in preference of any other Sect, but I would not have it managed by any Sect. For that reason I would have no Charter from the Crown, but an Act of Assembly for the Purpose. Nor, for the same Reason should Divinity be taught at College because whoever is in the Chair will obtrude his own Notions for Theology. Let the Students follow their own Inclinations in the Study of Divinity and read what Books they please in their Chambers or apply themselves to it after they leave the College. Their religious Exercises should consist of reading the Scriptures and hearing a Prayer in which all Protestants may join. I know that if it falls into the hands of Churchmen, it will either ruin the College or the Country, and in fifty Years, no Dissenter however deserving, will be able to get into any office.[81]

If Livingston's crusade against an Anglican college had any political motivations, as was later charged, he concealed them from his most intimate correspondent, and no political overtones are apparent in the six issues of the *Reflector* in which Livingston expounded his views (March 22 to April 26, 1753). His overriding objection to the Anglican scheme was that it would make the college "a contracted Receptacle of Bigotry," unduly strengthen the Anglican Church, and even lead to a full Episcopal establishment. Aware of popular sensitivity about the Assembly's power, he argued his case on political as well as religious grounds: a royal charter would represent a gubernatorial encroachment on a legislative preserve. Cloaked in the trenchant exposition and the florid rhetoric of the *Reflector,* Livingston's essays transformed the college question into a burning issue of broad political and religious consequence.

"Had a new government, tyrannical, arbitrary, and despotic, been erected, the popish religion established, the presbyterians burned at the stake and the Episcopalians their persecutors," Thomas Jones recalled in amazement, "more noise could not have been made, than was now excited about this charter." For the next two years, the coffee houses and taverns were alive with the subject, and only the imminent war with France competed with the college controversy as the "Grand topheck" of public discussion.[82] The followers of James De Lancey, who constituted the party in power in the legislature, were placed in an embarrassing position. Their leader, Chief Justice De Lancey, became acting governor in October; and since his strongest patrons in England were members of the Episcopal hierarchy, the De Lanceyites were compelled to support the Anglican charter proposal. Secretly, however, they cursed the *Reflector* for raising the issue, since the De Lanceyites in the Assembly were largely Dissenters and in sympathy with the *Reflector's* stand. The chief justice's own ambivalent behavior weakened his hold on his followers and helped ultimately to bring about his downfall; but this was not until 1758. Meanwhile, Anglican clergymen carried on the war against the *Reflector* with great vigor.

The *New-York Mercury* remained the Anglican forum, and from April to October, 1753, its pages were filled with the polemics of the "anti-Reflectors." When they were not assailing Livingston and his coeditors as "furious" bigots, "Champions of Ribaldry," and "a sly insidious, restless Set of Men," they were actively defending the charter plan as legitimate, justifiable, and financially desirable. While they insisted on the necessity for a "Church-college," they assured Dissenters that their religious liberties would not be endangered. Paradoxically, the Anglicans simultaneously denied that any "perfect Equality" of religious privilege existed in either New York or England. The triumvirate's real motive, it was alleged, was to prevent the establishment of *any* New York college in order to assure the prosperity of the Presbyterian College of New Jersey. At other times, they charged Livingston with seeking to destroy both the Anglican and Dutch Churches in order to raise the Presbyterian on the ruins and to organize a new party—a "most abject Republican Party, both in Politics and Religion," at that.[83]

"Madd[en]ed . . . not a little" by these Anglican insinuations, Livingston hewed to a line he had announced earlier of not engaging his opponents in face-to-face combat in the columns of the *Reflector.* This did not prevent him, however, from using its pages to respond to the Anglican position indirectly. Essays on priestcraft, church establishments, natural rights, the compact theory of government, and the right of resistance all dealt with subjects raised by his Anglican critics, and the *Reflector's* burlesques of orthodoxy and religious credulity were grist for his mill in arguing the anti-Anglican case. Despite this, the triumvirate was at a disadvantage in the continuing press warfare through lack of a regular outlet. To solve their dilemma, they launched a new periodical.[84]

The new journal, *The Occasional Reverberator,* first appeared in September, 1753. Its title described with considerable accuracy its character and purpose. It was not conceived with the forethought and care that went into the *Reflector,* and it is not likely that the editors expected it to last very long. They probably hoped it would prod Hugh Gaine, printer of the *Mercury,* or Parker, of the *Gazette,* into opening their papers to the *Reflector's* supporters; it could then die a quiet death. Only the latter expectation was realized. The *Reverberator* expired after its fourth number. Its reverberations proved even more offensive to Anglican clergymen than the *Reflector.* William Smith, Jr., was its nominal editor, and his pen was more vituperative and more personal than Livingston's.

Livingston employed the paper's columns to answer directly the "foul-mouthed Invectives" which were "perpetually disgorged" against him in the *Mercury.* In the *Reverberator* he assumed the role of polemicist, permitting himself a style less impersonal and more abusive than he employed in the *Reflector.* In stigmatizing his Anglican opponents as "wilful Calumniator[s]" and "fulminating Ecclesiastic[s]," Livingston did little to clarify the issues in dispute and only provoked the clergymen to direct action. Their pressure on Parker, the printer of the *Reverberator,* brought about its demise on October 5, 1753. Incensed, Livingston denounced the printer for his "irresolution or corruption" and returned to the *Reflector* for his literary cannonading.[85]

The most effective of the remaining essays was a caustic burlesque on all clerical pretensions to theological infallibility, to which Livingston added a personal religious "creed" in mock imitation of those for which he had repeatedly professed his repugnance. The language of this number, however entertaining to the triumvirate, proved too strong for either Parker or the Episcopal clergy. Six weeks later, the printer discontinued publication without notice to either Livingston or his associates. Their surprise is attested by the fifty-second and last issue of the journal, which contained no hint of its prospective demise; indeed, the next week's issue was already written.[86]

William Smith, the Anglican penman, celebrated the *Reflector's* end with a jubilant epitaph, but Livingston was infuriated. Parker's "singular" action he found reprehensible: "it shewed that some of those who ought to be the guardians of our liberties, were ready to become the authors of our vassalage, when ever a spirit of freedom interfered with their politics." Two months earlier Livingston had received the printer's promise to continue publishing at least until June, 1754, or to provide timely notice to the editors if financial considerations dictated an earlier discontinuance. In quitting, Parker had honored neither promise. He had informed subscribers of the paper's forthcoming demise only through the newsboy who delivered it.[87]

Asked for an explanation, Parker admitted that "he had been threat[e]ned with the loss of the public business" unless he ceased publication of the offending periodical. To Livingston this appeared as a plain case of suppression arising from "a villainous Collusion" between the printer and the Anglican-De Lanceyite coalition. De Lancey's role was enacted in the Assembly, which his party controlled. Parker's danger was loss of position as public printer, a position determined by the Assembly.[88] De Lancey was happy to assist the Anglicans in suppressing the *Reflector,* whose death restored his political peace. Its campaign against a charter college had placed him in the awkward position of having to take sides on the delicate question of royal versus legislative incorporation when he was simultaneously leader of the Assembly and acting governor.

The pressure on Parker was so severe that he even declined to print for the triumvirate a supplement to the *Reflector,* which the editors intended as a kind of final vindication. For the next few months

Livingston sought unsuccessfully to secure a printer in Philadelphia and Boston. Finally, he induced Henry De Foreest, the publisher of the defunct *New-York Evening Post,* to come out of retirement for the purpose. De Foreest did not enjoy a good reputation for craftsmanship, and Livingston was not happy about the choice, but he had no alternative.

The vindication took the form of a thirty-one-page *Preface,* which appeared in February, 1754. Since neither Parker nor Gaine would permit it to be advertised in their newspapers, Livingston was compelled to announce its appearance in a broadside.[89] He promised buyers a full exposé of the arbitrary and wicked craft by which "some *Episcopal Bigots*" had silenced him, and a full refutation of all the "vile Calumnies" of his adversaries. When the *Preface* appeared, however, it proved to be a disappointment. Written in haste, it contained none of Livingston's characteristic vigor and eloquence; its contents were merely a rehash of ideas already expressed in the *Reflector.* The only novelties were the account of Parker's treachery in suspending the journal so precipitously and Livingston's charge that "insidious and indirect practices" had been employed by the Anglicans to secure that end. The title page of the *Preface* bore the ominous inscription: "The Independent Reflector . . . Printed (until tyrannically suppressed) in MDCCLIII." The publication assailed priestcraft in general and the "scurrilous scribblers" of the *Mercury* in particular; defended Livingston's peculiar brand of "unadulterated" Christianity, free of the "voluminous rubbish and pious villainy of ecclesiastics"; disavowed any hostility to religion as such; disclaimed any intention of promoting Presbyterianism at the expense of either the Episcopal or Dutch Reformed faiths; and reiterated the *Reflector's* opposition to the "unreasonable encroachments" of the Church of England and not to its religious tenets.

The college came in for extended discussion. Livingston reviewed the entire affair, renewing his demand for a "public academy" and charging the Anglicans with responsibility for slowing progress on the project. Anglican pretensions had aroused his opposition, and Anglican obstinacy would assure a continued fight for a "free" college, where children of all Protestant persuasions would possess a "perfect parity of privileges" and where superstition would not make its "gloomy abode" nor persecution "unfurl his bloody standard."[90]

Anglican clergymen were neither impressed nor disturbed by the appearance of Livingston's latest diatribe, and none considered it worth a reply. They decided, in fact, to terminate their paper warfare. For the next ten months, the columns of both the *New-York Mercury* and the *New-York Gazette* were silent on the college affair. The Anglicans were confident that the battle was won and that Lieutenant Governor James De Lancey would grant the desired charter on the terms outlined by spokesmen of the Church.

Livingston confessed in private that the first round had been lost. The lottery trustees had invited the Episcopal cleric, Dr. Johnson, to accept the presidency of the college, and Trinity Church had added an offer of an assistancy at £150 per annum more. Only the *Reflector's* "gallant Opposition" had prevented churchmen from monopolizing the governance of the academy. There were some grounds for optimism, however. The Dissenters were beginning to rouse themselves; the Church's "unreasonable Encroachments" had been exposed; the residents of Queens County were preparing a legal challenge to the local Episcopal parson's right to a salary from public funds. To yield in the face of apparent defeat was not even remotely in Livingston's thoughts. The battle for a "free generous and Catholic" academy would go on; and if the conflict required weapons more sturdy than a quill, they would be found. "If a Man must be knocked down," Livingston wrote his brother, "at all rates he may as well fall fighting, as running away."[91]

The contest over the founding of King's College was even more protracted and more exciting than the controversy over the *Reflector,* but it is a tale worth telling independently.[92] For the next two years the battle was waged in the chambers of the lottery trustees, the Assembly, the Council, and "out of doors"—in the taverns, the streets, and "the fields." Nor were the printing presses silent for very long. In addition to broadsides and pamphlets, two new essay series were set off by the controversy. The first was a serialized column in the *New-York Mercury* titled "The Watch-Tower." Its authors were, like those of the *Reflector,* shrouded in the familiar anonymity of obscure signatures, but the camouflage fooled no one. Episcopal penmen had no doubt that "whatever new Names they have since been pleased to take, whether Philo-Reflector, Reverberator, Watch-Tower, or Querist, still you may read the Reflector in all."[93] The Anglicans responded with a shorter-lived paper, titled *John Englishman, In Defence of the English Constitution;* and what they could not crowd into its two-page issues, they included in separate communications to the *Mercury*.[94] That newspaper became so filled with contentious articles by both disputants that Gaine, its publisher, was frequently compelled to print a supplement to carry the regular news and advertising!

The Anglicans ultimately received their charter, but Livingston's political strength in the Assembly was sufficient to deny them the lottery funds or legislative approval. The Episcopalians opened the college in July, 1754, but as a "child of bitterness," it remained weak and insecure in the face of the triumvirate's continuing assault. Lieutenant Governor De Lancey expected that his grant of the charter would increase his political influence with churchmen both at home and abroad, but his action only harvested him a bitter crop of political animosity. Anglicans criticized him for failing to silence the *Reflector* coterie or to secure the lottery funds for the charter college. The Livingstons were able to employ the college issue as the rallying point around which to unite dissident Dutch, Presbyterian, and anti-gubernatorial elements into a new political party, the most formidable the De Lanceys had ever faced. There was good reason why De Lancey, with considerable asperity, refused to attend meetings of the King's College Trustees. He had already contributed enough to their cause, he remarked sharply, in the loss of his reputation and "the breaches upon his popularity without doors."[95]

The official end of the controversy came in December, 1756, when a political deal resulted in a division of the lottery funds between King's College and the Corporation of the City of New York. The latter would use its half of the money for erecting a new jail and house of detention for the crews of infected ships. William Smith, Sr., could not miss the wry humor of the situation: the financial compromise rid the province of its bone of contention by dividing the money "between the two pest houses."[96] Dr. Samuel Johnson was sanguine that the compromise would permit the college to flourish free of political factionalism; De Lancey expected the settlement to reunite his party in the Assembly; the legislators were eager to eliminate an issue that had "kindled such a flame" in the province.[97] Honors were about even. The Anglicans secured their charter college but without public support. The Livingstons failed to secure their free college but denied the Episcopalians legislative sanction for their own.

Only William Livingston remained unreconciled and unsatisfied. He viewed the compromise as a defeat, and he found its memory too odious to recall a year later. To Welles he wrote:

> Relative to the affair of the Coledge; we stood as long as our legs would support us, and, I may add, even fought for some time, on our Stumps; but to recount, at present, the particular manner in which we were vanquished, *Animus meminisse Horret Luctuque refugit.*[98]

A decade later, Livingston could remember the affair with less rancor, but the passage of time did nothing to moderate the intensity of his earlier convictions. Writing to his son, he observed:

> You are very severe on our famous New York College, but I believe not more sarcastical than it deserves. It makes indeed a most contemptible Figure, and I rejoice that I have been so greatly instrumental in giving it the *betale vulnus* in its first origination. The partial bigotted and iniquitous plan upon which it was constructed deserved the opposition of every Friend of civil and religious Liberty, and the clamour I raised against it in conjunction with two or three friends when it was first founded on its present narrow principles, it has not yet and probably never will totally silence.[99]

Livingston's suspicions of the college were not shared by other members of his family. Some served on the college Board of Trustees, and others sent their sons to it; but until the Revolution, the public at large viewed the institution as the ill-begotten offspring of the De Lancey-Church "interest." It did not receive popular support, and it did not exert much influence. Yet in many respects King's College was more liberal than Yale. Dr. Johnson at the outset assured New Yorkers that students would not be compelled to attend Episcopal services on the Sabbath nor would the faculty impose on the scholars "the peculiar Tenets of any particular Sect of Christians." The same could not be said of the New Haven institution, where students were required to attend Congregational services and received heavy doses of its theology in the classroom.[100] Nevertheless, the New York college continued to carry the stigma of illiberality and narrow sectarianism which the *Independent Reflector* first affixed to it in 1753. When a writer in a journal of 1790 remarked that the college did not flourish before the Revolution because of the "contracted" plan upon which it was first founded, he was paying high tribute to Livingston's skill as a propagandist.[101]

The *Reflector's* contemporary popularity is more readily inferred than demonstrated. No subscription list has been located, but if the names inscribed in sets that survive are any measure, the journal's audience was wide. Franklin, among other Philadelphians, received both the *Reflector* and the *Reverberator*. Bostonians read the paper and its printers found some of the essays attractive enough to reprint in their own magazines.[102] John Adams knew of the triumvirate as the authors of the *Reflector* long before he met them in 1774, and Princeton students, on the eve of the Revolution, were using the paper's essays as models for their undergraduate declamations, finding them admirable for "energy and eloquence." The *Reflector's* popularity survived the Revolution, even though Episcopal clergymen dismissed the essays as the "fleeting foibles of their day." When Mathew Carey launched the *American Museum* at the end of the war, essays from the *Reflector* found a ready place among its contents.[103] Even in the twentieth century, the editor of a small Minnesota paper could find in the "honest old type" of the *Reflector* cause for admiration; and when a reader compared the modern periodical to its colonial forebear, the Minnesota editor accepted the compliment, observing: "However successful The Bellman may be in emulating the high principles, the courage, the truth and fidelity of the Independent Reflector, it can never hope to equal it in the use of elegantly polite language."[104]

The *Reflector's* importance stemmed from its substance far more than from its style. Its essays on education helped to plant the seed of revolt against the traditional system of church-controlled schooling which bore final fruit in 1787 with the establishment of the University of the State of New York. The plan of a Board of Regents, nonsectarian in character, appointed by the legislature, and charged with the civic responsibility of supervising the education of all of the state's youth bears a striking similarity to Livingston's proposals.[105] In the essays on religion and government the colonists found a textbook in Whig political theory especially adaptable to American use. New Yorkers employed the principles two decades later to good advantage; and if they voiced these principles with particular ease, it was because their schooling in "popular" theories had begun early.[106] Livingston was no democrat, but his political philosophy was broad enough to appeal to both future Sons of Liberty and landholding aristocrats. He could not, of course, foresee the dilemma his radical Whiggism would pose two decades later for many of these "dilettante democrats" of the 1750s. Ultimately they would have to decide whether the bold principles and the high-flown rhetoric of the *Reflector* were worth the price of treason. William Smith, Jr., for one, decided they were not; and when the Revolution came, he remained loyal to the Crown. Livingston chose otherwise. He not only joined the patriot cause but helped to lead it. As a member of the Continental Congress, commander of New Jersey's militia, governor of the state throughout the Revolution, and one of the ablest and most effective propagandists on the American side, he gave convincing proof that the fervid language of the *Independent Reflector* and its "independent" theories of government were not those of a "sunshine soldier" or a "summer patriot."

Notes

1. New York's second experiment in periodical literature was Samuel Loudon's *American Magazine* (Dec. 1787 - Nov. 1788).

2. *The American Magazine, or Monthly Chronicle,* published by William Bradford and edited by Rev. William Smith, Provost of the Philadelphia College. The earliest American magazines are analyzed comprehensively in Lyon N. Richardson, *A History of Early American Magazines, 1741-1789* (New York, 1931) and discussed more generally in Frank Luther Mott, *A History of American Magazines, 1741-1850* (New York and London, 1930).

3. Mott, *American Magazines,* 40, 79; Richardson, *Early American Magazines,* 34, 37-46. For the earliest English prototypes of American magazines, see Walter Graham, *English Literary Periodicals* (New York, 1930), chap. 5.

4. *The New-England Magazine* (Boston), I (Aug. 1758), 8.

5. *The Boston Weekly Magazine,* March 2, 1743; *The American Magazine, or Monthly Chronicle* (Philadelphia), I (Oct. 1757), Preface, 4; announcement of Bradford's *American Magazine* (Philadelphia) in his newspaper, *The American Weekly Mercury,* Nov. 6, 1740, quoted in Anna J. DeArmond, *Andrew Bradford: Colonial Journalist* (Newark, Del., 1949), 225.

6. Richardson, *Early American Magazines,* chap. 2; DeArmond, *Bradford,* 223-239. Andrew Bradford was the publisher of the *American Magazine* and Benjamin Franklin of the *General Magazine.* Franklin thought so little of his journal that he did not mention it in his *Autobiography.*

7. Richardson, *Early American Magazines,* 45, 58-73; Elizabeth C. Cook, "Colonial Newspapers and Magazines" in the *Cambridge History of American Literature,* 4 vols. (Cambridge and New York, 1918-1921), I, 121.

8. The subtitle of the journal, in the *Preface* published early in 1754, was "Weekly Essays on Sundry Important Subjects. More particularly adapted to the Province of New-York."

9. Richardson, *Early American Magazines,* 74, 77; Robert Spiller et al., *The Literary History of the United States,* 3 vols. (New York, 1948-1949), I, 94.

10. Jones, *History of New York,* I, 7.

11. Livingston was born on Nov. 30, 1723. Theodore Sedgwick, Jr., *A Memoir of the Life of William Livingston* (New York, 1833), 45 note. Sedgwick gives this as the "probable" date. It is confirmed by an entry in the Family Bible of Mrs. Catherine Livingston, William's daughter, in the Massachusetts Historical Society.

12. Livingston to Alida Hoffman, Oct. 29, 1782, Livingston Papers, Mass. Hist. Soc.

13. The sole biography of the founder of the family, Leder's *Robert Livingston,* deals only incidentally with the manor and its management. There is no biography of Philip, the second manor lord.

14. The first composition was published in the *New-York Weekly Post-Boy* on Aug. 19, 1745; the second, in the same paper, on March 3, 1746.

15. On Livingston as a lawyer, see Chap. 6 below.

16. Livingston to Noah Welles, May 1742, Livingston-Welles Correspondence, Johnson Family Papers, Yale University (hereafter cited as JFP, Yale).

17. Livingston to Welles, June 16, 1747, April 16, 1748, JFP, Yale. Stopping in New Jersey in 1774, en route to the First Continental Congress, John Adams was told that Livingston even then was regarded as a good writer but a "bad speaker." John Adams, "Diary," in *The Works of John Adams,* ed. Charles F. Adams, 10 vols. (Boston, 1856-1866), II, 356.

18. Livingston to James Pemberton, Dec. 21, 1788, Etting Papers, "Washingtonia," Historical Society of Pennsylvania. Long before, Livingston had admitted his "prolixity" in a letter to Noah Welles (July 26, 1745, JFP, Yale).

19. Livingston to Welles, March 17, April 12, 1746, JFP, Yale. The MS of the prayer is in the Livingston Papers, Mass. Hist. Soc. Livingston's biographer and great-grandson, Theodore Sedgwick, Jr., discovered the original among some old family papers. He endorsed it: "I have never met with it before but often seen and heard it mentioned." Livingston's son, William, Jr., identified it as his father's. (William Livingston, Jr., to William Paterson, May 29, 1801, Livingston MSS, New York Historical Society.) The poem to Eliza appears in part in Sedgwick, *Memoir,* 117-118; the complete manuscript is in the Livingston Papers, Mass. Hist. Soc. The playwriting effort was disclosed to Miss E— T—, Nov. 17, Dec. 29, 1744, in Letter Book, 1744-1745, Sedgwick Papers, Mass. Hist. Soc.

20. See Edwin T. Bowden, "Benjamin Church's *Choice* and American Colonial Poetry," *N. Engl. Qtly.,* XXXII (1959), 170-184; also Stanley T. Williams, *The Beginnings of American Poetry* ([Uppsala, Sweden, 1951]), 42-49.

21. *Philosophic Solitude* (New York, 1747), vi. For uncomplimentary estimates, see Spiller et al., *Literary History,* I, 94; Moses C. Tyler, *A History of American Literature,* 2 vols. (New York, 1878), II, 219; and Charles Angoff, *Literary History of the American People,* 2 vols. (New York, 1931), I, 358-359. By a curious standard of judgment, a recent anthology of early American poetry omits Livingston's poem entirely, despite its typicality in genre and theme, on the ground that it was "less American" than other early verse attempts. See Kenneth Silverman, comp., *Colonial American Poetry* (New York and London, 1968), 1-3, 354.

22. Livingston to Welles, Sep. 19, 1747, JFP, Yale.

23. The unkind comment appeared in a review of Sedgwick's *Memoir* in the *American Quarterly Review,* XIV (1833), 5-6. A few years earlier, however, one of the first efforts to evaluate critically American writing praised the poem as "full of thought and point, and not destitute of elegance." Samuel L. Knapp, *Lectures on American Literature* (New York, 1829; reprinted, Gainesville, Fla., 1961), 169. For more recent favorable estimates, see Max Savelle, *Seeds of Liberty: The Genesis of the American Mind* (New York, 1948), 408-409, 417; and Louis B. Wright, *The Cultural Life of the American Colonies* (New York, 1957), 172.

24. A partial investigation reveals, in addition to New York editions of 1747, 1769, and 1790, a Boston edition of 1762 and a Trenton edition of 1782. The poem was reproduced in part in *The New-England Magazine,* I (Aug. 1758), 50-51; reprinted serially in the *Boston Magazine,* II (March-June

1785), 107-109, 147-148, 189-190, 227-228; and included in the *Columbian Muse, A Selection of American Poetry, from Various Authors of Established Reputation* (New York, 1794), 16-33; *American Poems, Selected and Original* (Litchfield, Conn., 1793), 154-175; and the *Young Gentleman and Lady's Monitor* . . . (New York, 1790), 325-342.

25. This extremely rare pamphlet, printed by John Zenger, Jr., was advertised for sale in the *New-York Weekly Journal,* March 20, 1749. There is a copy in the Columbia University Library. The most recent and comprehensive inventory of early American printing does not properly ascribe authorship to Livingston. (Clifford K. Shipton and James E. Mooney, *National Index of American Imprints through 1800: the Short Title Evans,* 2 vols. [Worcester, Mass., 1969]). Livingston disclosed his authorship in a letter to Noah Welles, Feb. 18, 1749, JFP, Yale. The pamphlet does not appear to have sold well. Six months after its appearance, the printer was still advertising copies for sale. See *New-York Weekly Journal,* Sep. 25, 1749.

26. *The Colonial Laws of New York,* 5 vols. (Albany, 1894), III, 607-616, 679-688, 731-732.

27. The target of Livingston's attack was camouflaged as "Selyn Molouck," and Livingston's own pseudonym was "Solomon Bensirach." The pamphlets are referred to in the *New-York Evening Post,* Nov. 14, 1748. A manuscript version of one is in the Livingston Papers, Mass. Hist. Soc. For his rejoinder Livingston selected another pseudonym, "Don John Ferdinando Scribblous." The defense, signed "G. B.," appeared in the *Evening Post,* Nov. 14; the author may have been Goldsbrow Banyar, Governor Clinton's secretary. Livingston's "Answer to a paper signed G. B." is in the Livingston Papers, Mass. Hist. Soc.

28. Clinton to the Duke of Newcastle, Nov. 18, 1745, *N. Y. Col. Docs.,* VI, 286; Philip Livingston to Jacob Wendell, Feb. 13, 1747, Livingston Papers, Museum of the City of New York.

29. The pamphlet was dated Aug. 22, 1750. The only copy located is that of the Library of Congress. The attribution of authorship is somewhat circuitous. In October 1750, there appeared a publication titled *A Reply to A Letter from a Gentleman in New-York, To his Friend in Brunswick* also signed "Tribunus Populi." The writer acknowledged himself to be the author of the earlier *Letter to the Freemen.* James Alexander identified the author of the *Reply,* in private correspondence, as "W— L—." See Alexander to Robert Hunter Morris, Oct. 26, 1750, Stevens Family Papers, New Jersey Historical Society, Newark, N.J. (formerly in the Stevens Institute of Technology, Hoboken, N.J.); and Alexander to Cadwallader Colden, Jan. 2, 1751, *The Letters and Papers of Cadwallader Colden, 1711-1775,* 9 vols. (N.Y. Hist. Soc. *Collections,* 1917-1923, 1934-1935), IV, 249-250.

30. "Political Bill of Mortality for the Month of August in the Year 1750, in a Certain Quarter of the Town near the Bowling-green," printed in Sedgwick, *Memoir,* 65. The manuscript is in the Livingston Papers, Mass. Hist. Soc. For the facts in this case, see Julius Goebel, Jr., and T. Raymond Naughton, *Law Enforcement in Colonial New York* (New York, 1944), 304-306.

31. *New-York Gazette,* Sep. 3, 1750; *A Letter to the Freemen and Freeholders* . . . ([Feb., 1752]). No copy of the latter publication has been located, but it was advertised in the *New-York Gazette* for Feb. 10 and 17, 1752. Livingston's authorship is suggested by the similarity in title to the *Letter* of 1750 and by Philip Livingston's broad hint to his brother Robert that the pamphlet was "wrote . . . by a relation of ours." Philip to Robert Livingston, Feb. 15, March 25, 1752, Livingston-Redmond Papers, Hyde Park, N.Y.

32. On these activities, see Chap. 6 below.

33. Peartree Smith was graduated from Yale in 1742, one year after Livingston. He was related to William Smith, Jr., through his grandfather, the elder Smith's uncle. See Franklin B. Dexter, ed., *Biographical Sketches of the Graduates of Yale College,* 6 vols. (New Haven, 1885-1912), I, 719-720; Maturin L. Delafield, "William Smith, Judge of the Supreme Court of the Province of New York," *Magazine of American History,* VI (1881), 264-282, especially 264, 271, 273-274; Thomas J. Wertenbaker, *Princeton, 1746-1896* (Princeton, 1946), 14-15.

34. The only book that treats the three as a group is Dorothy R. Dillon, *The New York Triumvirate: A Study of the Legal and Political Careers of William Livingston, John Morin Scott, William Smith, Jr.* (New York, 1949). Its emphasis is on the trio's later collaboration rather than their activities in the mid-18th century.

35. Colden to the Secretary of State and the Board of Trade, Dec. 6, 1765, *Colden Letter Books,* II, 71; Johnson to Thomas Secker, March 1, 1759, *Samuel Johnson, President of King's College: His Career and Writings,* eds. Herbert and Carol Schneider, 4 vols. (New York, 1929), I, 283.

36. Livingston to Welles, Oct. 6, 1745, Feb. 10, 1746, JFP, Yale; Livingston to Chauncey Whittelsey, Aug. 23, 1744, Letter Book, 1744-1745, Sedgwick Papers, Mass. Hist. Soc.

37. Livingston to Welles, Nov. 27, 1746, Jan. 27, 1747, JFP, Yale; Smith, *Some Critical Observations upon A late Poem, entitled The Breeches . . .* (New York, 1750). For this and Smith's other early writings, see Beverly McAnear, "American Imprints Concerning King's College," *Papers of the Bibliographical Society of America,* XLIV (1950), 306-307 note.

38. For the critical view, see Jones, *History,* I, 4; also Roger Wines, "William Smith, the Historian of New York," *N.Y. Hist.,* XL (1959), 3-17, particularly 5-6. The most perceptive appraisal of Smith's character is by Michael Kammen in his introduction (I, xvii-xxxvii) to the new edition of Smith's *History,* 2 vols. (Cambridge, Mass., 1972).

39. Edwin B. Livingston, *The Livingstons of Livingston Manor* (New York, 1910), 19-20, 54-55, 540; Maria S. B. Chance and Mary A. E. Smith, eds., *Scott Family Letters* (Philadelphia, 1930), 11, 318, 335; Delafield, "William Smith, Judge," *Magazine of American History,* VI (1881), 276, "William Smith—The Historian," *ibid.,* 418-439, particularly 431.

40. On the religious affiliations of the triumvirate, see Jones, *History,* I, 4, 41 note; "Memoir of the Honourable William Smith," in Smith, *History,* I, x, xiv-xv; Livingston to Rev. Aaron Burr, May 29, 1754, Letter Book A, 1754-1770, Livingston Papers, Mass. Hist. Soc.; Dillon, *New York Triumvirate,* 18 note.

41. The club's existence was disclosed by a newspaper controversy with its critics. See *New-York Weekly Journal,* Feb. 13, 27, March 20. April 3, 1749, Oct. 8, 1750; "To the Publick," n.d., William Smith Papers, New York Public Library.

42. Livingston to Welles, Feb. 18, 1749, JFP, Yale. Thomas Jones' characterization of the Philosophic Society as a Whig Club (*History,* I, 5-6, 221) is repeated in Charles H. Levermore, "The Whigs of Colonial New York," *Am. Hist. Rev.,* I (1896), 242; Becker, "Nominations in Colonial New York," *ibid.,* VI (1901), 273; Wilbur C. Abbott, *New York in the American Revolution* (New York and London, 1929), 44; and Richard B. Morris, ed., *The Era of the American Revolution* (New York, 1939), 269-270. The charge that the *Reflector* was launched to inaugurate a new political party appears in Beverly McAnear's writings: "Politics in Provincial New York, 1689-1761" (unpublished Ph.D. dissertation, Stanford U., 1935), 775-777; "Mr. Robert R. Livingston's Reasons against a Land Tax," *Journal of Political Economy,* XLVIII

(1940), 68 note; and "American Imprints Concerning King's College," *Papers of the Bibliographic Society,* XLIV (1950), 307.

43. *New-York Gazette,* Jan. 6, 1755. On Parker's difficulties in 1747, see *Journal of the Votes and Proceedings of the General Assembly of the Colony of New-York,* [1691-1765], 2 vols. (New York, 1764-1766), II, 173-180, 192-193, 202, 272; on the 1752 incident, *New-York Gazette,* April 27, May 11, 1752; Goebel and Naughton, *Law Enforcement,* 153-154; Franklin to Cadwallader Colden, May 14, 1752, *Colden Papers,* IV, 324-325.

44. Jones, *History,* I, 5.

45. The draft of the first issue of the *Reflector,* bearing the "Guardian" title, is in the William Smith Papers, New York Public Library. *The Guardian* in England began in March, 1713, three months after the demise of the *Spectator,* and continued until October.

46. Clinton Rossiter, in his *Seedtime of the Republic* (New York, 1953), called attention to the enormous impact of Gordon's and Trenchard's writings in colonial America, but it took almost another decade for historians to spell out the implications of his observation. This has more than adequately been done since by Caroline Robbins in her *Eighteenth Century Commonwealthman* (Cambridge, Mass., 1959), 115-125, and by Bernard Bailyn in his *Ideological Origins of the American Revolution* (Cambridge, Mass., 1967), 35-36 and *passim.* The writings of Gordon and Trenchard have been made available to modern American audiences by David L. Jacobson's edition of their works, *The English Libertarian Tradition* (Indianapolis, 1965). Biographical information is available in Jacobson, introd.; *Dictionary of National Biography,* VIII, 230-231, and XIX, 1125-1126; and in Charles B. Realey, *The London Journal and Its Authors, 1720-1723* (University of Kansas Humanistic Studies, 1935), 237-274.

47. The tangled publication history of both the *Whig* and *Cato's Letters* is treated in Jacobson, introd., lxi-lxiii. The eighth edition of the *Whig* is dated 1752, but there appear to have been at least eight before then. The figures given in the text above are from Realey, who is in error, however, in noting a French edition. The text was in French, but the edition was published in Holland. The two American editions of the *Whig,* both published in Philadelphia, were in 1724 and 1740. *Cato's Letters* first appeared in a collected version in 1721 and thereafter was reprinted in other editions, perhaps as many as eight, by 1753.

48. DeArmond, *Bradford,* 16-17, 166-170; Elizabeth C. Cook, *Literary Influences in Colonial Newspapers, 1704-1750* (New York, 1912), 81-83 and *passim;* Hennig Cohen, *The South Carolina Gazette* (Columbia, S.C., 1953), 217-218; *New-York Weekly Journal,* Dec. 10, 1733; Samuel Johnson to the Archbishop of Canterbury, June 29, 1753, *N.Y. Col. Docs.,* VI, 777. Miss Robbins properly calls the essays of Gordon and Trenchard "the most famous" occasional political papers of the early 18th century (*Eighteenth Century Commonwealthman,* 392). Rossiter says that Gordon and Trenchard were more often invoked in defense of colonial liberties than was John Locke (*Seedtime of the Republic,* 141); and Bailyn documents the generalization (*Ideological Origins,* 36).

49. *New-York Gazette,* Feb. 19, 1753; *The Craftsmen: A Sermon from the Independent Whig . . .* (New York, 1753). The latter was a republication by the triumvirate of a work by Gordon, to which they added a new preface, "Suitable to the peculiar Malignity of the present Day." The allusions to Gordon and Trenchard are in the preface, ii. xxvi. Livingston quoted *Cato's Letters* in the *Reflector,* No. XLIII (Sep. 20, 1753) and made more frequent complimentary references to Gordon and Trenchard in his later newspaper series, "The Watch-Tower," *New-York Mercury,* Jan. 13, March 3, Sep. 15, 1755.

50. *Independent Reflector,* No. LI (Nov. 15, 1753).

51. See *ibid.,* No. VI (Jan. 4, 1753) and *Preface,* 3; Livingston to Rev. John Mason, May 29, 1778, in Sedgwick, *Memoir,* 288-290; Livingston to Henry Laurens, Feb. 5, 1778, Laurens Papers, South Carolina Historical Society.

52. Livingston to Welles, July 23, 1747, Dec. 15, 1753, JFP, Yale. See Alexander J. Wall, "The Controversy in the Dutch Church in New York concerning Preaching in English," N.Y. Hist. Soc. *Quarterly Bulletin,* XII (1928), 39-58; and Nelson R. Burr, "The Episcopal Church and the Dutch in Colonial New York and New Jersey, 1664-1784," *Hist. Mag. P. E. Church,* XIX (1950), 90-109, especially 103-107. Livingston himself left the Dutch Church because he could no longer understand the sermons preached in Dutch, even though he could still read the language. As a Presbyterian, he continued to lament the decline of the Dutch Church and to urge the appointment of an English-speaking minister. On the language question in the Dutch Church, see Corwin, ed., *N.Y. Ecclesiastical Records,* IV, 2582-2583, 3037-3038; and James Tanis, *Dutch Calvinistic Pietism in the Middle Colonies* (The Hague, 1967), 73-78.

53. Livingston to Welles, July 23, Dec. 18, 1747, JFP, Yale; *Independent Reflector,* No. VI (Jan. 4, 1753). Like his contemporaries, Livingston was intensely anti-Catholic, but his hostility was more often expressed in political terms—by attacking French power in America—than by direct attacks on Catholic ritual or theology. See Sister Mary Augustina (Ray), *American Opinion of Roman Catholicism in the Eighteenth Century* (New York, 1936).

54. Livingston to Welles, July 23, Sep. 19, Dec. 18, 1747, March 12, April 16, 1748, JFP, Yale. The pamphlet was an English publication, Micaiah Towgood, *The Dissenting Gentleman's Answer to the Reverend Mr. White's Three Letters; in which The Church of England and the Church of Jesus Christ, are . . . found to be . . . of a quite Different Nature* (New York, 1748). The London edition had been published in 1746. The exchange in England was being carried on with Rev. John White, Fellow of St. John's College, Cambridge.

55. Livingston to Welles, Feb. 18, 1749, [March, 1751?], April 7, 1751, JFP, Yale. The second phase of this literary warfare was carried on between Noah Hobart, the Congregationalist minister at Fairfield, Conn., and James Wetmore, the Episcopal rector at Rye, New York.

56. The Ministry Act of 1693 provided for public support of "a good sufficient Protestant Minister" in the counties of New York, Queens, Westchester, and Richmond. (*Colonial Laws of New York,* I, 328-331.) Elected vestries of six parishes were empowered to levy local taxes for this purpose. Although the intention of the Assembly had not been to establish the Episcopal Church by this plan, the interpretation of successive royal governors produced that effect. When the Anglican Trinity Church in New York City received its charter in 1697, it enjoyed the exclusive benefits of the Ministry Act in the county of New York, and its minister was supported by public taxation. See R. Townsend Henshaw, "The New York Ministry Act of 1693," *Hist. Mag. P. E. Church,* II (1933), 199-204; Charles C. Tiffany, *History of the Protestant Episcopal Church in the United States of America* (New York, 1895), 165-166; Morgan Dix, *A History of the Parish of Trinity Church in the City of New York,* 4 vols. (New York, 1898), I, 80-88, 91-92; John W. Pratt, *Religion, Politics, and Diversity: The Church-State Theme in New York History* (Ithaca, N.Y., 1967), 39-48.

57. *N.Y. Ecclesiastical Records,* IV, 2392, 2547, 2565, 2601, 2624, 2635-2636, 2645-2646; Richard Webster, *History of the Presbyterian Church in America* (Philadelphia, 1857), 328-329; Ezra Hall Gillett, *History of the*

Presbyterian Church in the United States of America (Philadelphia, 1864), I, 10-16, 38; Samuel Miller, *Memoirs of Rev. John Rodgers* (New York, 1813), 136, 141-142; Charles W. Baird, "Civil Status of the Presbyterians in the Province of New York," *Magazine of American History*, III (1879), 593-628. After the failure of the last Presbyterian incorporation effort, William Smith, Jr., complained bitterly about "this unreasonable Instance of prelatic Partiality." Smith to Eleazar Wheelock, Jan. 30, 1768, Wheelock Papers, Dartmouth College.

58. Livingston to Welles, Jan. 3, 1756, JFP, Yale; Smith, *History*, I, 56.

59. The full title of the English periodical was *The Reflector: representing human affairs, as they are; and may be improved*. It was edited by a physician, Peter Shaw. Articles from the *Reflector* were reprinted in the *New-York Evening Post* on March 25, April 15, June 24, Sep. 2, 1751; and one appeared in the *New-York Gazette* on Feb. 10, 1755. Selections from it also ran in the *Boston Evening-Post* late in 1752 and early in 1753. For parallels between the *Independent Reflector* and the *Independent Whig*, see *Independent Reflector*, ed. Klein, Appendix III.

60. The first number of the *Reflector* was reproduced in the *New-York Gazette*, Dec. 4, 1752; the disparaging remarks appeared in the *New-York Mercury*, April 30, 1753.

61. The differences in the two printings may be readily observed by comparing the two sets of the *Reflector* at the Henry E. Huntington Library, San Marino, California (107794 and 107797). They include variations in ornamentation in Nos. III, IV, and VI, the colophon at the end of No. IV, and the pagination of No. III. See McAnear, "American Imprints Concerning King's College," *Papers of the Bibliographical Society*, XLIV (1950), 308 note.

62. Samuel Johnson to the Archbishop of Canterbury, Oct. 20, 1759, in *Samuel Johnson Writings*, IV, 51.

63. Clarence S. Brigham, *Journals and Journeymen: A Contribution to the History of Early Newspapers* (Philadelphia, 1950), 19-20; Arthur M. Schlesinger, *Prelude to Independence: The Newspaper War on Britain, 1764-1776* (New York, 1958), 54, 303-304; Mott, *History of American Magazines*, 14.

64. The population of New York City in 1749 was 10,926 whites and 2,368 Negroes. It is estimated that half the white population was adult. See *N.Y. Doc. Hist.*, I, 695.

65. Livingston to Welles, Jan. 17, Feb. [19?], 1753, JFP, Yale; David Marin Ben Jesse, *A Letter to the Independent Reflector* (New York, 1753). The author's name was a pseudonym for the Reverend Theodore Frelinghuysen. For this identification, see McAnear, "American Imprints Concerning King's College," *Papers of the Bibliographical Society*, XLIV (1950), 327-328 note. The controversial sixth number, Jan. 4, 1753, was "A Vindication of the MORAVIANS, against the Aspersions of their Enemies."

66. Livingston's vindication of himself appeared in the *Reflector*, No. XI, Feb. 8, 1753. The Anglican response was in the *New-York Mercury*, Feb. 12, 1753, and Smith's defense in the *New-York Gazette, or Weekly Post-Boy*, Feb. 19. Additional defenses of the *Reflector* appeared in Nos. XV (March 8, 1753) and XXXI (June 28, 1753).

67. *A Scheme for the Revival of Christianity* (New-York, 1753), and Francis Squire, *An Answer to some late Papers, Entitled, The Independent Whig* (New-York, 1753). The latter was a reprint of a 1723 English publication. On these and other pamphlets issued during this phase of the contest, see McAnear, "American Imprints Concerning King's College," *Papers of the Bibliographical Society*, XLIV (1950), 311-313.

68. *The Craftsmen: A Sermon from The Independent Whig. Suitable to the peculiar Malignity of the present Day . . .* (New York, 1753). The preface was dated Aug. 22, and the publication appeared in September. The manuscript of the preface is in the William Smith Papers, New York Public Library. It was written by Livingston and Smith and corrected by Scott.

69. Livingston to Welles, Feb. [19?], 1753, JFP, Yale.

70. *Independent Reflector, Preface,* 14.

71. Livingston to Welles, Jan. 13, 1746, JFP, Yale; *Some Serious Thoughts on the Design of erecting a College in the Province of New-York* (New York, 1749), 1. Livingston's complaint was reiterated by men like Cadwallader Colden, who informed the English authorities that nothing had been more neglected in New York than education and that the "only Principle of Life propagated among the young People is to get money," men being "esteemed only according to what they are worth, that is, the money they are possessed of." [Cadwallader Colden] to [Rev. Hezekiah Watkins], [December 12, 1748], SPG MSS, B-20, 86-88, Archives of the Society for the Propagation of the Gospel in Foreign Parts, London.

72. See Beverly McAnear, "College Founding in the American Colonies, 1745-1775," *Miss. Valley Hist. Rev.,* XLII (1955), 24-55. A recent study suggests that the college founders were also motivated by anxiety that colonial values were being destroyed by rising affluence and declining piety. See Margaret W. Masson, "The Premises and Purposes of Higher Education in American Society" (unpublished Ph.D. dissertation, U. of Washington, 1971).

73. "The Watch-Tower," XLII, *New-York Mercury,* Sep. 8, 1755.

74. *Colonial Laws of New York,* III, 607-616, 679-688, 731-732, 842-844. The trustees announced that they would meet regularly at the City Hall to receive requests for loans and proposals for the location of the college. *New-York Gazette,* Jan. 20, March 23, 1752.

75. Samuel Johnson to Cadwallader Colden, April 15, 1747, *Colden Papers,* III, 374-375; Johnson to Bishop George Berkeley, Sep. 10, 1750, Thomas B. Chandler to Johnson, Feb. 6, 1753, *Samuel Johnson Writings,* I, 137, 166; James Wetmore to the SPG, June 25, 1753, quoted in W. W. Kemp, *The Support of Schools in Colonial New York by the Society for the Propagation of the Gospel in Foreign Parts* (New York, 1913), 42 note. The number of Anglicans in New York at the mid-century can only be estimated. Smith (*History,* I, 284) gave their number as one-fifteenth of the total population, but this is probably an underestimate. About 13 percent of the churches in 1750 were Anglican. (See Edwin S. Gaustad, *Historical Atlas of Religion in America* [New York, 1962], 167.) The 10 percent figure used in the text is Corwin's in *N.Y. Ecclesiastical Records,* V, 3612.

76. Lewis Morris to the Secretary of the SPG, [1702], SPG Archives, I, 171 (transcript), College Papers, I, Columbia University; Dix, *Trinity Church,* I, 141, 145. The Queen's Farm property was first leased to Trinity by Governor Benjamin Fletcher in 1697 and finally deeded to the church by Lord Cornbury eight years later.

77. Dix, *Trinity Church,* I, 258. The value of the property has been estimated at £7–8,000. See Arthur P. Middleton, "Anglican Contributions to Higher Education in Colonial America," *Pennsylvania History,* XXV (1958), 259.

78. Vestry of Trinity Church to the SPG, Nov. 3, 1755, SPG MSS, B–2, No. 315, SPG Archives, London. Trinity's expectation of preferential status in the college in the light of its offer is plainly conceded by historians of the college. See, for example, Nathaniel F. Moore, *An Historical Sketch of Columbia College* (New York, 1846), 8–9; John B. Pine, "King's College and the Early Days of Columbia College," New York State Historical Association *Proceed-*

ings, XVII (1919), 110; John B. Langstaff, "Anglican Origins of Columbia University," *Hist. Mag. P. E. Church,* IX (1940), 257–260. There was certainly no question in Samuel Johnson's mind that the school over which he was asked to preside was to be an "Episcopal College" and "a Seminary of the Church." See *Samuel Johnson Writings,* I, 137; *N. Y. Col. Docs.,* VI. 777.

79. "The Watch-Tower," I, *New-York Mercury,* Nov. 25, 1754.

80. *New-York Mercury,* Nov. 6, 1752; *New-York Gazette* (Supplement), Nov. 7, 1752.

81. Livingston to Welles, Feb. [19?], 1753, JFP, Yale. A few weeks later, Livingston similarly informed James Alexander of his intended college essays, changing the anti-Episcopal temper of his words in deference to Alexander's membership in the Anglican Church. The chief objection stated was to the management of the college by "any particular religious Sect." "Independent Reflector" to Alexander, March 8, 1753, Rutherfurd Collection, III, New York Historical Society.

82. Jones, *History,* I, 12; Robert Livingston to Jacob Wendell, Dec. 13, 1754, Livingston Papers, Museum of the City of New York. A concurrent controversy, carried on with less heat, revolved around the location of the college—in the city or the country. On this, see David C. Humphrey, "Urban Manners and Rural Morals: The Controversy over the Location of King's College," *N. Y. Hist.,* LIV (1973), 5-23.

83. Samuel Johnson to the Bishop of London, June 25, 1753, King's College, Letters and Documents, 1753-1762, Columbia University. See particularly the following issues of the *New-York Mercury:* April 30, June 4, 11, July 9, 23, 30, Sep. 10, 24, Oct. 8, 15, 22, 1753.

84. By now, James Parker had closed the *Gazette* to both disputants, and Hugh Gaine, the printer of the Anglican *Mercury,* refused to allow the triumvirate to publish in his paper. Livingston assailed Gaine for his conduct in the *Reflector,* No. XL (Aug. 30, 1753), which was titled "Of the Use, Abuse, and Liberty of the Press." On this, see Paul L. Ford, ed., *The Journals of Hugh Gaine, Printer,* 2 vols. (New York, 1902), I, 9-10, 65.

85. *Independent Reflector, Preface,* 14. For a literary evaluation of the *Reverberator,* see Richardson, *Early American Magazines,* 89-91. The *Reverberator* appeared on Sep. 7, 14, 21, and Oct. 5, 1753. The manuscript of the first issue is in the William Smith Papers, New York Public Library.

86. The offensive number was titled "Of CREEDS and SYSTEMS, together with the Author's Own Creed" (Oct. 11, 1753). The manuscript of the 53rd issue, entitled "On the Importance Privileges and Duty of Gran[d] Juries," is in the William Smith Papers, New York Public Library.

87. William Smith, "An Epitaph on the Independent Reflector," n.d., in "List of old Papers written by W[illiam] S[mith]," William Smith Papers, Historical Society of Pennsylvania; *Independent Reflector, Preface,* 2, 26.

88. Livingston to Welles, Dec. 15, 1753, JFP, Yale; *Independent Reflector, Preface,* 2–3. By 1753, colonial printers were relatively immune to all threats except that of legislative action. Financial pressure, as in the case of the *Reflector,* was even more unusual. See Harold L. Nelson, "Seditious Libel in Colonial America," *Am. Journal Legal Hist.,* III (1959), 160–172; and Leonard W. Levy, *Legacy of Suppression* (Cambridge, Mass., 1960), chaps. 2, 4.

89. Dated Feb. 29, 1754, the broadside is bound with the New York Public Library set of the *Reflector.* There is another copy in the Peters Papers, III, Historical Society of Pennsylvania, and a reproduction in I. N. P. Stokes, *The Iconography of Manhattan Island,* 6 vols. (New York, 1915-1928), IV, 647. Livingston was also under the necessity of selling the *Preface* through a local bookbinder, Robert McAlpine, since De Foreest no longer had a shop of his own.

90. *Independent Reflector, Preface,* 2-3, 14-22, 24-25, 30-31.

91. Livingston to Welles, Feb. 1, 1754, JFP, Yale; to Robert Livingston, Feb. 4, 1754, Livingston-Redmond Papers, Hyde Park, N. Y.

92. There is no full account of the college controversy in print. Chapter 4 below provides a brief treatment. Histories of Columbia University are rather thin on the events surrounding its inception. The most comprehensive treatment of the literature of the controversy is McAnear, "American Imprints Concerning King's College," *Papers of the Bibliographical Society,* XLIV (1950), 301-339.

93. *New-York Mercury,* Dec. 30, 1754. *The Querist* was the title of one of the pamphlets born of this later phase of the controversy. Written by Livingston and Smith, it appeared late in 1754 and raised forty-eight questions concerning the Anglican-proposed charter. The "Watch-Tower" series ran from Nov. 25, 1754, to Nov. 17, 1755. A fifty-third number was published separately on Jan. 16, 1756.

94. *John Englishman* ran from April [9?] to July 5, 1755. Its principal authors were the Episcopal clergymen Thomas Bradbury Chandler, Samuel Auchmuty, and Samuel Seabury. On the authorship of this journal, see Bruce E. Steiner, *Samuel Seabury* ([Athens, Ohio], 1971), 93-94.

95. Smith, *History,* II, 238-239.

96. *Colonial Laws of New York,* IV, 104-105, 160-162; *Assembly Journal,* II, 512-513, 520; Smith, *History,* II, 238.

97. *Samuel Johnson Writings,* I, 35-36, 268, IV, 44.

98. Livingston to Welles, Aug. 8, 1757, JFP, Yale. The quotation is from *Aeneid,* II, 12: "My mind at the remembrance shudders, and from the grief recoils."

99. Livingston to William Livingston, Jr., July 15, [1768?], Livingston Papers, Mass. Hist. Soc.

100. *New-York Mercury,* June 3, 1754, Dec. 7, 1772; Louis L. Tucker, "The Church of England and Religious Liberty at Pre-Revolutionary Yale," *Wm. and Mary Qtly.,* XVII (1960), 314-328.

101. *The New-York Magazine,* I (May 1790), 256. The Reverend Andrew Burnaby, on his travels through New York in 1760, found the college to be "far from . . . flourishing"; and when Eleazar Wheelock sought in 1769 to secure a royal charter for Dartmouth, he expressed the hope that its provisions would be more liberal than that of King's, which he considered a "party college." Burnaby, *Travels through the Middle Settlements,* ed. Rufus R. Wilson, 117; Wheelock to Hugh Wallace, Sep. 30, 1769, in Frederick Chase, *A History of Dartmouth College* (2nd ed., Brattleboro, Vt., 1928), 115. Ironically, the college never became the Episcopal "seminary" intended by its founders: only one Episcopal priest was graduated from King's between 1761 and 1775 compared to eleven produced by Yale and Harvard. After the Revolution, the Episcopal Church lost interest in King's and in 1817 established the General Theological Seminary in New York City to train its ministers. See Frederick V. Mills, "Anglican Expansion in Colonial America, 1761-1775," *Hist. Mag. P. E. Church,* XXXIX (1970), 315-324, particularly 322; and John S. Whitehead, "The Separation of College and State: The Transformation of Columbia, Dartmouth, Harvard, and Yale from Quasi-Public to Private Institutions, 1776-1876" (unpublished Ph.D. dissertation, Yale, 1971), 34-35.

102. Franklin's sets of both journals are in the Princeton Library. The Library of Congress's set of the *Reflector* was owned by another Pennsylvanian. *The New-England Magazine* (Boston, 1758) reprinted No. XL of the *Reflector* in its first issue (August, pp. 33-38) and part of No. XLVI in its second (October, pp. 19-22).

103. *The Works of John Adams,* ed. C. F. Adams, II, 349; Sedgwick, *Memoir,* 96; James Madison to Theodore Sedgwick, Jr., Feb. 12, 1831, in *The Writings of James Madison,* ed. Gaillard Hunt, 9 vols. (New York, 1900-1910), IX, 441. No. XIII of the *Reflector* appeared in the *American Museum,* VIII (Oct. 1790), 176-178, and No. IX in VIII (Nov. 1790), 233-235.

104. William C. Edgar to William H. Dunwoody, Jan. 31, 1907; *The Bellman* (Minneapolis), Feb. 9, 1907; both bound with the copy of the *Independent Reflector* in the William L. Clements Library, Ann Arbor, Mich.

105. Sidney Sherwood, *The University of the State of New York: History of Higher Education in the State of New York* (Washington, D.C., 1900), 49-88, 92-99.

106. Rossiter, *Seedtime of the Republic,* 108; Bailyn, *Ideological Origins of the American Revolution,* 53, 250; Bailyn, *The Origins of American Politics* (New York, 1968), 128-130.

4.

Church, State, and Education: Testing the Issue in Colonial New York

FEW CONTEMPORARY issues have so painfully touched the raw nerve of American society as that of religion in education. The question of religion in the schools has been argued most bitterly and emotionally on the elementary and secondary level, but the colleges and universities have not escaped the controversy. Perhaps the only undebatable element of the question is the consensus that public funds should not be used to establish or support colleges which exclusively promote the interests of a single religious denomination. However ill-defined the character of the wall separating church and state may be, there is not much disagreement that a theological seminary cannot claim financial support from the public purse. To paraphrase somewhat Marshall's language in McCulloch v. Maryland, Let a college be founded under sectarian auspices, let its governing board be filled with clerics, let its curriculum be heavily larded with theology, let its students be compelled to attend compulsory denominational chapel services, and let its end be the advancement of the interests of a particular church—then it forswears all expectation of state patronage and endowment.

The principle of governmental nonsupport of church seminaries and its corollary of legislative support of civic-oriented, nondenomina-

Reprinted from *New York History*, XLV (October 1964), 291-303, by permission of the New York State Historical Association.

tional colleges did not spring full-blown from the American soil. Not until the American Revolution were colleges founded by state legislatures and in an atmosphere of public hostility to denominational education.[1] The colonial colleges were not molded entirely in the European pattern, but they were similar to their English counterparts in their religious orientation.[2] Recent studies have called attention to the civic as well as the religious purpose which motivated the founding of Harvard, Yale, and William and Mary.[3] The charters of these institutions did speak of the intention to advance "all good literature, arts and sciences" and to educate youth "in good Letters and Manners," but the ultimate end of the colonial colleges, by and large, was the propagation of the orthodoxy of a particular denomination.[4] In a heterogeneous society, each sect sought security for its members from the false dogmas of its competitors by a college that would aggressively and deliberately promote its own tenets. Only thus, it was believed, could each sect survive in the peculiarly cosmopolitan American climate.[5]

By 1750, four colleges had been founded in America, and each represented the religious zeal of a particular sect: Harvard and Yale, of varying shades of Puritanism; William and Mary, of the Church of England; and the College of New Jersey, of the New Side Presbyterianism that emerged from the Great Awakening. The first great challenge to the time-honored pattern of clerically dominated collegiate education came in New York in 1753. It was prompted by Anglican attempts to found a college of the traditional type under church auspices—the future King's College. The furious "clamour" raised by a trio of Presbyterian lawyers set the entire colony by its ears for three years, resounded from Boston to Philadelphia, subverted the Anglican proposal partially, and in the process gave colonial America a new ideology of higher education: public, civic, and liberal.

What these New York critics of traditional education proposed was a "free" rather than a "party" college, incorporated by the legislature, publicly supported and under legislative supervision, open to students of all Protestant denominations, without religious tests for its president or teachers or compulsory church attendance for its students. As if this departure from the conventional pattern were not enough, the New Yorkers added a philosophy of learning that was even more radical:

> The true Use of Education, is to qualify Men for the different Employments of Life, to which it may please God to call them . . . to improve their Hearts

and Understandings, to infuse a public Spirit and Love of their Country; to inspire them with . . . a fervent Zeal for Liberty, and a diffusive Benevolence for Mankind; . . . in a word, to make them more extensively serviceable to the Common-wealth. . . . [and] better Members of Society. . . .[6]

The novelty of these liberal sentiments would have jolted readers in any colony, but in New York they proved particularly inflammatory because of the already explosive religious situation. The seedbed of religious (and political) contention in the province was the heterogeneity of its population and the growing pretensions to power of the Anglican minority. New York had long developed a notoriety among Crown officials for the diversity of its religions. They were "of all sorts," Governor Andros reported in some irritation in 1678. A decade later, Governor Dongan reiterated the complaint, noting that there were only a few Anglicans and Catholics but an abundance of Quakers, Sabbatarians, Anti-sabbatarians, Jews, and Presbyterians—"in short of all opinions . . . some, and the most part of none at all."[7]

By the mid-eighteenth century, the Anglicans had not become much more numerous, but this had not prevented them from securing preferential treatment. A Ministry Act of 1693 and its subsequent interpretations by royal governors "established" the Church of England in the counties of New York, Richmond, Queens, and Westchester. Dissenting ministers had been arrested for preaching without gubernatorial license. New York City's Presbyterian Church had three times sought a charter of incorporation, and each time the opposition of Anglican churchmen had frustrated the design. Presbyterians, in turn, had managed to prevent Anglican churchmen from securing the exclusive right to perform marriages and had irritated the Episcopalians by helping to organize the College of New Jersey, which Anglicans regarded as simply another "engine to play against the church."[8] In 1750, Anglicans and Presbyterians eyed each other with suspicion. Churchmen stigmatized the Presbyterians as "republicans" in politics and "freethinkers" in religion. Dissenters viewed each Anglican victory as evidence of a "lust for dominion" which would ultimately lead to the suppression of all dissenting sects and a full Anglican church establishment.

Anglican churchmen could not have selected a more unlikely place to promote the idea of an Episcopal college than New York City in 1750. Not only were the Anglicans outnumbered by Dissenters in a ratio of nine to one, but they faced here an opposition leadership of intellectual talent and literary eloquence unequaled in any other colony. The anti-Anglicans were led by three Yale graduates dubbed "the triumvirate": William Livingston, William Smith, Jr., and John Morin Scott. All three were lawyers—and soon to be leaders of the New York bar—but they were also men of broad intellectual interests and literary ability. There was scarcely a single project for cultural improvement in mid-eighteenth-century New York in which they were not active: the organization of a "Society for the Promotion of Useful Knowledge"; the establishment of the New York Society Library; the codification of the New York laws; the founding of a law society, "The Moot"; the publication of New York's first magazine, *The Independent Reflector*.

Besides their common affection for the belles lettres and their desire to raise the cultural level of the colony, these three young men shared an intense suspicion of the Anglican Church and its encroachments on the rights not only of their own Presbyterian sect but of all the dissenting denominations in the colony. The Reverend Samuel Johnson, future president of King's College and a leading Episcopal churchman, vouchsafed the sting of their collective pen when he complained that arguing with them was like "fencing against a flail," so persistent were their efforts to oppose and discredit the Church. Johnson could not, however, dismiss them lightly: they were, he admitted, "a notable set of Young gentlemen of figure" in the province.[9]

Leadership of this talented triumvirate was provided by its eldest member, William Livingston, thirty years of age at the time of the college controversy. Livingston was the ablest and also the most unorthodox member of his family, the prominent owners of one of the largest manors in colonial New York. His deviations from the socially accepted norms of aristocratic society were already marked before he embarked on his crusade against King's College. He shocked his family by proposing a career as an artist rather than a lawyer. He publicly criticized the established system of legal apprenticeship so sharply that he was dismissed from his clerkship in one law office. He married without parental consent, escaping to New Jersey for a secret ceremony with a young lady already on the way to motherhood. But his opposition to the Anglican scheme to found a sectarian college was not the product of literary or social quixoticism.

Livingston was a true child of the Enlightenment. Nominally a New Side Presbyterian, he was by intellectual conviction a freethinker, or at least a rationalist, primitive Christian. "I am a sincere professor of the religion of Jesus," he informed his public, but he considered "the several distinctions amongst Protestants as more or less convenient, but no ways essential."[10] He had little use for forms, creeds, or rituals. He transferred his church affiliation from the Reformed Dutch to the Presbyterian simply because he regarded as absurd the continued use of Dutch as the language of the Reformed service. He rejected Old Side Presbyterianism as rigid, cold, and narrow; but he was equally hostile to the New Side evangelism spawned by the Great Awakening because of its extreme emotionalism. New York had long represented for him the politico-religious ideal, because its diversity of sects and its legal toleration assured everyone liberty of conscience. His proudest boast to a Connecticut confrere—a dissenting minister—was that in New York "a Man . . . may Serve his Maker after his own fashion without running the Risque of fine or imprisonment."[11] More generous than most of his coreligionists, he would extend such freedom to eccentric sects like the Moravians and even to the Deists. He was unsympathetic to the Deists on philosophical and theological grounds, but he welcomed their presence as a challenge to Christians to vindicate by argument their own belief in the Saviour and the divinity of Christianity.[12] Religious diversity and the free exchange of ideas represented for Livingston both spiritual and political desiderata. No one sect could secure political control of the colony, and no orthodoxy could gain acceptance as every pretended one was subject to the critical inquiry of unbelievers. "I believe," he wrote, "that if the Whole Kingdom professed one Religion, it would be of no Religion; and that the Variety of Sects in the Nation, are a Guard against the Tyranny and Usurpation of one over another."[13] Here is a theory of balanced government not unlike Madison's in *The Federalist* or of countervailing power espoused by modern economic theorists. Its expression in New York in the 1750s is remarkably prescient.

Livingston's hostility to the Anglican college proposal stemmed directly from his fear that it would be a nursery of religious orthodoxy, weaken the spirit of free inquiry in matters of faith, and strengthen the political influence of the Church of England. But his wholesale involvement in the debate over the New York college was not merely a partisan reaction to an Anglican proposal. Livingston was himself genuinely interested in education, and this interest antedated the King's College scheme. He complained frequently after leaving Yale of the poverty of New York's cultural resources, remarking that its young people were blockheads, loudmouths, or drunkards, and that its neglect of education was "shameful." He approved the establishment of the College of New Jersey in 1746—his brother was one of its original trustees, and its second president was an intimate friend of the Livingston family—and hoped that it would stimulate New York to follow the example. He applauded the several public lotteries authorized by the New York Assembly between 1746 and 1748 to raise funds for a college; and when he discovered that public interest in the project was flagging, he published a spirited essay on "the Advantages of a liberal Education" in order to encourage "so useful an undertaking."[14]

It was quite natural that when the monies raised by the lotteries—some £3,443—were vested by the legislature in a board of trustees, Livingston should be named one of its members.[15] His pleasure at this recognition of his reputation and interest in learning was quickly mixed with dismay when he discovered that no less than seven of the ten trustees were Anglicans. Two were of the Dutch Church; the tenth was Livingston himself. The suspicions which Livingston inferred from this unequal distribution of representation were confirmed by two public events of the next year. In March, 1752, the Anglican Trinity Church offered part of its property—the King's Farm—as the site of the proposed college, and an Episcopal spokesman proposed, in letters to the press, that the college be founded by royal charter, that Dr. Samuel Johnson, the Anglican pastor of Stratford, Connecticut, be named its president, and that Johnson be simultaneously designated a rector of Trinity Church.[16]

Livingston immediately took alarm. He confided his fears to his friend and classmate, Noah Welles, the Congregational minister at Stamford, Connecticut. A college chartered by the Crown and managed by Episcopal clergymen and trustees, as seemed likely, would infect the province with "Priestcraft and Bigotry" in less than fifty years. Not only would the college be ruined, but so would the colony, as its public offices became monopolized by the college's graduates. The only alternative, in Livingston's view, was a non-sectarian college, with no chair in divinity and no compulsory denominational prayers for the students. If theology needed to be studied, it should be done by the students privately.[17]

As Livingston appraised events, he concluded that the Anglican scheme would reproduce all the worst features of the existing denominational colleges and would also set a dangerous political precedent.

Anglicans were already claiming that the Church of England was legally established in New York, and a few years earlier they had made a determined effort to have bishops sent to America. Only the strength of the English Dissenters had frustrated the project.[18] Livingston and his Presbyterian cohorts feared that a concession to the Anglicans on the New York college would represent tacit acquiescence in the larger Episcopal contention that the Church deserved preferential treatment by law in the colony.

Anglicans vigorously denied that the college was part of a larger Church scheme or a precursor to the establishment of an American episcopate, but to Livingston the elements seemed distinctly present. The proposed charter for the college was to be requested by an Anglican-dominated board of trustees from an Anglican governor and an Anglican-controlled Council. It would be located on Episcopal church property and headed by a rector of Trinity Church, and its students would be subjected to compulsory church services in the Anglican liturgy. The latter aspect of the Anglican scheme was made public in a pamphlet which blandly argued the propriety of the prayer proposal because the Church of England already had "a preference by the Constitution of the Province."[19]

Livingston might well have chosen to contest the Anglican proposal along purely sectarian lines, as a threat to the rights of Dissenters, but he chose to argue his case on the broader grounds of popular rights, religious liberty, and liberal education. As such, his words commanded an intercolonial audience and assumed transcendent importance.

The battle which Livingston, Smith, and Scott launched against the King's College charter design was of three years' duration, and it was waged with an intensity that stunned Churchmen. "Had a new government, tyrannical, arbitrary, and despotic, been erected, the popish religion established, the presbyterians burned at the stake, and the Episcopalians their persecutors, more noise could not have been made, than was now excited about this charter." So recalled one Anglican, Thomas Jones, the historian of Revolutionary New York.[20] The juxtaposition of the college, episcopacy, civil liberty, and religious freedom in Jones's complaint is a tribute to Livingston's success in elevating the controversy to one of high principle.

The warfare between the Livingston group and its Anglican opponents was waged in two forums: the public prints and the legislative chambers. For the literary side of the campaign, the triumvirate had a ready-made weapon of public appeal in the *Independent Reflector,* the essay-journal founded by Livingston in November 1752. In six issues of this periodical, from March 22 to April 26, 1753, Livingston reiterated in pungent and passionate language the arguments against a traditional state-church college as proposed by the Anglicans and in favor of nondenominational and publicly controlled higher education.[21]

The starting point of Livingston's educational philosophy was the sensationalist psychology of John Locke. The youthful mind was tender and flexible, "like the ductile Wax," susceptible to almost any impression. The principles implanted in schools were difficult to eradicate, becoming a kind of "second Nature." Colleges were especially important, because of the variety of impressions received there. Harvard and Yale were perfect illustrations of the dangers of a "party college." The students received the dogmas of their teachers and instead of subjecting them to critical inquiry, spent all their time mustering evidence to support the college's orthodoxies. Such narrowly contracted seminaries would not only corrupt the minds of the students, but by a kind of diffusion destroy the civil and religious liberties of the whole community. The orthodoxy of the college would become the orthodoxy of the province's officialdom—drawn largely from the college's graduates—and ultimately of the colony itself.

Of all the prejudices to be feared, the worst was that implanted in tender minds by religious sectaries. Their partiality and bigotry would disseminate "blind Precepts, contracted Opinions, [and] inexplicable Mysteries" to students too innocent and raw to contest them. Freedom of thought would never penetrate the "contracted Mansions of systematic Learning" controlled by religious sectaries. The practical consequences of a "party college" were equally fearful. The jealousy of New York's myriad other sects would inevitably be aroused by that one which secured control of the college. Apart from the "general Discontent and Tumult" that would ensue, the college would not attract students. Parents of the sects excluded from the college's superintendency would send their sons elsewhere and would surely not contribute to the college's support.

In place of a privately chartered and denominationally controlled seminary, Livingston proposed a legislatively incorporated college under public management with a nondenominational constitution. The underlying premise of his argument for a public college was that society as a whole had the "indisputable Right to direct the Education of their youthful Members." A college should be a "mere civil Institution"; its aim, to make youth more "useful Members of the Community." It followed, therefore, that the teaching of religion had no place in such an academy—this was the province of the pulpit—and that the supervision of the college could not "with any tolerable Propriety be monopolized by any religious Sect."

The logic of his argument led Livingston straight to the conclusion that a public college could only be entrusted to the control and inspection of the legislature. *First,* because public money had been raised for the college's support, and only the legislature could properly determine and account for its use. *Second,* because only the legislature, representing the consensus of the community, could ensure that the college would not become a tool in the hands of one sect for the advancement of its own interest and the suppression of all others:

> For as we are split into so great a Variety of Opinions and Professions; had each individual his Share in the Government of the Academy, the Jealousy of all Parties combating each other, would inevitably produce a perfect Freedom for each particular Party.

Third, because the advancement of science and the improvement of literature were too important to be entrusted to any but the elected guardians of the public welfare. And, *fourth,* because only a legislatively incorporated college, in the hands of the people or their representatives, could prevent those "Attacks upon the Liberty and Happiness" of the citizens which might with impunity be perpetrated by trustees of a chartered college who were beyond the reach of the people's power.

Livingston did not confine himself to general principles. He outlined, in some detail, the constitution of a public academy. Its trustees would be elected by the legislature, with gubernatorial assent. The trustees would select the college president and, with him, make the college's by-laws, subject always to legislative confirmation. No religious profession in particular would be established, no professor of divinity appointed, and no religious test applied which might bar any Protestant from holding college office. Students should be free to attend their own churches on the Sabbath, and the daily chapel services would be nondenominational in character. Finally, Livingston insisted that "the Officers and the Collegians have an unrestrained

Access to all Books in the Library, and that free Conversation upon polemical and controverted Points of Divinity, be not discountenanced."

Moderate, and indeed limited, as these ideas appear today, they provoked a bitter response from Anglican proponents of a charter college. For the next two years, the press was filled with heated and intemperate charges and countercharges by the two sides. Each issued pamphlets in defense of its position; both launched weekly papers to carry on the running press war.[22] The torrent of words merely reiterated the viewpoints already set forth by each of the contestants; they add little to our understanding of the broad educational issues at stake. In the heated contest, Livingston's educational ideas were often lost to view as he shifted his ground from the college and the advancement of learning to the dangers of priestly domination, Episcopal Church establishment, and the extension of royal prerogative. In at least one additional instance, however, he managed to demonstrate that his concern for public control of education was not merely anti-Anglican in nature. One of the last issues of the *Independent Reflector* —it was "tyrannically suppressed" in late 1753—argued for a system of county grammar schools, managed by elected local boards of guardians, with the teachers paid from local taxes.[23]

Despite the literary eloquence and the intellectual force with which Livingston and his friends asserted their views, they failed to secure either the public grammar schools or the public college. The lower school proposal never even reached the stage of legislative consideration. The "free college" plan was introduced in the Assembly by Livingston's brother Robert, but it died there. Its principal tactical value was that the possibility of its passage prevented King's College from pressing for transfer of the lottery funds to its own coffers. Not until the end of 1756 was the affair finally terminated, under pressure of the approaching French and Indian War. A compromise divided the lottery money between the college and the City of New York, the latter to use its share for building a new jail and a house of detention for the crews of infected ships. As one wag put it, the settlement rid the Assembly of a troublesome bone of contention by dividing it "between the two pest houses."[24]

The indecisive finale should not obscure the significance of the King's College controversy in the educational history of New York. The college itself suffered until after the Revolution the stigma of the "partial," "bigoted," and "Church-interest" labels attached to it by Livingston and his coterie.[25] But the impress of the educational ideas expounded in the *Independent Reflector* was much more indelible. Nowhere in America had so powerful a plea for public education, from grammar school to college, yet appeared. Both the Dutch and the English in New York had employed public funds to establish grammar schools, but the appointment of teachers and the supervision of instruction had been delegated to the churches. The *Reflector's* proposal to vest such responsibility in elected, lay officials was strikingly original and remarkably liberal. The "free college" idea was equally novel for its time, even if limited in conception by modern standards. "Free" higher education, to Livingston, did not mean compulsory, universal, or tuition-free schooling. The liberality of education he contended for was in the spirit of instruction, and its freedom represented escape from narrow, sectarian domination.

Perhaps the most significant aspect of Livingston's proposals was his contention that supervision of the community's schools should not be abrogated to any private group but must be exercised by the community itself, through its elected representatives. It is this assumption which underlay the establishment of the University of the State of New York after the Revolution. New Yorkers did not have to look abroad to French educational philosophers for their models; they had theirs in Livingston's old "free college" idea. When, in 1787, New York accepted the principle that the Regents should exercise general powers of incorporation, visitation, and supervision over all the schools and colleges of the state, it vindicated Livingston's contention, three decades earlier, that

> If . . . it belongs to any to inspect the Education of Youth, it is the proper Business of the Public, with whose Happiness their future Conduct in life is inseparably connected. . . .[26]

With the establishment of a state supervisory body, New York rejected the last vestiges of the European spirit in education by removing the churches from control of the state's educational policy. The republican society which emerged from the Revolution was not yet ready to make a full commitment to the democratic ideal in education, but it had made a giant step forward by its recognition of the primacy of education among the responsibilities of a free society. The rationale for the decision was no different from that laid down in the *Independent Reflector* when it embarked on the King's College controversy: "When Men know their Rights, they will at all Hazards defend them. . . ."[27]

Notes

1. Frederick Rudolph, *The American College and University: A History* (New York, 1962), 35-36.

2. *Ibid.,* 18, 24, 26; Daniel J. Boorstin, *The Americans: The Colonial Experience* (New York, 1958), 171-172; Bernard Bailyn, *Education in the Forming of American Society* (Chapel Hill, 1960), 40-41; Richard Hofstadter and Walter P. Metzger, *The Development of Academic Freedom in the United States* (New York, 1955), 114.

3. Rudolph, *American College and University,* 6-7, 12; Hofstadter and Metzger, *Development of Academic Freedom,* 115-116; Richard Hofstadter and Wilson Smith, eds., *American Higher Education: A Documentary History,* 2 vols. (Chicago, 1961), I, 1-2; Lawrence A. Cremin, *American Education: The Colonial Experience* (New York, 1970), 212, 219-220.

4. See the Harvard Charter of 1650 and the Charter of the College of William and Mary, 1693, in Hofstadter and Smith, eds., *Documentary History,* I, 10, 33.

5. Bailyn, *Education in the Forming of American Society,* 40-41; Boorstin, *Colonial Experience,* 179; Hofstadter and Smith, eds., *Documentary History,* I, 4.

6. Livingston et al., *Independent Reflector,* ed. Klein, 172 (March 22, 1753).

7. *N.Y. Col. Docs.,* III, 262; *N.Y. Doc. Hist.,* I, 186.

8. Bridenbaugh, *Mitre and Sceptre,* chap. 5; Smith, *History,* I, 285, 294; Wertenbaker, *Princeton,* 13-23; *Samuel Johnson Writings,* I, 166.

9. *Samuel Johnson Writings,* I, 283; Johnson to the Archbishop of Canterbury, June 29, 1753, *N.Y. Col. Docs.,* VI, 777.

10. *Independent Reflector, Preface,* 31.

11. Livingston to Noah Welles, Sep. 17, 1746, JFP, Yale.

12. On the Moravians, see *Independent Reflector,* ed. Klein, 89-95; on Deism, *ibid.,* 396 note 3. For Livingston's religious objections to Deism, see Livingston to Welles, March 21, 1759, JFP, Yale.

13. *Independent Reflector,* ed. Klein, 391.

14. *Some Serious Thoughts on the Design of erecting a College in . . . New-York* (1749). On the authorship of this pamphlet, see Chap. 3, note 25 above. It was printed by John Zenger, son of the famous John Peter Zenger, and sold for nine pence.

15. *Colonial Laws of New York,* III, 842-844.

16. *New-York Mercury,* Nov. 6, 1752; *New-York Gazette* (Supplement), Nov. 7, 1752. The spokesman was William Smith, future Provost of the Philadelphia Academy. He also wrote a non-controversial essay on the subject of the college, *Some Thoughts on Education* (New-York, 1752).

17. Livingston to Welles, Feb. [19?], 1753, JFP, Yale.

18. Bridenbaugh, *Mitre and Sceptre,* 90-97; F. L. Hawks, "Efforts to Obtain the Episcopate before the Revolution," *Collections of the Protestant Episcopal Historical Society for the Year 1851* (New York, 1851), 145; Tiffany, *History of the Protestant Episcopal Church,* 269-270.

19. William Smith, *A General Idea of the College of Mirania* (New-York, 1753).

20. Jones, *History of New York,* I, 12.

21. The college essays were Nos. XVII-XXII. See *Independent Reflector,*

ed. Klein, 171-214. For a brief, interesting analysis of the college essays see Hofstadter and Metzger, *Development of Academic Freedom,* 188-191; for their political import, see Bailyn, *Origins of American Politics,* 128-129.

22. The fullest discussion of the literary phase of the controversy is in McAnear, "American Imprints Concerning King's College," *Papers of the Bibliographical Society,* XLIV (1950), 301-339.

23. *Independent Reflector,* ed. Klein, 419-425. This issue of the *Reflector* appeared on Nov. 8, 1753.

24. Smith, *History,* II, 191-192, 199-201, 231, 238-239; *Samuel Johnson Writings,* I, 35-36.

25. *New-York Mercury,* Nov. 9, 16, 1772; *The New-York Magazine,* I (May 1790), 256; McAnear, "American Imprints Concerning King's College," *Papers of the Bibliographical Society,* XLIV (1950), 335-338. In 1763, Samuel Bard expressed fear that if a medical school were founded and linked with King's College, that "alone would be sufficient to make the Presbeterian partie our Enimys"; and in 1770, Myles Cooper, the college's president, conceded ruefully that "we have enemies in Abundance . . . every Dissenter of high principles, upon the Continent is our Enemy" because of the charter which placed control of the institution "in the Hands only of Churchmen." The opposition to the college, he admitted, was "coeval" with its founding and had continued "without Interruption, to this very Day. . . ." Samuel Bard to John Bard, Dec. 29, 1763, quoted in Brooke Hindle, *The Pursuit of Science in Revolutionary America, 1735-1789* (Chapel Hill, 1956), 117; Myles Cooper to Jonathan Boucher, March 22, 1770, *Columbia University Quarterly,* XXIV (1932), 140-141.

26. *Independent Reflector,* ed. Klein, 191; Frank C. Abbott, *Government Policy and Higher Education* (Ithaca, N.Y., 1958), 10-16; Sherwood, *University of the State of New York,* 49-57.

27. *Independent Reflector,* ed. Klein, 419.

5.

The Cultural Tyros of Colonial New York

WHEN THE Reverend Andrew Burnaby, an English parson, visited New York in 1760, he remarked that arts and science had made little progress in that colony; but he made the same observation after visiting Virginia, New Jersey, Pennsylvania, and Rhode Island. Only Massachusetts escaped his critical eye. Here, he noted, arts and sciences were "undeniably forwarder" than in New York or Pennsylvania. The public buildings were more elegant, and there was a "more general turn for music, painting, and the belles lettres."[1]

Burnaby's observations are not surprising. It would have been even more astonishing if he had discovered in the year 1760 a da Vinci in New York, a Shakespeare in Pennsylvania, a Newton in Virginia, or a Beethoven in New Jersey. Colonial America was a frontier of European civilization, and Americans were busy conquering the wilderness. It was, in the words of Benjamin Franklin, only after the first cares for the necessities of life were attended to that Americans could come to think about "the Embellishments"—or what we call culture.[2] That Massachusetts could receive even the small accolade of having begun to develop an intellectual culture was a tribute to its Puritan origins, its large population, and its relative social homoge-

Reprinted from *The South Atlantic Quarterly*, LXVI (Spring 1967), 218-232, by permission of the Duke University Press.

neity. Writing of the generation following the Revolution, the historian Henry Adams commented somewhat smugly that the difference between the cultures of Massachusetts and New York was much like the gulf that separated England from Scotland. Neither the Scots nor the New Yorkers esteemed wisdom or virtue! Yet even Adams had to concede that as late as the year 1800, the American mind (except in politics) wallowed in a condition of "unnatural sluggishness," with learning superficial "in a shameful degree," colleges destitute of books and scientific apparatus, libraries scarce and imperfect, and ignorance widespread. The labor of the hand, Adams concluded, took precedence over the life of the mind throughout the United States.[3]

What was true in 1800 was even more so in the year 1750; and perceptive New Yorkers were themselves quick to voice the criticisms which outside observers only echoed. "The want of a liberal Education has long been our Reproach and Misfortune," lamented one New Yorker in 1749.[4] His remedy was the establishment of a college in New York City. Seconding the proposal, another native of the province remarked that there had been less care taken to propagate knowledge and learning in New York than in any other colony. The fault, in his view, was the community standard by which "men are Esteemed only according to what they are worth, that is, the money they are possessed of." Young people merely followed the bad example of their elders.[5] William Smith, Jr., New York's contemporary historian, publicly acknowledged in the 1750s that no colony had been as "culpably inattentive" to public education as New York. What disturbed him most about the low order of the schools was that it contributed to the shameful neglect of all the arts and sciences and to the corruption of the "common speech."[6]

The complaint about the corruption of the English language had particular relevance in New York, because here English was, in the middle of the eighteenth century, still contesting with Dutch for universal acceptability. No other English colony in America faced the challenge of conquering, replacing, or absorbing an already established European culture. The presence of the Dutch, already a minority by 1750, undoubtedly gave New York a flavor that was unique among the mainland colonies. The continued use of the Dutch language was the most visible and persistent evidence of New York's foreign origin. Dr. Alexander Hamilton, a Maryland physician, traveled through the province in 1744. He journeyed by boat down the Hudson from Albany to New York City. "I never was so destitute of conversation in my life as in this voyage," he recorded in his diary. "I heard nothing but Dutch spoke all the way."[7]

Other visitors to New York had the same experience. Albany was almost entirely Dutch in population, religion, and manners; and Dutch influence was strong all along the Hudson River Valley. Children played games in the Dutch style, women wore what Englishmen called "comicall head dress," homes were heavily furnished with colorful tiles, and kitchens were hung with delft plates and dishes. Everywhere, visitors were impressed with the Dutch *haus vrouw's* penchant for cleanliness. Floors were scrubbed so many times during the week that they became as smooth as though planed. "They keep their houses cleaner than their bodies, and their bodies cleaner than their souls," was the tart observation of an English Puritan; and a visiting Frenchman quipped that the floors in a Dutch house were so clean that he was afraid to spit.[8]

New York City was much less Dutch in character, but the houses mirrored the influence of old Holland. Even new buildings were erected in the Dutch manner: brick construction; stepped gable ends facing the street; a narrow garret serving as a warehouse; and a crane extending from it to use in hauling up the goods.[9] While many homes were still furnished in the Dutch style and Dutch words like "boss" virtually incorporated into the English language, the city was otherwise succumbing to English influence by the mid-century. Public buildings like Trinity Church were built in "exactly English fashion," and prominent Dutch merchants who aspired to a place in New York City's society quickly followed suit.[10] It was London styles which the city's high society imitated, not Amsterdam's; and Georgian architecture, Chippendale furniture, and Queen Anne silver marked the houses of influential New Yorkers by the mid-eighteenth century.[11] The Dutch Reformed Church was the last stronghold of the influence of old Holland, but in 1763 it surrendered to the demands of its parishioners in New York City for preaching in English. The surrender was hastened by the exodus from the church of large numbers of young people who, despite their Dutch parentage, could no longer follow the service in that language. Willing to humor the older generation by observing some Dutch customs at home, they spoke English almost exclusively and resented being referred to publicly as Dutch.[12]

Local critics of New York culture found in the Dutch influence a convenient justification for the province's backwardness. The judicial process was corrupted, it was alleged, because in the country courts the jurors were unable to understand the proceedings in English.[13] For those who attributed the colony's cultural impoverishment to the preoccupation of the inhabitants with business affairs, the Dutch again were to blame. "Their whole thoughts," it was charged, were "turned upon profit and gain." They were too frugal, industrious, and parsimonious to expend money or energy on purely intellectual pursuits.[14] If medical practice was not much beyond quackery, it was because Albany's doctors were all Dutch and lacked knowledge of medicine other than that which they acquired by "bare experience."[15] (In New York City, after their inexperience had led to several "grave mistakes," some of the ships' barbers in port who also doubled as surgeons were commanded to stick to shaving heads and trimming beards and not to "dress any wounds" or "bleed . . . any one on land" without express permission.)[16]

While many of these criticisms were ungenerous, there is little doubt that the cultural impress of New Netherland was slight. The residents of Knickerbocker New York were lusty, convivial, and bibulous folk, but they were not a bookish people. They learned to drink, it was said, before they were able to lick a spoon. With seventeen tap houses in New Amsterdam in the year 1647, it was not difficult for them to begin their self-education so early.[17] The Dutch colony had no printing press, no newspapers, no public libraries, and few private libraries of any consequence. In 1642, the library of the huge Van Rensselaer estate consisted of seventeen books. One Dutch merchant left an estate in 1665 which included five hundred volumes, but most of them were schoolbooks. New Netherland had its native poets, but even the most sympathetic of modern critics concedes that their verse was not "highly imaginative." It had portrait painters, too, but none of their work has survived.[18]

New Netherland's cultural deficiencies do not, however, explain those of English New York. The century that elapsed between the English conquest and the opening of the Revolutionary era allowed ample time for the English to remedy the defects of the Dutch; but they did not. The reasons are not extraordinary. They reflect the deterrents to cultural progress that existed in all the colonies, and the principal obstacle was the exacting, persistent task of mastering the physical environment. Despite 130 years of settlement, New York in the mid-eighteenth century was still largely wilderness. English land policy, which conferred vast estates upon a handful of individuals, did not encourage the migration of small farmers. One million acres were owned by eighteen manor lords who reigned over their lands in semifeudal splendor and who leased rather than sold the lands within their manors. The irksome and demeaning dues and services exacted from the leaseholders provoked some to outright rebellion and discouraged newcomers from becoming tenants. "What man," queried one of New York's governors, "will be such a fool to become a base tenant to Mr. Dellius, Colonel Schuyler, [or] Mr. Livingston . . . when for crossing Hudson's river that man can for a song purchase a good freehold in the Jersies?"[19]

The governors and other royal officials did little to alter the pattern of land ownership. They preferred to share in the spoils. They acquired huge estates themselves and granted others to speculator friends. By 1732, 2,500,000 acres had been taken up by governors; and in 1763, there were three grants each comprising 1,000,000 acres.[20] It was little wonder, then, that by 1770 New York was surpassed in population not only by large colonies such as Pennsylvania and Virginia, but also by such smaller ones as Massachusetts, Maryland, and Connecticut.[21]

In a colony so poorly inhabited, labor was at a premium. New York could not afford the luxury of devoting manpower exclusively to literature, painting, architecture, or even law. Until the first quarter of the eighteenth century, it was not uncommon to find merchants and landlords acting as their own lawyers, and judges in the local courts often possessed no legal training except that which they acquired on the job. New Yorkers echoed the sentiment of a New Englander who moralized that "the Plow-man that raiseth Grain, is more serviceable to Mankind, than the Painter who draws only to please the Eye." In sharper language, a prominent New York lawyer advised Englishmen that "we want hands . . . more than heads. The most intimate acquaintance with the classics, will not remove our oaks; nor a taste for the *Georgics* cultivate our lands."[22]

The plea for hands rather than heads was not entirely honest. It was made in 1768, and by then New York had become sufficiently prosperous and civilized to afford both hands and heads. Yet the very prosperity which in later years served to foster intellectual culture discouraged it in the mid-eighteenth century. The Dutch had long given New York a reputation for aggressive pursuit of wealth, and their successors carried on the tradition. The colony's magnificent commercial opportunities could not easily be ignored by its inhabitants. The Hudson River provided a natural channel for the flow of furs and farm produce from the agricultural hinterland via Albany to New York City and thence to Europe, the West Indies, and every colony from Nova Scotia to Georgia. The great landed estates along the Hudson complemented the commercial economy of Albany and New York City; and the union was visibly demonstrated by the large number of wealthy New Yorkers—such as the De Lanceys and the Livingstons—who were at the same time landlords and merchants.

Prosperity merely begot the desire for more prosperity. New York's landed and mercantile magnates did not rest on their laurels, nor did they lead a life of genteel leisure. Indeed they were constantly reproached by their neighbors for their preoccupation with the "Art of getting Money." In New York, it was said, the wisest man without a fortune was neglected and despised, while the "greatest Blockhead with one [was] caress'd and honour'd." New Yorkers hotly denied the charge as the product of envy of their "flourishing Circumstances," but they were compelled to confess that the seduction of material prosperity had resulted in the neglect of learning.[23]

The professional theater received only sporadic support from New Yorkers. A company of Engish players expressed public dismay in 1753 over the hostile reception accorded to them "in a city [New York] to all appearances so polite as this." Ten years later, the players had more reason to complain. Someone in the gallery was "so very rude" as to throw eggs upon the stage, splattering the ladies and gentlemen in the boxes and interrupting "in some measure" the performance. Professional musicians had better success than actors. New York City had a number of music teachers, and concerts were a popular form of entertainment. Yet even in this field, there were complaints from the artists that Americans had no musical taste and were unwilling to support professional musicians. Perhaps the only art which New York's wealthy merchants and landed proprietors were willing to support enthusiastically was painting. They were happy to commission limners to paint portraits of themselves and their families.[24] But when the youngest son of one of New York's manor lords professed a desire to study painting in Europe, the idea was dismissed by his father as utterly frivolous.

New York, like other colonies, could not afford the luxury of a professional elite. The scarcity of labor which led tradesmen and artisans to be jacks-of-all-trades compelled the craftsmen of culture to be similarly unspecialized. Gerardus Duyckink and his son advertised in the 1730s and 1740s that they painted portraits, but this was only a sideline. Their principal business consisted of selling paints, looking glasses, and pictures and performing all sorts of varnishing, painting, glazing, and gilding.[25] New York's first poet, William Livingston, was also one of its most prominent lawyers. William Smith, Jr., the colony's principal historian, was a lawyer and a judge. Cadwallader Colden was New York's lieutenant governor and surveyor general; but he was also the colony's leading physicist, mathematician, botanist, anthropologist, and astronomer. The first play written in the colony was the handiwork of its then governor, Robert Hunter.[26]

In addition to their own amateurish contributions to the colony's cultural development, men such as these strove energetically to organize community enterprises to achieve the same end. In 1748, a few of the province's intellectuals formed a literary club which they named the "Society for the Promotion of Useful Knowledge." Its purpose, they announced somewhat pretentiously, was to provide an antidote to New York City's infamous drinking clubs. The "Sage Philosophers" —as they were dubbed by cynics—would substitute serious discussions of philosophy, science, and morality for the bawdy stories and idle gossip that occupied the usual tavern crowds. Its founders expected their discussion group to become an American counterpart of the Royal Society in London.[27]

The aspiring philosophers made little headway among the city's bumpermen, and they spent their brief life fending off newspaper attacks from their doubting critics. Eight years later, the same men had better success in organizing the New York Society Library, a subscription library open to the public. The society survived—it exists, indeed, today; but the hopes of its founders that it would become the nucleus of a larger research institution, including a museum and an observatory, proved futile. There is something pathetically naive about the bookplate designed for the society in 1758 by one of its more optimistic members. It showed New York City as the American Athens.[28]

The same coterie of intellectuals was active in launching New York's first essay-journal, the *Independent Reflector,* in 1752, and in sponsoring a movement for the establishment of a college in the colony at about the same time. Neither enterprise came to full fruition. The essay-journal lasted only one year,[29] and the college, established by royal charter in 1754 as King's College, had a precarious existence up to the Revolution. The charter failed to secure legislative approval, its delivery to the college's governors was held up for many months, and only half of the public monies raised for the institution were ever delivered to it. The governors were not very interested in its progress, its enrolment remained small, and the absence of good grammar schools in the colony meant that its students were "very raw" when they entered. Critics ridiculed its educational program, and even its first president conceded, nine years after its establishment, that it was not held in high public repute.[30] Perhaps one reason for the college's poor reputation was the fact that the entrance used by the students was through the street where the most notorious prostitutes lived. Since New York City was reported to have at least five hundred ladies of pleasure at the time, the college, one had to agree, was "a little unlucky" in its location.[31]

The men who engaged so actively in all these literary and educational projects were an impressive group of individuals. They would have been leaders in any colony. In New York, they stood high within the circle of the ruling families. Cadwallader Colden, James Alexander, William Smith, Sr., James De Lancey, William Livingston, and William Smith, Jr., were all men of outstanding ability. They were prominent in their professions and held important positions of political power. Most of them were graduates of American colleges or British universities. Why, then, did their intellectual efforts not make a more profound impact on New York's cultural development? Why did they not provide the leadership for the colony's cultural efflorescence? Simply because they preferred to channel their capacious energies and intellectual talents into the arenas of politics and religion rather than to devote themselves fully to belles lettres.

Few colonies provided the attraction which politics held for New York's aristocracy of talent. Unlike Massachusetts, where it was charged that politics engaged chiefly men of "Middling or low Rank," New York's politics attracted men of education, wealth, and social position.[32] The political structure in New York was tailor-made for their participation. Ever since 1689, there had been in the colony two fairly well developed factions or parties, contesting for control of the government: Leislerians and anti-Leislerians, Cosbyites and anti-Cosbyites, Coldenites and De Lanceys, De Lanceys and Livingstons. New Yorkers not only accepted these divisions as healthy safeguards of popular liberties, but they reveled in the excitement generated by political contests. Nor were these private affairs between rival aristocratic families against a backdrop of a silent and passive populace. New York's electorate was broad, the suffrage liberal, and participation in electoral contests extensive.[33]

By the mid-eighteenth century, New Yorkers had developed a high degree of political sophistication and a remarkable mastery of the art of politics. Elections were fought over issues rather than personalities. In the 1720s, the issue was governmental policy with respect to the fur trade; in the 1730s, it was the right of the governor to establish juryless courts and the right of the press to criticize his conduct. Ten years later, the parties clashed over New York's role in the war with France, and in the 1750s and 1760s, the alleged encroachment of the Anglican Church upon the rights of Dissenters colored almost every electoral battle. In waging campaigns, the parties employed many of the techniques of the modern political process: balanced tickets, slogans and catch-phrases, appeals to minority groups, mass meetings, and torrents of campaign literature.

Leaders and followers enjoyed these spectacles, but the hectic contests left little time or energy for the reflective arts or the life of the intellect. The reading public came to expect and demand not belles lettres but political oratory, pamphleteering, and satire. And they received it, with a vengeance. New York's newspapers were particularly contentious in tone. Sometimes supplements had to be issued to carry the news and advertisements, so filled were the regular columns with political and religious polemics. In number of newspapers alone, New York led all of its neighbors well into the nineteenth century. Between 1725 and 1776, twenty-two newspapers were published in the colony, all but one in New York City.[34] And the very men who were seeking to elevate the colony's cultural level were the principal authors of the disputatious pieces that filled the press. With their talented pens so heavily engaged in preparing essays of a timely character, they had little time to produce literature of a timeless quality.

New York had still another distraction for its intellectual leadership in the colony's religious tensions, which were the product of its denominational diversity. No other colony was of such polyglot character. The Dutch set the pattern with their tolerance of Lutherans, English Protestants, Baptists, and Jews. As early as 1643, a visitor reported in astonishment that eighteen languages were spoken in New Netherland.[35] English rule legalized the freedom that had developed under the Dutch as an economic expedient. With liberty of conscience thus assured to all Christians—Papists always excepted—New York became the most cosmopolitan colony in English America. "There are religions of all sorts," one governor reported in 1678; another remarked somewhat facetiously about ten years later that there were in the province some "of all opinions" but the most of no opinion at all![36] The English traveler, Burnaby, confessed that his stay in the colony in 1760 left him baffled as to how to describe New Yorkers. "Being . . . of different nations, different languages, and different religions, it is almost impossible to give them any precise or determinate character."[37]

Out of this diversity grew toleration, not only as a legal prescription but as a social necessity. Some New Yorkers viewed the diverse religious situation as a genuine virtue. The variety of sects in the colony ensured that no one sect would gain a "Tyranny and Usurpation" over the others.[38] To religious liberals, any orthodoxy that sought to command universal assent was suspect. New Yorkers had learned from the Dutch not to take the externals of religion too seriously. Frontier living had shorn off much of the formalism of Dutch Calvinism. The inhabitants of New Netherland were less interested in articles of faith than in faith itself. Visitors to New York City at the beginning of the eighteenth century were shocked to find the Dutch "not very strict in Keepeing the Sabath." The taverns were filled as usual, women worked at their regular household chores, and even the children played their games without change.[39] A later visitor reaffirmed the casualness of the Dutch. "As to religion," observed one in 1744, "they have little of it . . . and of enthusiasm not a grain." But a perceptive English woman added that if New York's Dutch lacked the enthusiasm of the zealot, they were also without the bigotry of the doctrinaire.[40]

The raw edges of religious dogmatism were further worn smooth by the continued influx of new religious persuasions into the colony: French Huguenots, Scottish Presbyterians, Moravians, Quakers, and, of course, Anglicans. In the fluid religious atmosphere produced by such variety, persons moved easily from one church affiliation to another. Some Livingstons, originally Presbyterians, joined the Dutch Reformed Church, then shifted back to the Presbyterian. Others became Anglicans. The De Lanceys left the French Reformed Church and joined the Church of England. The latter liked to consider itself the official church of the colony, but it never managed to secure such a preferment; the one thing that all Dissenters could agree upon was that the Anglican Church must not be permitted to secure official status. The religious ideal for dissenting Protestants was an equilibrium in which each sect could freely profess its principles without fear of interference by the state. This situation could be assured only if the Anglican Church were kept from securing political privileges that would elevate it above the other churches. New York's Protestants might take their own religions lightly, but they were in dead earnest in their resistance to any attempt to upset the religious balance of power.

The most forceful opponents of an Anglican church establishment in the mid-eighteenth century were the very same men who sought to promote the colony's cultural progress—William Smith, Sr., William Livingston, William Smith, Jr.; their political opponents—the De Lanceys—were regarded as spokesmen of the Episcopal Church "interest." Political contests became charged with religious overtones. Even innocuous literary and educational enterprises foundered on the rock of religious contention. The establishment of King's College provoked a furious battle because the Presbyterians resented the charter which gave control of the trustees and the presidency to the Anglicans.[41] The founding of the Society Library became embroiled in the same religious quarrel as Dissenters and Anglicans vied for control of the institution's board of trustees. The literary society of 1748 was accused of harboring anti-Church designs. The colony's first essay-journal was killed by Anglican pressure on its printer.

The energies that might otherwise have been diverted into the intellectual and cultural life of New York were thus drained off by the powerful attraction of politics and religion. The literary heritage left by these contests was not inconsiderable in quantity—a veritable mountain of tracts, pamphlets, handbills, broadsides, and newspaper essays—but most of these papers are of greater interest to the historian of political thought than of literature. And herein lies both the tragedy and the triumph of the lawyer-politicians who comprised colonial New York's intellectual leadership.

The principles of civil and religious liberty which they espoused in the course of their contests with political and ecclesiastical foes became so well understood by New Yorkers that they could easily be offered as "self-evident truths" in the larger struggle with Britain in 1776. The game of politics to which colonial New Yorkers were introduced with such skill and sophistication continued to fascinate the citizens of the later Empire State; and if they later displayed more political literacy than their neighbors, it was because of their expert schooling in the colonial period. In religion, too, colonial New York set an example to the American Republic of the virtues of creedal competition in a state where the government acted the role of neutral.

Long experienced in the practice of living amidst diversity of religious beliefs, New Yorkers gave the lie to the conventional argument that sectarian discord could produce only social confusion and religious decline. In New York, the reverse was true. It was freedom which was strengthened by creedal competition, not bigotry or atheism.

If "New York remained a cultural fief of Great Britain and western Europe throughout the colonial period," it was perhaps not too great a price to pay for the principles of civic consciousness and religious freedom which the colony developed so effectively while its arts and science languished.[42] New York's contribution to the reflective arts could wait; after all, England and western Europe had a rich cultural heritage upon which the new American nation could draw. But Europe could not furnish the young republic with a model of a free, popular government built upon the foundation of social diversity. This was to be a uniquely American innovation, and toward the achievement of this objective, colonial New York with its 150 years of successful experience made a significant contribution.

Notes

1. Burnaby, *Travels through the Middle Settlements,* ed. Rufus R. Wilson, 52, 109, 116, 127, 139. After visiting the northern colonies in 1744, Dr. Alexander Hamilton, a Maryland physician, concluded that only in Boston were the inhabitants "civilized." *Gentleman's Progress: The Itinerarium of Dr. Alexander Hamilton, 1744,* ed. Carl Bridenbaugh (Chapel Hill, 1948), 199.

2. Quoted in Rossiter, *Seedtime of the Republic,* 118.

3. Henry Adams, *History of the United States of America,* 9 vols. (New York, 1889-1891), I, 62-63, 108, 130.

4. [William Livingston], *Some Serious Thoughts on the Design of erecting a College in . . . New-York* (1749), 1.

5. [Cadwallader Colden] to [Rev. Hezekiah Watkins], Dec. 12, 1748, SPG MSS, B-20, 86-88, Archives of the SPG, London.

6. Smith, *History,* I, 278; Livingston et al., *Independent Reflector,* ed. Klein, 420 (Nov. 8, 1753).

7. Hamilton, *Itinerarium,* ed. Bridenbaugh, 79.

8. *Ibid.,* 72; *The America of 1750: Peter Kalm's Travels in North America,* 2 vols. (London, 1770; new edition, ed. Adolph B. Benson, New York, 1937), I, 343, 346, II, 614-615; James T. Flexner, *American Painting, First Flowers of Our Wilderness* (Cambridge, Mass., 1947), 52.

9. Wayne Andrews, ed., "A Glance at New York in 1697: The Travel Diary of Dr. Benjamin Bullivant," *N.Y. Hist. Soc. Qtly.,* XL (1956), 65.

10. Abraham de Peyster, for one, built his house in the late 17th century in "the newest English fashion." *Ibid.,* 10-11.

11. Esther Singleton, *Social New York under the Georges* (New York, 1902), Parts II and III, *passim;* Thomas J. Wertenbaker, *The Golden Age of Colonial Culture* (Ithaca, N.Y., 1949), 42-43, 58-59.

12. Edward T. Corwin, *A Manual of the Reformed Church in America* (New York, 1902), 116.

13. Smith, *History,* I, 277.

14. Hamilton, *Itinerarium,* ed. Bridenbaugh, 73; Burnaby, *Travels,* ed. Wilson, 117.

15. Hamilton, *Itinerarium,* ed. Bridenbaugh, 65.

16. Ellis L. Raesly, *Portrait of New Netherland* (New York, 1945; reprinted, 1965), 156.

17. *Ibid.,* 209; Bayrd Still, *Mirror for Gotham* (New York, 1956), 10.

18. Flick, ed., *History of the State of New York,* IX, 47; Raesly, *Portrait of New Netherland,* 255-256, 330; Flexner, *American Painting,* 57.

19. Earl of Bellomont to the Lords of Trade, Nov. 28, 1700, *N.Y. Col. Docs.,* IV, 791. Peter Kalm, the Swedish visitor, remarked in 1750 that so many parts of New York were still uncultivated that the province "has entirely the appearance of a frontierland." Kalm, *Travels,* ed. Benson, I, 143, II, 615-616.

20. Spaulding, *Critical Period,* 47.

21. Clifford L. and Elizabeth H. Lord, *Historical Atlas of the United States* (rev. ed., New York, 1953), 198.

22. William Livingston, *A Letter to the Right Reverend Father in God, John, Lord Bishop of Llandaff . . .* (New-York, 1768), 23-24. Livingston added: "Many of our young people are knocking their heads against the *Iliad,* who should employ their hands in clearing our swamps, and draining our marshes. Others are musing, in cogitation profound, on the arrangement of a syllogism, while they ought to be guiding the tail of a plough."

23. [Livingston], *Some Serious Thoughts,* 1; Kalm, *Travels,* ed. Benson, I, 344, II, 615.

24. Flexner, *American Painting,* chap. 3; Singleton, *Social New York,* 272-300; Rita S. Gottesman, *The Arts and Crafts in New York, 1726-1776* (New York, 1938), 286-287; Savelle, *Seeds of Liberty,* 529-530; Hugh Rankin, *The Theater in Colonial America* (Chapel Hill, 1960, 1965), 23-25, 31-36, 60-65, 77-79, 96-98, 108-110.

25. Flexner, *American Painting,* 60-61.

26. Wright, *Cultural Life of the American Colonies,* 186; Lawrence H. Leder, "Robert Hunter's *Androborus,*" *Bulletin of the New York Public Library,* LXVIII (March 1964), 153-190.

27. *New-York Weekly Journal,* Feb. 13, 27, March 20, April 3 (Supplement), 1749.

28. Smith, *History,* II, 171-172; Austin B. Keep, *History of the New York Society Library* ([New York], 1908), 166-168.

29. On the history of the *Reflector,* see Chap. 3 above.

30. *Samuel Johnson Writings,* IV, 56, 94, 98, 109-110; McAnear, "American Imprints Concerning King's College," *Papers of the Bibliographical Society,* XLIV (1950), 335-336; pp. 84 and 106 above.

31. Patrick McRobert, *A Tour through Part of the North Provinces of America . . . in the years 1774, and 1775* (Edinburgh, 1776; reprinted with notes by Carl Bridenbaugh, Pamphlet Series, *Narratives and Documents,* No. 1, Historical Society of Pennsylvania, 1935), 3, 5.

32. Francis Bernard to Lord Barrington, Feb. 7, 1768, Channing and Coolidge, eds., *Barrington-Bernard Correspondence,* 142.

33. See pp. 37-42 above.

34. Harry B. Weiss, "A Graphic Summary of the Growth of Newspapers in New York and other States, 1704-1820," *Bulletin, New York Public Library,* LII (April 1948), 182-196, particularly 182 and 188; Flick, ed., *History of the State of New York,* III, 85-86.

35. *N.Y. Doc. Hist.,* IV, 21.

36. The remarks are those of Governor Edmund Andros in 1678 and Governor Thomas Dongan in 1687. See *ibid.,* I, 186, and *N.Y. Col. Docs.,* III, 262.

37. Burnaby, *Travels,* ed. Wilson, 117.

38. Livingston et al., *Independent Reflector,* ed. Klein, 391.

39. Bullivant, "Diary," ed. Andrews, 66; Sarah Kemble Knight, *Private Journal of a Journey from Boston to New York in the Year 1704* (Albany, 1865), 69.

40. Hamilton, *Itinerarium,* ed. Bridenbaugh, 74; Mrs. Anne Grant, *Memoirs of an American Lady,* 2 vols. in one (New York, 1901), I, 70.

41. See Chap. 4 above.

42. The estimate of New York's cultural condition appears in David M. Ellis and others, *A Short History of New York State* (Ithaca, N.Y., 1957), 70.

III

Law and Politics

More than a century ago, the French observer Alexis de Tocqueville remarked that "scarcely any political question arises in the United States that is not resolved, sooner or later, into a judicial question." In colonial New York, the converse appeared true: every judicial question became a political issue. None touched the sensitivities of New Yorkers more than the issues of the tenure of judges and the right to trial by jury. As the colonists came increasingly to see themselves as possessing the same rights as Englishmen in the mother country and the empire as a federation of separate sovereignties with equal rights and mutual commitments, they correspondingly resented any variations from English practice that implied colonial inequality. The spokesmen for the American position in these matters were, not unnaturally, members of the lawyer class, which by the mid-eighteenth century had achieved a high degree of professional respectability and social recognition. The nature of this transformation, from an earlier period in which lawyers were held in low repute, is illustrated in the first essay by the legal career of one of New York's prominent attorneys, William Livingston. The second essay describes the leadership of these men of the bar in two struggles with Lieutenant Governor Cadwallader Colden. In one, New Yorkers challenged the right of the chief executive to appoint judges without granting them the same permanency of tenure that had assured English jurists independence from royal intimidation; in the other, the colony challenged the governor's right to review the substantive issues in a jury decision as compromising the traditional inviolability of the judgment of one's peers. In each contest, the lawyers led the opposition to Colden, and in the process they not only enunciated principles that were later incorporated in the protests of the united colonies against the New Imperial Policy but also contributed to the climate of colonial fears that persuaded Americans a conspiracy was afoot to deprive them of their liberties.

6.

The Rise of the New York Bar: The Legal Career of William Livingston

ON THE EVE of the American Revolution, the legal profession in New York possessed both social prestige and political power. The terms "lawyer" and "merchant," Crèvecoeur noted in his *Letters from an American Farmer,* were the two "fairest titles" in colonial urban society. In New York, the "Dominion of the Lawyers" was a ceaseless complaint of one loyal servant of the King. Lieutenant Governor Cadwallader Colden warned the English authorities that the New York bar, with their landlord allies and their friends in the Assembly, comprised a "faction" that was at once "formidable and dangerous to good Government" and a major threat to the "Powers of the Crown."[1]

During the earlier years of the eighteenth century, however, both bench and bar had been generally held in low repute. Merchants regarded lawyers jealously as potential rivals for political power; the rural population eyed them with suspicion as agents of the hated landlord class; and the great proprietors themselves were resentful of legal experts who could find flaws in long-accepted land titles and transform a peaceful countryside into a bedlam of litigation. Both merchants and landlords, accustomed to handling their own legal affairs or to entrusting them to lay colleagues, protested the professionalization of

Reprinted from the *William and Mary Quarterly,* XV (July 1958), 334-358, by permission of the Institute of Early American History and Culture, Williamsburg, Virginia.

the law into a "Mysterious Business"; and they denounced it as a "System of confounding other People and picking their Pockets."[2]

The legal community helped to provide ammunition for its critics. Many of its members were poorly trained; legal fees were high; barratry was not uncommon. Even members of the profession conceded the charges. One young law clerk, disgusted with the subject matter of his studies—a "dry and insipid Science"—and with the apprenticeship system of training lawyers, confessed publicly: "There is perhaps no Set of Men that bear so ill a Character in the Estimation of the Vulgar, as the Gentlemen of the Long Robe."[3] A few years later, the same critic, now a lawyer himself, expressed his contempt for the "unletter'd Blockheads of the Robe" in stronger language and with a literary scalpel that had been honed by experience:

> Some Lawyers at the op'ning of a Cause,
> Set out with mighty Pomp to gain Applause,
> But finding instantly their Want of Skill,
> With *Hums* and *Haws,* their Declamations fill.
> * * * *
> While others blund'ring fearless of Disgrace,
> Recite in *Trespass,* and join *Debt* and *Case.*
> Thus want of Learning, join'd with want of Sense,
> Is the most certain Source of Impudence.[4]

The transformation of the law in colonial New York took place about the middle of the century, coincident with a period of marked business expansion. Heightened commercial activity produced an astonishing increase in litigation, and this, in turn, created an enlarged demand for legal services. The minute books of the provincial courts mirror the intensification of legal activity. In the Supreme Court of Judicature, the apex of the colony's common law structure, some fifty-one cases were on the docket for the summer term of 1724. Ten years later, the number had risen to 107; and by 1751, the figure was 144.[5] The New York City Mayor's Court, a court of petty jurisdiction in which most of the city's civil litigation was settled, showed a corresponding expansion. During the month of June in 1720, for example, the court had forty-six cases before it; in June of 1730, ninety-eight; and in the same month during 1751, no less than 268.[6]

At about the same time, the legal system itself underwent a metamorphosis, becoming so much more disciplined and specialized that laymen could no longer master it without professional training. As the bar became financially more attractive, men of greater ability and education entered its ranks; and by their achievements and their learning they helped to overcome much of the public hostility formerly directed against the profession.[7]

The representatives of the new bar were young men of talent and education. Many of them held baccalaureate degrees from colonial colleges, and all received training in the offices of able attorneys. Among the newcomers were William Smith, Jr., future historian of New York; John Morin Scott, subsequently a leader of the Sons of Liberty; Whitehead Hicks, later mayor of New York; and William Livingston. As the most important and influential member of the emergent lawyer class, Livingston's legal career warrants attention in its own right and as an illustration of the rising power and prestige of the entire bar in the second half of the eighteenth century.

Livingston entered the legal profession with advantages not shared by all of New York's young attorneys. Born in Albany in 1723, the youngest of the six sons of Philip Livingston, the second lord of the Livingston Manor, William Livingston was reared in "ease and affluence." He secured his formal education in Albany grammar schools and at Yale, from which he graduated in 1741. His legal apprenticeship was served under the two most prominent attorneys of the province, James Alexander and William Smith, Sr., both of whom were on intimate personal terms with the Livingston family. Livingston's apprenticeship under two attorneys was not a matter of choice. He began his clerkship under Alexander, but two intemperate publications which he sent to the New York press resulted in his peremptory discharge. One was a withering indictment of the legal apprenticeship system and the other an equally devastating personal attack on Mrs. Alexander for her social pretentiousness. Livingston was then sent to Smith's office to complete his legal studies.[8]

Livingston fretted about the inadequacy of the training he received as a law clerk, but his masters were men of broader learning and greater legal knowledge than any other attorneys in the colony. They both possessed libraries of more than ordinary size and breadth, and Smith offered his apprentices a set of "Directions relating to the Study of the Law" which provided the rudimentary framework of a law course.[9] Livingston was so impressed with it that he later adopted it for the training of his own clerks.[10]

As a member of a socially prominent and wealthy family, Livingston possessed the further advantage of a ready-made source of legal business among his own kinsmen, all active as merchants and landowners. His family was linked by blood or marriage with virtually every name in the provincial aristocracy: Schuyler, Van Rensselaer, Van Cortlandt, Beekman, Cuyler, Van Brugh, Bayard, De Peyster, and Ten Broeck; and his own marriage in 1747 to Susanna French brought him new family connections in New Jersey as well as New York: with the Philipses, Reades, Van Hornes, and Brockholsts.

Despite these impressive advantages, Livingston suffered the same early disappointments as beginning lawyers of a later day. Prospective clients beat no busy path to his door. His first business consisted largely of drawing up wills, indentures, deeds, and bonds—chiefly for relatives and close friends. A week after receiving his license to practice,[11] he entered the first receipt in his account book: "For drawing several deeds between Volkert Pothout and Robert Benson—£3.8.0." The entry was the sole one for the month. It was followed by others of a similar nature: "For drawing Aunt Vetch's will—£2.10"; "From Mother Livingston for sundries—£9.0.3"; "From Brother Robt. for sundries—£5.10." For November 1748, his first month as a lawyer, Livingston's receipts added up to less than five pounds; for December they totaled only one. Not until three months after receiving his license did Livingston make his first appearance in the Supreme Court; seven months later he pleaded his first case in the Mayor's Court.[12] After two years of practice, his earnings averaged only about eight pounds a month.[13]

With characteristic impatience, Livingston attributed his slow start to the defects of his clerkship, which had emphasized the theoretical at the expense of the practical side of the law, and to the competition of "pettifoggers." There was more justification to the latter complaint than the former, although Livingston probably exaggerated the extent. The courts had prescribed rather exacting qualifications for the admission of lawyers, but these efforts—designed to limit the size of the profession as much as to raise its level—were frustrated by legislative enactments, the necessity of accepting lawyers who had been licensed in other colonies, and open defiance of the courts' rulings, particularly in the rural districts. When an Albany colleague complained in 1755 of the large number of "Mountebank Lawyers" in that city, Livingston expressed his sympathy, adding that New York, too, was "crowded with practitioners."[14]

Livingston voiced his irritation in the medium he knew so well, the press. With William Smith, Jr., he addressed a series of letters to the *New-York Gazette* castigating the "Low Characters" who were tarnishing the reputation of the entire legal profession and excoriating the men who sat on the bench of the rural courts. Two years later, the charges were repeated in an essay on "Abuses in the Practice of the Law" which appeared in Livingston's newspaper-magazine, the *Independent Reflector*.[15] In verse, Livingston burlesqued the "Geniusses" who had suddenly emerged from "Obscurity and Silence" as "sage and infallible Oracles of the Law" without benefit of schooling or experience; and with grim humor he warned prospective barristers to

> Avoid, avoid, the inextricable Snare,
> Nor madly venture to approach the Bar;
> But instant clipping vain Ambition's Wing,
> Turn *Carman, Cobbler, Fiddler,* any Thing.[16]

By 1752 Livingston should have had considerably less cause for complaint, for by then both his reputation and his business had been well advanced. Two years earlier the New York Assembly had commissioned him and William Smith, Jr., to revise the laws of the province, offering £280 for the editorial job.[17] The appearance of the work in 1752 brought the compilers the approbation not only of their colleagues at home but also of the Board of Trade in England. The Board had been critical of the confused state of the colony's statutes and long urged a revision. The new volume was such a success that when the Board's secretary wrote to New York some years later for three or four copies, he was told that the whole edition had been "sold off."[18] A second volume, also prepared by Livingston and Smith, brought the codification up to 1762.[19]

Family business of a larger nature than an occasional will or bond soon raised Livingston's spirits and fattened his purse. In 1751 he was offered a general retainer by his cousin, Robert G. Livingston, and the latter's father-in-law, Colonel Henry Beekman, to serve as their general counsel "in every action to be commenced or defended concerning the[ir] premises" in Ulster and Dutchess Counties.[20] James Alexander retained him in important litigation, and Mrs. Alexander forgot Livingston's unseemly behavior during his clerkship sufficiently to employ him to dispose of her first husband's estate.[21] His brothers, Peter, John, and Philip, all prominent New York merchants, engaged him in debt-recovery actions against other local tradesmen; Cousins Robert and James Livingston of New York City and Cousin

Henry Livingston of Poughkeepsie contributed additional business; and from the distaff side of the family, Aunt Mary Brockholst, Aunt Joanna Philipse, and brothers-in-law David Van Horne and David Clarkson provided still other cases. The Livingston Manor itself offered a lucrative source of law business, but after 1759 this had to be shared with Robert Livingston's son-in-law, James Duane.[22] With his sources of practice thus enlarged, Livingston's income rose to £217 by 1751, and a year later it mounted further to £358.[23]

Like most New York lawyers, Livingston undertook some practice outside the city. He appeared in the higher county courts—Sessions, Common Pleas, and the Mayor's Court of Albany—and accompanied the judges of the Supreme Court as they rode the circuit, once in the spring and again in autumn. These excursions into the country were tiring to the bench and to the bar,[24] and Livingston enjoyed circuit riding only when he could visit boyhood friends in Albany or on the manor or when, during a political campaign, he could mix his law work with electioneering. As his reputation and his practice grew, he declined to accept cases in the rural courts unless old clients insisted on his services.[25]

It was in New York City, however, that ambitious lawyers secured the bulk of their business. Here were concentrated the ablest of the colony's lawyers and the most important courts. The presence of the governor and his Council, the Assembly, the Supreme Court of Judicature, the Mayor's Court, and the Court of Vice-Admiralty lent to the provincial capital an air of political as well as judicial distinction. The city's many tribunals provided opportunities for a varied practice, and Livingston's was of just such a diversified nature.

Civil rather than criminal cases occupied most of his professional attention. As in other colonies, a New York attorney's practice involved largely matters of real estate, probate, trade, and business; and Livingston was most frequently engaged in actions to collect debts, compel the enforcement of contracts, punish recalcitrant tenants, solve land titles, and clear estates in the process of administration.[26] Then, as now, much of a lawyer's business was performed outside the courtroom. Wills were drawn, deeds prepared, and indentures written, all for relatively small fees. Court costs were usually high, but popular hostility to the legal profession kept counsel's fees at a level that lawyers considered "niggardly."[27] Fees were fixed by the legislature and the courts, and the schedules were enforced strictly. In the Supreme Court, for example, no more than six shillings was permitted as a retainer, three shillings for drawing up a plea, and a like sum for making out a writ. A maximum of four pounds was allowed for all attorney's charges in normal proceedings, five pounds in the case of special verdicts or special pleadings. In the lower courts, the fees were smaller: only twenty shillings for prosecuting an action to judgment, less if the case terminated in some other way.[28]

Livingston's law papers help to establish the extent of his practice but disclose little concerning the nature of his cases or his working methods. Briefs were rarely prepared; few have survived. Many cases were settled out of court, the New York judicial system making frequent use of the Dutch institution of arbitration which obviated court proceedings by referring the case to the decision of an impartial third party. Livingston, like other New York lawyers, was employed on such occasions as court-appointed referee, and at other times his own cases were settled in the same way.[29]

The high cost of justice served to discourage court proceedings. A hostile critic of the legal profession estimated in 1764 that the "Expense of Law suits in the Province yearly amounts to more than four times the support of Government."[30] Merchants used informal methods to collect debts from delinquent customers in order to avoid disagreeable and costly lawsuits. Livingston took pains to assure his merchant clients that they could depend on his prosecuting no one "while there is any Probability of recovering the Debt without the Trouble and Expence of an Action at Law." The latter was a "troublesome" business that ought to be avoided if there were "any apprehensions of not succeeding in the prosecution of the Action." He had given his London clients complete satisfaction over a two-year period "tho' I never actually sued but one Man." But, he warned his English clients, they had better not depend on their New York friends to act in their behalf. Merchants were not likely to use strong measures against their own colleagues in the business community. Lawyers could press for payment more vigorously since "People do not expect the same Complaisance from Gentlemen of our Profession whose peculiar business it is to put the Law in full force."[31]

During the course of his practice, Livingston gave ample evidence of his effectiveness in prosecuting recalcitrant debtors as well as in conciliating them. The years from 1753 to 1755 witnessed a rash of debt-recovery actions. Trade fell sharply during this period; both English and colonial merchants were caught with overextended credits.

London business houses dunned their New York correspondents for payment, and the latter, in turn, pressed the local tradespeople for settlement. Livingston profited doubly from the squeeze, being retained by merchants in England and in New York. "Times are so bad with us," he wrote to an Albany colleague in the spring of 1754, "that I have letters of attorney . . . against no less than twelve merchants."[32] Forty-three of Livingston's fifty appearances in the Supreme Court during the spring, summer, and fall terms of 1754 were on behalf of merchants seeking debt recoveries.[33] His receipts reflected the volume of this type of litigation, amounting in 1754 to almost £450, the peak income of his legal career thus far.[34]

Lawyers benefited from the flood tide as well as the ebb of commerce, and the years of the French and Indian War proved especially remunerative to the legal community. New York City became the hub of the imperial supply line to the colonies, and the upsurge of business ended the city's "bad times." Lawyers reaped the harvest of maritime litigation that followed, much of it stemming from ship seizures, captured cargoes, and the suppression of the illicit trade with the French and Dutch West Indies. Maritime cases were heard in the Court of Vice-Admiralty, which sat in New York City. Livingston was among the few attorneys who virtually monopolized the practice of this court.[35] Although maritime cases constituted but a small portion of Livingston's total practice, the financial returns were disproportionately large since the established schedules of fees did not apply in the Vice-Admiralty Court. The value of the ships and cargo in dispute determined counsel's fees. In one privateering case alone, Livingston earned £196 3*s.* 8*d.* Great issues were seldom debated in the Vice-Admiralty Court, but on one occasion Livingston's arguments resulted in narrowing the interpretation of the unpopular Acts of Trade and in removing jurisdiction over certain maritime cases from the admiralty to the common-law courts.[36]

Next to commercial litigation, suits involving real property comprised the bulk of Livingston's law practice. His dockets were filled with the names of wealthy landowners whom he represented in ejectment proceedings against their tenants: the Livingstons, Morrises, Philipses, Robinsons, Van Rensselaers, and De Lanceys. That Oliver De Lancey, a political archfoe of the Livingston family, should retain William as his legal counsel merely demonstrated the degree to which political antipathies could be submerged when common economic interests were at stake.[37] During the large-scale agrarian disturbances on the great Hudson Valley estates in the late 1760s, Livingston made over fifty appearances in the Supreme Court as counsel for landlords in actions against defiant tenants.[38] Not infrequently, he acted on his own behalf, for by this time he was not only an ally of the landed aristocracy but a landowner as well.

Livingston's propertied clients included Jerseyites as well as New Yorkers. James Alexander, his old law teacher, was one of the East Jersey Proprietors, and these landowners were almost constantly engaged in litigation with small holders who refused to acknowledge the title of the proprietary group. Livingston, with William Smith, Jr., was frequently engaged by the proprietors in suits against tenants and squatters. One such action, in 1754, arose from the near-armed warfare that developed between New Yorkers and Jerseyites along the border between the two colonies. Jersey officials representing the proprietors sought to evict settlers from land claimed by the Alexander group. The settlers secured assistance from New York courts, which ordered the arrest of the Jersey process servers. Livingston successfully defended the proprietary agents, challenging the jurisdiction of the New York courts on the ground that the locus of the alleged offense was in New Jersey. Since the boundary was in dispute, Livingston's plea was valid, and his challenge had the effect of terminating the New York proceedings.[39]

Clients did not always reflect the political, religious, or social interests of their counsel. Thus while Livingston feuded bitterly with Lieutenant Governor Colden in the political arena, the latter's son employed Livingston as his attorney in Ulster County land actions.[40] And while Livingston acted on behalf of the Jersey proprietors in some cases, he represented small holders against the proprietary group in others.[41] The most prominent such case was the famous suit in chancery of "John, Earl of Stair, and others v. Benjamin Bond and others." This action, prolonged and involved, was begun in 1745 and continued in litigation for over three decades. At issue was the ownership of the lands in and around Elizabethtown, New Jersey. Livingston and his colleague, William Smith, Jr., entered the case in 1750 as counsel for the "Elizabethtown Associates," the small holders who challenged the claims of the East Jersey Proprietors.

The proprietors based their title on claims from Berkeley and Carteret; the small holders had Indian deeds to prove their ownership.

When common-law actions, petitions to the New Jersey legislature, and an appeal to the Crown all failed to validate the proprietors' claim, in 1745 they instituted a proceeding in the juryless chancery court, confident of the outcome because the incumbent governor and chancellor, Lewis Morris, was himself one of the proprietary group.[42] The bill in chancery filed by James Alexander and Joseph Murray on the proprietors' behalf was an awesome document of over 160 pages which had been three years in preparation. Livingston and Smith required almost two years to write their reply, a more modest effort of only forty-eight pages.[43]

The mass of laws, deeds, patents, indentures, and maps included in these two prolix documents did little to clarify or simplify the issues in dispute. To complicate matters further and to harass their opponents, Livingston and Smith filed their reply on behalf of about 450 defendants, although only sixty had been named in the original bill. The purpose of this bit of legal legerdemain was to put the proprietors to "an Immense Charge to Serve all of them with the Future Necessary proofs of the Court," a trick which Alexander was quick to recognize but which he could not readily circumvent. In addition, the defense counsel challenged the jurisdiction of the chancery court on the ground that it had been erected without royal warrant.[44]

Haggling between the opposing counsel over pretrial proceedings, demurrers, petitions, motions, and replies dragged the case out for years.[45] Parties to the original suit died; Morris was replaced by Governor Jonathan Belcher, who was known to be sympathetic to the Elizabethtown Associates; the French and Indian War diverted attention from the litigation; and despite the immense labors that had gone into the preparation of the case, it was never brought to trial.[46] Had the suit been revived after the Revolution, it would have been heard by the then governor of the state of New Jersey, William Livingston.

Criminal cases were as exceptional as outstanding civil suits in Livingston's practice. The high cost of justice deterred the employment of counsel in most criminal actions, and judicial procedure limited the role of the participating lawyers. There were few opportunities for forensic contests or the display of clever courtroom tactics. Livingston's law records reveal few criminal cases of significance. In an illustrative, if not typical, Supreme Court term, that of January 1768, Livingston made thirty-five appearances. Twenty-three were ordinary debt actions, four were ejectments, seven were testamentary causes, and one a suit for restitution. Not one of the cases was of a criminal character. During his entire career at the bar, Livingston was employed in only sixteen criminal proceedings out of a Supreme Court total of some six hundred.[47]

The few criminal cases of record in which Livingston was engaged attracted public attention because of the prominence of the defendants or the nature of the crime. In a celebrated rape case in 1754, Livingston was retained by four gay blades who were charged with criminally assaulting a fourteen-year-old girl. The attorney general's information alleged that the foursome "with fforce and Arms . . . did make an Assault . . . beat wound and illtreat so that of her life it was greatly dispaired . . . Mary Anderson . . . a young Girl at the time of the Violence . . . but barely turned 14 years of Age." The Crown made a strong appeal for conviction, denouncing the crime as "reprehensible" and warning that failure to punish the offenders would threaten the chastity of every woman in the city—"No mans wife or Daughter would be long secure from the brutal Attempts of lustfull and licentious people."[48]

Not content with their first offense, the defendants proceeded—according to the attorney general—to arrange a "frame-up" against the girl's mother in order to bar her testimony at the expected trial. A trumped-up charge of stealing a petticoat brought Mrs. Anderson before the city's magistrates, who adjudged her guilty and sentenced her to public whipping. Although Livingston appears to have had no part in the alleged plot, he made a vigorous attempt at the trial to bar the mother's testimony on the ground that "Having undergone a publick punishm[en]t by whipping . . . she is thereby infamous and disqualified to be a Witness." Although the Crown managed to answer this argument satisfactorily, Livingston apparently cast sufficient doubt upon Mrs. Anderson's credibility to weaken her testimony. The trial on April 18, 1755, resulted in a verdict of not guilty.[49]

Still another of Livingston's criminal cases bears the dubious distinction of being the most confused and complicated prosecution in the colony's legal history. It arose from the Crown's efforts during the French and Indian War to curb the vast illicit trade with the enemy carried on from New York. A corps of paid informers was recruited for the purpose, and one of the most notorious of these agents was one George Spencer. To prevent his testimony from being used in future proceedings, some of the city's merchants arranged a plot designed to bring Spencer into public disgrace. The plot was executed neatly. An organized mob raided Spencer's home on the evening of November 2, 1759, dragged him outside, plied him with liquor until he was drunk, and then hauled him through the streets in a cart, showering him with blows, "filth, and offal" along the route.[50]

To protect Spencer and other informants, the attorney general, John Tabor Kempe, immediately secured indictments for riot against seven persons, almost all of whom were leaders of the city's mercantile community. Livingston was retained by two of the defendants, James Duane by the others. Through successive postponements, they managed to delay the case for over a year. Kempe, irritated almost to the point of hysteria by the defense's dilatory tactics, managed to use the intervening time to pile up additional charges against the accused, adamant in his refusal to drop the prosecutions. When the first of the trials took place, in 1761, Livingston's client was acquitted; and although Kempe moved for a new trial, the court records show no evidence that his motion was granted. The other defendants presumably were the beneficiaries of Livingston's successful defense, since their cases seem never to have been tried.[51]

A few of Livingston's cases excited popular attention because important political or constitutional issues were at stake; and in such suits Livingston usually acted in association with William Smith, Jr., and John Morin Scott. Dubbed the "triumvirate" because of their joint leadership of the Livingston-Presbyterian "party," the three did not constitute a formal legal partnership; but in cases bearing political or religious overtones, they worked together. Their first public appearance as a team was made in 1754, in what appeared to be a minor debt action, but in arguing the case they transformed it into a challenge to the constitutional structure of the British Empire in America.

The suit of John Obriant *v.* William Bryant originated inauspiciously enough in the New York Mayor's Court in March 1752. The plaintiff sued to compel payment by Bryant of a seven-year-old debt, amounting with interest to about £60. Livingston, as counsel for the defendant, secured removal of the case to the Supreme Court, where, after preliminary legal maneuvering, it was tried on October 24, 1753, judgment being rendered for the plaintiff.[52] Livingston now sought, by "writ of error," to carry the case on appeal to the governor and Council, based upon certain defense exceptions to the bench's ruling on the admissibility of some evidence. Despite objections from Lambert Moore, Obriant's counsel, the writ was granted, returnable before the governor in December 1754. During the interim, both sides enlisted additional counsel, Smith and Scott joining Livingston for the defense and Benjamin Nicoll assisting Moore.[53]

Obriant's lawyers introduced the broader implications of the suit in arguing that the writ of error should be quashed because the most recent royal instructions to the governor forbade appeals beyond the Supreme Court in cases involving less than £300.[54] In their rebuttal, the triumvirate protested that adherence to such instructions would virtually eliminate all appeals beyond the Supreme Court since "not one personal action in a Thousand in this Infant Country" was above £300 in value. The judges of the Supreme Court would thus be "unaccountable for their Errors and in a Vast Degree the absolute Master of the Property of his Majesty's subjects."[55] But the trio also attacked Obriant's position at its constitutional root. A writ of error, they insisted, was a writ of right; and although it may have originated by, it did not depend upon, royal instructions but was rather "part of the Political Constitution and State of this Province necessary to the Peace of his Majesty's government and advantageous to the Rights of his Subjects."

The triumvirate challenged the validity of the royal instruction on the ground that it was neither sanctioned by common law nor confirmed by act of Parliament or of the New York legislature. No mere instrument of imperial administration could "Destroy nor Restrain inlarge nor Abridge" a right that was "interwoven with and part of the Political Frame and Constitution of this Province." The instruction in question was a "most mischievous" one, and if upheld it would vest the judges with an "uncontrollable, absolute, and formidable despotism" over the property of British subjects and would deny the latter a constitutional right of "having Recourse where Error hath intervened."[56]

Livingston and his associates lost their case when the Council, in March 1755, sustained the validity of the royal instruction, declined to accept jurisdiction of the suit, and ordered the writ of error vacated and the original judgment affirmed.[57] The principles they invoked in arguing the case, however, were scarcely lost, for the challenge to government by instruction, the attack on arbitrary acts of imperial administration, and the presupposition of a colonial constitution formed the essence of the legal position taken by the colonists on the eve of the Revolution. In their perception of this basic weakness in the imperial system, the triumvirate anticipated the later analyses of more vigorous critics like Otis, the Adamses, Dickinson, and Jefferson.[58]

The triumvirate again raised the same constitutional question a few years later, in the celebrated case of Forsey *v*. Cunningham. This suit arose in 1763 from an altercation between two of the city's merchants, Thomas Forsey and Waddel Cunningham, in which the former was severely wounded. Forsey instituted two actions for assault and battery against Cunningham, one civil and one criminal, winning both. The civil suit became the *cause célèbre* when Cunningham, failing to have the £1500 judgment against him set aside as excessive, appealed for a review of the case to Lieutenant Governor Colden.[59]

The Supreme Court judges refused Colden's request for the minutes of the trial on the ground that since no errors of law were involved, "no proper writ" for sending up the record existed. Colden insisted on his right to review the facts in the case as well as the law; bench and bar almost to a man opposed Colden's action as a threat to the inviolability of jury trials; and Colden exacerbated public suspicion by insisting that, as the Crown's representative, he could virtually erect courts at will and define their jurisdiction and procedure.[60] Coinciding with the news of the approaching Stamp Tax, Colden's "unseasonable Effort" to introduce a judicial innovation was viewed by the triumvirate as evidence that "the Crown is aiming to deprive the Subject of his most valuable Rights."[61]

While the legal profession pleaded the case in court, Livingston sounded the alarm in a series of newspaper essays in which he warned that Colden's "scandalous abuse of the King's name and authority" would subvert the ancient right of trial by jury and destroy the "excellency" of the British constitution. The New York Assembly added its own protest, and the Board of Trade ultimately upheld the Livingston position.[62] The triumvirate's victory had political as well as legal repercussions. The clamor over the Forsey case helped to raise public tempers and set the stage for the Stamp Act disorders. New Yorkers viewed Colden's attitude and the new British taxes as two sides of the same coin: a tightened imperial administration; and they were as vocal in protesting the one as the other.

Commonplace rather than distinguished cases provided the measure of Livingston's professional success. An examination of his law registers for the period 1750-1763 discloses a total of 1,150 cases, fully half of which were undertaken during the years of the French and Indian War, a period of intense activity for the entire legal fraternity. The contrast between the prewar and the war years is shown in the following table.

	Total cases	*Average annual case load*
1750-1753	170	43
1753-1759	433	72
1759-1763	547	137

In the New York Supreme Court, Livingston's activity increased similarly. During the period 1753-1759, he appeared in the Supreme Court an average of eighteen times each term; during 1759-1763, that figure increased to twenty-five. From 1750 to 1760, Livingston's appearances averaged about seventy-two a year; during the three-year period 1763-1765, the number almost doubled.[63]

Nevertheless, Livingston's practice was both less extensive and less lucrative than that of his colleagues of the triumvirate. During his first ten years as a lawyer, Livingston handled 257 cases in the New York Supreme Court; William Smith, Jr., had 362 during his own first decade in the law.[64] From 1760 to 1768, Livingston appeared in the Supreme Court about twenty-six times each term; Smith, forty-one; and John Morin Scott, forty-three. All three reached their peak of activity in the Supreme Court during the years 1763-1765, and again the junior partners outstripped Livingston in the volume of their practice. Their appearances during this period were:

	1763	*1764*	*1765*	*Total*	*Annual average*[65]
Livingston	146	127	141	414	138
Smith	211	167	176	554	185
Scott	167	182	226	575	192

The account book which Livingston maintained from 1748 to 1773 discloses the extent of his professional income. Although he maintained it with fidelity throughout his legal career, it may well err in understating his earnings. He was often lax in recording receipts and was generally haphazard about collecting debts, pressing clients for payment, and keeping straight his personal finances. The reason was his professed "aversion to Figures." "Of all Things," he once confessed, "I hate to keep Accounts." Finances represented to him a subject "more intricate" than "all the hieroglyphics of Egypt."[66]

Livingston's income paralleled his practice, although receipts often lagged behind litigation. Prior to 1752, Livingston's earnings from the law amounted to an average of about £200 a year; during the next four years, they doubled.[67]

1748-1749	£ 70.9.0	1752-1753	£336. 0.0
1749-1750	145.3.3	1753-1754	442. 8.0
1750-1751	217.5.9	1754-1755	406.17.11
1751-1752	358.0.0	1755-1756	354.12.2

The increase in litigation accompanying the outbreak of the French and Indian War was reflected in the receipts of the year 1757. For the first time, Livingston's income rose to over £1000.[68] It never sank below that level for the next decade, except during the year of the Stamp Act's operation. The closing of the courts following the enactment of the law interrupted the prosperity of the entire legal profession, and Livingston suffered with the rest of his colleagues. His income dropped precipitously from a high of £1472 during 1765-1766 to a meager £425 the following year. Livingston marked the loss by the rueful comment in his "Account Book": "The small am[oun]t of this years profit owing to the Stamp Act."[69]

The reopening of the courts the next year, however, brought a "Luxuriant Harvest of Law" as the institution of long-delayed suits crowded the courts' calendars. Livingston reaped the fruit with the rest of the bar as his income rose over the £1000 mark.[70]

From 1769 to 1773, Livingston's practice declined steadily. The dislocations produced by the new British commercial restrictions upset normal business relations between mother country and colonies, and the law reflected the disturbance. In addition, Livingston found himself in competition with an increasing number of New Yorkers who had entered the legal profession. Finally, he had already begun a voluntary contraction of practice in anticipation of his forthcoming removal to Elizabethtown, New Jersey.

At the time of his retirement from active practice in 1772, Livingston had acquired an estate variously estimated at between £6000 and £8500, together with extensive property holdings of uneven value. This did not constitute great wealth in a city where commercial fortunes of £10,000 were not uncommon, but Livingston believed the sum sufficient to permit him "with justice to my dear children [to] go into the country, where the interest . . . would more than maintain me."[71] Other New York lawyers of the day profited more handsomely from their profession. During his five best years, Livingston's income from the law averaged £1287; James Duane's was over £1400. In his best year, Livingston earned £1472; Duane bested that figure by almost £400; William Smith, Jr., declined a place on the Supreme Court bench because its £500 salary would be less than half of his average income from private practice.[72] John Tabor Kempe, New York's attorney general from 1759 to the end of the Revolution, managed to average about £884 annually from his private law practice; Livingston, during twenty-four years at the New York bar, averaged only £695 annually.[73]

Some New York lawyers developed secondary economic interests. Smith held the positions of clerk in chancery and clerk of Queens County; Duane was deputy to the provincial attorney general; and both, along with John Morin Scott, speculated actively in land and accumulated vast holdings in New York and Vermont. Livingston neither sought nor secured judicial office, and although he was considered among the landed aristocracy of the colony, his property brought him few financial dividends. Even if such auxiliary enterprises had turned out more successfully, Livingston's carelessness would probably have dissipated the gains. "The truth is," he once wrote, that "I do not set a proper value on Money, and tho' I may soon be in the way of getting it, I dispair of ever attaining the Art of keeping it." Thirty years later he was forced to confess that "tho' it has been for many years my profession to manage other people's affairs, I never had any sagacity about my own."[74] The executors of his estate, struggling to repair the damage done by Livingston's lifetime of casual record keeping and over-indulgence with debtors, could well agree with his daughter Susan when she observed: "Papa was too lenient, he suffered every one to do as they pleased with his property."[75]

Neither the extent of his practice nor his income reflects adequately Livingston's influence in the law. He was active in every effort to raise professional standards and to improve legal education. He urged stricter requirements for admission to the bar—including a system of public examinations—in order to prevent the influx of untrained practitioners; he attacked the county courts for permitting unlicensed attorneys to practice before them.[76] He joined with other New York lawyers in 1756 in demanding a bachelor's degree of all future apprentices; and when this stipulation proved too stringent to enforce, he reluctantly agreed to relax the requirement to two years of college.[77] The requirements for admission to practice were ultimately fixed by the Supreme Court, and they were more liberal than Livingston would have liked: a five-year apprenticeship for those without college training, and a three-year clerkship for college graduates.[78]

With Smith and Scott, Livingston drew up a "Plan for a regulation of the several Rates of Business in the Profession" aimed at preventing fee-cutting wars among the city's better attorneys.[79] He urged reform of the rural courts and higher qualifications for justices of the peace, and when the New York Assembly passed legislation extending the jurisdiction of the local justices, he fought it unsuccessfully all the way to the Privy Council in England.[80] He criticized the delays in the chancery courts, demanded speedier trials in the Supreme Court and the Mayor's Court, and pleaded for improvement in the quality of juries.[81]

In his own office, Livingston provided his clerks with an elementary course of study and an extensive library, a double advantage not extended to most apprentices in colonial New York. The reading program was patterned after the one Livingston had used during his own clerkship. Its prescriptions for studying not merely law but also geography, history, divinity, and rhetoric were intended to "make a compleat Lawyer" and to "contribute their part to the perfecting a Scholar."[82] Livingston's library itself was evidence enough of the catholicity of his literary tastes and the breadth of his intellectual interests. The imperfect remnant which was inventoried in 1790, upon his death, showed over five hundred volumes. Law, political theory, and history made up about half of its contents; the remainder included the classics, poetry, contemporary English and French literature, essays, and science.[83]

The capstone of Livingston's efforts to improve the legal profession in New York was the law society which he helped to found in 1770 and of which he became the first president. It was "The Moot," patterned after the Moot of Gray's Inn in England. Meetings were professional rather than social, and its regular sessions were devoted to formal debates on technical questions in law and to discussions of large questions of professional policy. Younger members of the bar received there virtually the benefits of a graduate education in law, and veteran lawyers and even justices of the Supreme Court sought the collective judgment of the Moot on knotty legal questions. As a kind of seminar in legal education and an instrument for correcting defects in the province's legal system, the Moot was unique among colonial law societies.[84]

Had Livingston devoted his full energies to his profession, his place in American legal history would now be far more secure than it is. But he spread his abilities capriciously, shifting rapidly from one passionate attachment to another, giving each of his interests a large measure of his creative capacities, but neglecting to focus his full talents on any single one. He learned to paint and sketch; he studied foreign languages; he wrote and published poetry—of sufficient importance to make him colonial New York's leading poet; he was an accomplished essayist and journalist and an avid horticulturist; he was a vigorous early exponent of public education.

His liberalism propelled him into the political struggle between the Livingston-Whig party and the De Lancey-Tory faction, and his barbed pen became a potent weapon in the Livingston armory. His anticlericalism spurred him to lead two bitter contests against the Anglican Church, one over the attempts to found King's College under Episcopal control, the other over the proposal to establish an American Episcopate. His affection for the Empire made him a champion of the colonial forces which demanded vigorous prosecution of the French and Indian War; his attachment to America led him to resist, with equal vigor, the postwar measures to tighten the reins of imperial control. When he retired in 1772 to his country retreat at Elizabethtown, New Jersey, he paused only momentarily before embarking on yet another full career—as a delegate to the Continental Congress, commander of the New Jersey militia, first Governor of the State of New Jersey and its political chief through the Revolution, one of the ablest war propagandists on the American side during that conflict, and a member of the Constitutional Convention. And if his legal reputation suffered any neglect, it was merely the happy consequence of his distinction in so many other fields.

Notes

1. J. Hector St. John de Crèvecoeur, *Letters from an American Farmer* (London, 1782), 47; Colden to the Earl of Halifax, Feb. 22, 1765, *Colden Letter Books,* I, 469-471.

2. *Letter Book of John Watts, Merchant and Councillor of New York* (N.Y. Hist. Soc. *Collections,* 1928), 13; Anne Grant, *Memoirs of an American Lady,* II, 152. On the state of the law in early 18th-century New York, see Richard B. Morris, ed., *Select Cases of the Mayor's Court of New York City, 1674-1784* (Washington, D.C., 1935), 52-56, and Flick, ed., *History of the State of New York,* III, 34-36.

3. William Livingston to Noah Welles, July 24, 1745, JFP, Yale; *New-York Weekly Post-Boy,* Aug. 19, 1745.

4. [William Livingston], *The Art of Pleading, In Imitation of Part of Horace's Art of Poetry* (New York, 1751), 7-10. For the authorship of this anonymous publication, see Sedgwick, *Memoir,* 448 note, and William Livingston, Jr., to William Paterson, May 29, 1801, Livingston MSS, New York Historical Society.

5. Minute Book of the Supreme Court of Judicature, 1723-1727, 75-97; 1733-1739, 103-123; 1750-1754, 59-78; Hall of Records, New York City.

6. Mayor's Court Minutes, 1718-1720, 358-360; 1720-1723, 1-2, 8-10; 1729-1734, 76-86; 1750-1751, 321-333, Hall of Records, N.Y.C.

7. The same process was going on in other colonies. See Richard B. Morris, *Studies in the History of American Law* (New York, 1930), 62-66; Charles Warren, *A History of the American Bar* (Boston, 1911), 16-17; Paul M. Hamlin, *Legal Education in Colonial New York* (New York, 1939), 3-6, 115-116; Anton-Hermann Chroust, *The Rise of the Legal Profession in America,* 2 vols. (Norman, Okla., 1965), Vol. I, *passim.;* Lawrence M. Friedman, *A History of American Law* (New York, 1973), 45-49, 84-88.

8. The two articles appeared in the *New-York Weekly Post-Boy,* Aug. 19, 1745, and March 3, 1746.

9. Hamlin, *Legal Education,* 76-78, 80-82, 171-176, 182-192. Hamlin (61-62, 82) attributes this law course, erroneously, to William Smith, Jr., and dates it about 1756. Actually both Smith and Livingston were introduced to the program in the elder Smith's office much earlier. In 1747 the younger Smith sent it to a Connecticut friend who had sought help in studying law. See George C. Groce, Jr., *William Samuel Johnson: A Maker of the Constitution* (New York, 1937), 20 note.

10. Livingston's version may be found in his Lawyer's Book of Precedents, 139-142, New York State Library, Albany. With minor variations, it is the same as the one in the younger Smith's Commonplace Book, William Smith Papers, IX, Miscellania A, New York Public Library. Smith's version appears in Hamlin, *Legal Education,* 197-200.

11. Livingston secured his license on Oct. 14, 1748, and was admitted to the bar by the Supreme Court four days later.

12. Cost Books of Cases in which William Livingston Appeared as Counsel before the New York Supreme Court, I, 1-2, New York Public Library; Mayor's Court Minutes, 1749-1750, 197 (Aug. 29, 1749).

13. Account Book, 1748-1773, Livingston Papers, Mass. Hist. Soc. Livingston figured his receipts from October 1748 to September 1750 as £215 12*s.* 9*d.* and his expenses as £19 7*s.* 5*d.*

14. Hamlin, *Legal Education,* 35-36; Morris, ed., *Mayor's Court,* 53; Edwards, *New York as an Eighteenth Century Municipality,* 32-33; Livingston

to James Stevenson, April 18, 1754, March 28, 1755, Letter Book A, 1754-1770, Livingston Papers, Mass. Hist. Soc.

15. *New-York Gazette,* Feb. 18, April 1, 1751; *Independent Reflector,* ed. Klein, 299-305 (July 26, 1753).

16. *The Art of Pleading,* iv, 11.

17. *Colonial Laws of New York,* III, 832-835.

18. *Colden Letter Books,* I, 84; William Smith Papers, I, "1753," New York Public Library. The work bore the title *Laws of New-York, from the Year 1691, to 1751, Inclusive* (New York, 1752). The publisher was James Parker. See *New-York Gazette,* Jan. 28, 1751, April 27, Aug. 10, 1752.

19. *Laws of New-York, from the 11th Nov. 1752, to 22d May 1762 . . . Digested by William Livingston, and William Smith, Jun.* (New York, 1752). The publisher was William Weyman. For this supplement, Livingston and Smith received about £59 each. See Livingston Account Book, 1748-1773, entry of Jan. 12, 1764.

20. Livingston, Law Register, 1750-1762 [1753], 41, 51, Livingston Papers, Mass. Hist. Soc.; William Livingston to Peter Van Brugh Livingston, [August 1751], Vol. A, Livingston Papers, Mass. Hist. Soc.

21. Law Register, 1750-1762 [1753], 51, 53, 101-102; Livingston, Supreme Court Cost Books, I, 32-33, 48-49.

22. Edward P. Alexander, *A Revolutionary Conservative, James Duane of New York* (New York, 1938), 40, 42-46.

23. Account Book, 1748-1773.

24. In an illustrative year, 1754, the Supreme Court held sessions at Orange Town on June 1; at Poughkeepsie, June 3; at Kingston, June 6; and at Albany, June 11. In the fall, the court sat in Queens County on Sep. 3; in Suffolk on Sep. 10; in Kings on Sep. 17; and in Weschester on Sep. 24. Supreme Court Minute Book, 1754-1757, 18, 52.

25. Two such requests, in 1772 and 1773, were honored, even though Livingston had already moved to Elizabethtown, N.J. See Abraham Yates to Livingston, May 18, 1772, Beverly Robinson to James Duane, March 25, May 8, 1773, Duane Papers, New York Historical Society; Robinson to John Thomas, May 8, 1772, Robinson to Livingston, Aug. 27, 1773, Philipse-Gouverneur Family Papers, Columbia University.

26. An incomplete survey of litigation in seven American colonies, excluding New York, shows that in the mid-1730s matters of real estate, probate, and business comprised 47.4 percent of all cases of record. The percentage was probably greater during the next few decades. See Alfred S. Faught, "Three Centuries of American Litigation," *Temple University Law Quarterly,* XIII (1939), 501, 504.

27. In Livingston's Book of Precedents (410-436), the list of fees for various judicial officials took up twenty-seven pages. Included were fees of sheriffs, criers, clerks, judges, sergeants-at-arms, notaries, surveyors, doorkeepers, solicitors, coroners, masters, recorders, mayors, and the attorney general.

28. *Ibid.,* 412-414; Henry W. Scott, *The Courts of the State of New York* (New York, 1909), 143; Goebel and Naughton, *Law Enforcement in Colonial New York,* 731 ff.; Morris, ed., *Mayor's Court,* 169-171.

29. See, for example, Supreme Court Minute Book, 1756-1761, 229; 1757-1760, 153-154; "Report of Referees, McMillan ads. Lynch," Oct. 22, 1764, bound in the New York Historical Society copy of John W. Francis, *Old New York,* III, 429; Morris, ed., *Mayor's Court,* 551-565.

30. Colden to Lords Commissioners for Trade and Plantations, Aug. 9, 1764, *Colden Letter Books,* I, 342.

31. Livingston to John Strettell, April 17, 1754, to Joseph Richardson, May 8, 1754, to Timothy Forbes, June 7, 1755, Letter Book A, 1754-1770, Livingston Papers, Mass. Hist. Soc.

32. Livingston to James Stevenson, April 18, 1754, to Thomas Monkland, May 24, 1754, *ibid.*

33. Supreme Court Minute Book, 1754-1757, 33-35, 62-63, 73-75. See also William Livingston to Henry Livingston, Aug. 14, 1754, Letter Book A, 1754-1770, Livingston Papers, Mass. Hist. Soc.

34. Account Book, 1748-1773. Receipts for the period September 1753 to September 1754 were £442 8*s*. 9*d*.

35. Charles M. Hough, ed., *Reports of Cases in the Vice Admiralty of the Province of New York and in the Court of Admiralty of the State of New York, 1715-1788* (New Haven, 1925), xxiv-xxvi.

36. *Ibid.,* xx and 82-83. The incomplete record of admiralty proceedings published by Hough includes twenty-one cases between 1754 and 1762 in which Livingston acted as counsel.

37. See, for example, Supreme Court Minute Book, 1762-1764, 29.

38. *Ibid.,* 69-72, 85, 159, 228-230, 346-347, 403, 422, 424, 428; 1764-1767, 11, 38-39, 71-74, 90; 1764-1766, 224-226, 300; 1766-1769, 375-376. On the tenant uprisings of 1766, see Mark, *Agrarian Conflicts,* chap. 5.

39. The border controversy was an involved one. Not only were some settlers prosecuted by the Jersey landowners for trespass, but others who accepted Jersey title were harassed by demands for taxes from New York officials. The 1754 suit was fought in the Orange County courts. See James Alexander to Richard Gardner, Jan. 19, 1754, Alexander to David Ogden, Jan. 29, 1754, to William Alexander, July 25, 1754, "Account of the Expenses of William Livingston, William Smith and William Alexander to Orange County Court, April-May 1754," Stevens Family Papers, New Jersey Historical Society; Supreme Court Minute Book, 1754-1757, 44, 49; Goebel and Naughton, *Law Enforcement,* 314 note and 587 note.

40. Livingston to David Colden, April 27, 1762, Colden to Livingston, April 27, 1762, *Colden Papers,* VI, 155-156, IX, 184-185.

41. In 1753, for example, Livingston defended one small holder in a trespass and ejectment proceeding in which James Alexander represented the plaintiff. Livingston to James Alexander, Aug. 9, 1753, Alexander Papers, New York Historical Society.

42. On the background of the case, see Donald L. Kemmerer, *Path to Freedom: The Struggle for Self-Government in Colonial New Jersey, 1703-1776* (Princeton, 1940), 4-15, 187-196; Edwin F. Hatfield, *History of Elizabeth, New Jersey* (New York, 1868), 366-369; Edgar J. Fisher, *New Jersey as a Royal Province, 1738 to 1776* (New York, 1911), 176 ff.; Herbert L. Osgood, *The American Colonies in the Eighteenth Century,* 4 vols. (New York, 1924), IV, 27-31; Gary S. Horowitz, "New Jersey Land Riots, 1745-1755" (unpublished Ph.D. dissertation, Ohio State U., 1966), chaps. 1-3.

43. *A Bill in the Chancery of New-Jersey, at the Suit of John Earl of Stair, and others . . . against Benjamin Bond, and some other Persons of Elizabeth-Town . . .* (New York, 1747); *An Answer to a Bill in the Chancery of New-*Jersey . . . (New York, 1752). A bulky handwritten copy of the *Answer* is in the Stevens Family Papers, New Jersey Historical Society.

44. James Alexander to Livingston and Smith, March 3, 1752, Livingston Papers, Mass. Hist. Soc.; Richard S. Field, *The Provincial Courts of New Jersey* (New York, 1849), 122.

45. Alexander to Livingston and Smith, March 3, Nov. 29, 1752; Alexander and Murray, "Notice of Motions for rules," Dec. 15, 1752, "Brief to Point out the Indulgence of the Complainants and Dilatory Proceedings of the Defendants . . . ," Dec. 1752, "Notice of Motion for March 19, 1753," March 5, 1753; Livingston, Smith, and Nicoll to Alexander, Nov. 25, 1752; all in Livingston Papers, Mass. Hist. Soc.

46. Osgood, *American Colonies,* IV, 37; Kemmerer, *Path to Freedom,* 234-235; Hatfield, *History of Elizabeth,* 372; Field, *Provincial Courts,* 123; Fisher, *New Jersey,* 206-209.

47. Goebel and Naughton, *Law Enforcement,* 573-575; Supreme Court Minute Book, 1766-1769, 373-391; Livingston, Supreme Court Cost Books, I and II, *passim.*

48. "The King agt. John Lawrence, Jr., Charles Arding, Cornelius Livingston, and Hendrick Oudenard," Aug. 1, 1754, Supreme Court Pleadings, K-501, K-650, Hall of Records, N.Y.C.; Supreme Court Minute Book, 1754-1757, 53; Livingston to William Kempe, Aug. 26, 1754; Livingston Papers, Mass. Hist. Soc.

49. Supreme Court Pleadings, K-501; Supreme Court Minute Book, 1754-1757, 145-146. A discussion of the case and the text of the attorney general's information may be found in Goebel and Naughton, *Law Enforcement,* 262-263, 786-791.

50. Supreme Court Pleadings, K-930; Goebel and Naughton, *Law Enforcement,* 280-281.

51. Livingston, Supreme Court Cost Books, I, 358, 360, II, 1-7; Supreme Court Pleadings, K-926, 930, 962, 976; Supreme Court Minute Book, 1756-1761, 239, 1762-1764, 172; Goebel and Naughton, *Law Enforcement,* 282-283.

52. Mayor's Court Minutes, 1752-1753, 119; Supreme Court Minute Book, 1750-1754, 153, 177, 263, 312-313; Supreme Court Parchment Rolls, 228-D-1, Hall of Records, N.Y.C.

53. Supreme Court Minute Book, 1750-1754, 336. The triumvirate also secured assistance from William Smith, Sr. See Livingston, Supreme Court Cost Books, I, 86-87.

54. Supreme Court Parchment Rolls, 228-D-1. The figure had been raised from £100 to £300 in the instructions issued to Sir Danvers Osborn, who arrived as governor in October 1753.

55. Livingston, Smith, and Scott, "Wm. Bryant agt. John Obriant, In Error," [1754?], in William Smith Papers, II, 375-380, New York Public Library.

56. Smith, *History,* II, 204-205; Joseph H. Smith, *Appeals to the Privy Council from the American Plantations* (New York, 1950), 220-221.

57. Supreme Court Parchment Rolls, 228-D-1; *Calendar of Council Minutes, 1668-1783* (New York State Library Bulletin 58, March 1902 [Albany, 1902]), 399.

58. In this connection, see Leonard W. Labaree, *Royal Government in America: A Study of the British Colonial System before 1783* (New Haven, 1930), chap. 10; and Charles F. Mullett, *Fundamental Law and the American Revolution, 1760-1766* (New York, 1933), *passim.*

59. Livingston, Supreme Court Cost Books, II, 207; William Smith Papers, IV, "1764," New York Public Library; Supreme Court Minute Book, 1762-1764, 224-225, 308, 358-359; 1764-1767, 18, 32; Supreme Court Parchment Rolls, 21-A-8, 28-K-9, 186-K-3.

60. "Cadwallader Colden's Opinion on Appeals," [January 1765], *Colden Papers,* VII, 1-7.

61. William Smith, Jr., to Governor Robert Monckton, Dec. 3, 1764, Jan. 25, 1765, Chalmers Papers, New York, IV, 14-17, New York Public Library. On this case, see Chap. 7 below.

62. "The Sentinel," I, II, III, *New-York Gazette,* Feb. 28, March 7, 14, 1765; *Assembly Journal,* [*1691-1765*], II, 803-806; *New-York Gazette,* Dec. 26, 1765; *N.Y. Col. Docs.,* VII, 762-764, 815-816.

63. Supreme Court Minute Book, 1754-1757, 1757-1760, 1756-1761, 1762-1764, *passim.*

64. Livingston, Supreme Court Cost Books, I (1749-1760); William Smith, Jr., New York Supream Court Register A (1750-1760), New York Public Library.

65. James Duane, another active member of the New York bar, divided his energies between his private practice and Crown prosecutions in which he served as the attorney general's deputy. Yet he managed to handle almost as many private suits during this same three-year period as did Livingston, 338 to be exact. Supreme Court Minute Book, 1762-1764, 1764-1766, *passim.*

66. Livingston to Henry Laurens, April 27, 1778, Aug. 9, 1779, Laurens Papers, South Carolina Historical Society.

67. Account Book, 1748-1773. Livingston's personal fiscal year ran from October to September or from September to August.

68. The exact income for 1756-1757 was £1071 16*s.* 5*d.*

69. The courts held no regular sessions from November 1765 to May 1766. See Morris, ed., *Mayor's Court,* 48.

70. Livingston's Account Book shows an increase from £425 8*s.* 2*d.* in 1766-1767 to £1015 8*s.* 8*d.* the following year. Benjamin Kissam, one of Livingston's colleagues at the bar, expressed the sentiments of the entire legal fraternity in his observation: "As upon the Repeal of the Stamp Act, we shall doubtless have a luxuriant Harvest of Law, I would not willingly, after the long Famine we have had, miss reaping my part of the crop." Kissam to Jay, April 25, 1766, in *The Correspondence and Public Papers of John Jay,* ed. Henry P. Johnston, 4 vols. (New York, 1890-1893), I, 3.

71. Sedgwick, *Memoir,* 158 and note; Virginia Harrington, *The New York Merchant on the Eve of the Revolution* (New York, 1935), 19. The £6000 estimate was made in 1774 by Rev. Ezra Stiles; the higher figure was Livingston's own. See *The Literary Diary of Ezra Stiles,* ed. Franklin B. Dexter, 3 vols. (New York, 1901), I, 635-636.

72. Account Book, 1748-1773; Alexander, *James Duane,* 36-37; William Smith Papers, IV, "5 June, 20 July 1763"; Smith to Monckton, July 20, 1763, Chalmers Papers, New York, IV, 11, New York Public Library. Livingston's best five years were 1758-1759, 1759-1760, 1760-1761, 1763-1764, and 1765-1766. In the latter year, he reached his peak income, £1472 9*s.* 3*d.* Duane's in 1753 was £1860 13*s.* 3½*d.*

73. Catherine S. Crary, "The American Dream: John Tabor Kempe's Rise from Poverty to Riches," *Wm. and Mary Qtly.,* XIV (1957), 176-195, particularly 184.

74. Livingston to Noah Welles, Dec. 16, 1751, JFP, Yale; Livingston to Rev. John Witherspoon, May 10, 1781, Livingston Papers, Mass. Hist. Soc.

75. Susan Livingston Symmes to William Livingston, Jr., Sep. 3, 1802, Livingston Papers, Mass. Hist. Soc.

76. Livingston et al., *Independent Reflector,* ed. Klein, 299-305 (July 26, 1753).

77. "Articles of Agreement entered into by the Gentlemen of the Law . . . respecting Clerks," 1756, in Livingston's Book of Precedents, 493-494; "Law Society Agreement as to Clerks," July 1764, William Smith Papers, New York Public Library; Hamlin, *Legal Education,* 38, 160-161. Hamlin mistakenly believed the James Alexander copy of the 1756 agreement (New York Historical Society) to be the only one extant.

78. Supreme Court Minute Book, 1766-1769, 180 (May 1, 1767).

79. "New York City Bar Agreement Dated November 26, 1756," in Hamlin, *Legal Education,* 162; "A Regulation for the Taxation of Costs in the Supream Court . . . ," Aug. 1, 1757, William Smith Papers, IX, Miscellania A, New York Public Library.

80. Smith, *History,* I, 311; *Independent Reflector,* ed. Klein, 352-358 (Sep. 13, 1753); *Journal of the Legislative Council of the Colony of New-York* [*1691-1775*], 2 vols. (Albany, 1861), II, 1323-1326; David Jones to Robert Charles, April 26, 1760, "Draft of Protest agt. the Act to continue the £5 Act," n.d., William Smith Papers, New York Public Library.

81. *Independent Reflector,* ed. Klein, 250-256 (June 7, 1753), 299-305 (July 26, 1753); "The Watch-Tower," XXXVI, *New-York Mercury,* July 28, 1755.

82. "Some Directions relating to the Study of the Law," in Livingston's Book of Precedents, 139-142.

83. "List of Books found in the library of his late Excellency William Livingston, Esqr. . . . , [1790?]," Livingston Papers, Mass. Hist. Soc.

84. The constitution and the proceedings of the Moot are contained in the "Moot Debating Club Minutes," 1770-1775, in the New York Historical Society.

7.

Prelude to Revolution in New York: Jury Trials and Judicial Tenure

A GENERATION of historical reinterpretation of the causes and character of the American Revolution has brought us full circle back to the view that the conflict between England and her American colonies was primarily political and constitutional. At issue, wrote the Earl of Dartmouth to General Thomas Gage, the British commander in chief in North America, was the "Constitutional Authority of this Kingdom over its Colonies" and the assertion of its laws "throughout the whole Empire."[1] Americans accepted the challenge and argued the case on Britain's terms. The central question, responded Sam Adams, was whether the constitution of Great Britain permitted the Parliament to "rightly leap the bounds of it" in exercising unwarranted "power over the subjects in America."[2] American Tories, like Governor Francis Bernard of Massachusetts, agreed that patchwork solutions would not settle the basic question. What was needed was a definition of the constitutional relationship between Britain and the colonies and the establishment of an American government upon "fixed Constitutional Principles."[3]

The constitutional and legal grounds on which the great debate was conducted from 1763 to 1776 could scarcely have been better

Reprinted from the *William and Mary Quarterly,* XVII (October 1960), 439-462, by permission of the Institute of Early American History and Culture.

designed to serve the American cause: the colonists had both the ammunition and the generalship to fight a constitutional contest. They were well fortified with political theory borrowed from England and expounded, reformulated, reiterated, and perfected in the course of over a century of local conflict between assemblies and royal governors; and in each colony they possessed a first-rate corps of veterans to lead the constitutional defense, the lawyers.

The leadership of the American Revolution was drawn from many sources—the clergy, the merchants, the planters, and the newspaper editors—but no single group was better able to articulate the colonial position within the political, legal, and constitutional framework of the Anglo-American debate than the men of the legal profession. Curiously, modern historians have done them less credit than did their contemporaries. While there are excellent monographs on the roles of the merchants, the clergy, and the press in the Revolution, there is none on the lawyers.[4] Perhaps the fullness of the subject has discouraged systematic investigation. The roster of even the better-known lawyers who were active in the years before the Revolution is impressive: Jefferson, the Adamses, James Wilson, Patrick Henry, John Dickinson, Daniel Dulany, James Otis, John Jay, Alexander Hamilton, Josiah Quincy, William Livingston, Jared Ingersoll, William Smith, Jr., Richard Bland, George Mason, William Samuel Johnson, and James Iredell.

The colonial lawyer may not have been "deeply learned by . . . English standards," as Daniel J. Boorstin claims,[5] but this is somewhat irrelevant. Americans studied law widely if not deeply; their political theory was rooted in and fused with their knowledge of law; lawyers as a class, by the eve of the Revolution, possessed both social prestige and political power,[6] and they played a decisive role in many of the colonies in precipitating the Revolution. Friends of the Crown at least were in no doubt of the legal profession's pernicious influence. "The Lawyers are the Source from whence the Clamors have flowed in every Province," General Gage assured the home government during the Stamp Act disorders.[7] American Tories echoed the charge in their assertion that the lawyers were "cultivating, with unwearied Pains, the Seeds of Infatuation and Tumult."[8]

New York's lawyers were no exception. Their influence and power were recognized and feared by Tories and Churchmen. The Reverend Samuel Johnson, a staunch Episcopalian and the first president of King's College, vouchsafed the literary talents of three of New

York's legal fraternity—William Livingston, William Smith, Jr., and John Morin Scott—when he expostulated that it was "indeed fencing against a flail to hold any dispute with them as there is nothing that they will stick at, however so false and injurious, in opposing and discrediting the Church, and which they will not cease to repeat and inculcate over and over again, however so thoroughly it was answered."[9]

The irritated clergyman's compliment to the legal profession was only oblique. That of Cadwallader Colden, New York's ageless lieutenant governor, was more direct. In a long lament to the Board of Trade, diagnosing the source of New York's violent disorders in connection with the Stamp Act, Colden pictured himself as the helpless victim of the lawyers' near-diabolical power:

> The Gentlemen of the Law, both the Judges and principal Practitioners at the Bar, are either Owners Heirs or strongly connected in family Interest with the Proprietors. . . . the power of the Lawyers is such that every Man is affraid of offending them and is deterr'd from makeing any public opposition to their power and the daily increase of it. . . . many Court their Friendship, and all dread their hatred. . . . they rule the House of Assembly in all Matters of Importance. . . .
>
> By this association, united in interest and family Connections with the proprietors of the great Tracts of Land, a Domination of Lawyers was formed in this Province. . . . A Domination founded on the same Principles and carried on by the same wicked artifices that the Domination of Priests formerly was. . . . Every Man's character who dares to discover his Sentiments in opposition to theirs is loaded with infamy by every falsehood which malice can invent, and thereby exposed to the brutal Rage of the Mob. Nothing is too wicked for them to attempt which serves their purposes—the Press is to them what the Pulpit was in times of Popery. . . .[10]

Colden had personal reasons for his antipathy toward the legal profession, but other observers, without his hypersensitivity or his political myopia, conceded the accuracy of his judgment. General Gage ascribed New York City's Stamp Act troubles to the pervasive influence of the lawyers. "In this Province Nothing Publick is transacted without them." Without the instigation of the lawyers and their merchant-allies, "the inferior People would have been quiet." A young British engineering officer, stationed in the city during the disturbances, corroborated the impression. While many people of property participated in the "disloyal Insur[r]ection," he noted in his diary, the lawyers were "at the bottom" of it. They were the "Hornets and Firebrands. . . . The Planners and Incendiaries of the present Rupture."[11]

Neither New York's turbulent reaction to the Stamp Act nor the leadership assumed by the gentlemen of the law was entirely unexpected. The "seditious spirit" of which Colden complained so bitterly was the fruit of local political discontent as much as of resentment against imperial reorganization, and the political maturity exhibited by New York's lawyers in 1765 did not emerge full-blown in that year. It was rather the climax of a succession of local contests during the previous fifteen years, in each of which the lawyers managed to pose successfully as spokesmen of the "popular" cause against the extensions of royal prerogative. Two of these contests took place on the very eve of the Stamp Act's passage, between 1760 and 1765. Both were judicial in nature, involving, respectively, the tenure of judges and the traditional right of trial by jury. As matters of technical and professional interest, these disputes naturally engaged the attention of the legal fraternity; but by clothing their arguments in the twin dress of popular rights and constitutional privilege, the lawyers succeeded in making them issues of transcendent public interest. With the "grand Engine" of the press as their instrument and the doctrine that "all authority is derived from the People" as their theme, the lawyers created a climate of opinion that the Sons of Liberty turned to ready advantage in 1765. If the violence accompanying the Stamp Act marked the first act of the Revolution in New York, then the local contests over judges and jury trials constituted a fitting prelude.

The first of the judicial clashes came in 1760. It originated in the vacancy on the Supreme Court bench created by the death of James De Lancey, who had held that post since the days of the John Peter Zenger trial. During his long tenure as chief justice and, after 1753, lieutenant governor as well, De Lancey had built a powerful political machine which controlled the provincial government for more than a decade. De Lancey's prestige was due in no small measure to his success in championing the rights of the Assembly against the "encroachments" of Governor George Clinton, particularly over control of the purse. Clinton's strife-ridden ten-year administration (1743-1753), during which the governor failed first to secure from the De Lancey Assembly a permanent revenue for the support of the government and then to secure wholehearted legislative support for the prosecution of King George's War, left its mark on Cadwallader Colden. As Clinton's principal adviser, Colden shared his chief's frustrations in the losing struggle with De Lancey. Colden became convinced by this experience that a chief justice had "more influence on the public affairs in this Country" than a governor, and that the source of De Lancey's power was the number of lawyers whose "bread and fortune" depended on his "Countenance" and who served as "his emissaries and spies in every part of the Country."[12]

In 1760 Colden assumed command of New York's government, a responsibility that devolved upon him as the senior member of the Council. Seventy-three years old and a veteran of over forty years in the colony's politics, Colden had not mellowed one bit in his inordinate fear of the bench and bar or, indeed, of any disruptive element that threatened the stability of church and state. Colden had held royal office almost from the day of his arrival in New York in 1718. As "one of the most permanent of all permanent officials" in British North America, he was the archetype of the loyal servant of the Crown and the staunch defender of royal prerogative.[13] Temperamentally, the role suited him well. Vain, ambitious, petulant, inflexible, and unimaginative, this dour Scotsman saw government as a kind of irrepressible conflict between the insidious forces of republicanism and independency and the stabilizing influence of the British monarchy and the Anglican Church. During his active career in politics, Colden managed to secure a widespread reputation as a physician, botanist, philosopher, physicist, historian, and colonial savant, but the breadth of his intellectual interests never liberalized his political outlook.[14]

As the new chief executive of New York, Colden was still firmly persuaded that the lawyers were the most dangerous enemies to good government in the colony. The courts were their private domain, and there no honest citizen could expect redress unless he were initiated into the legal mysteries that the bar so jealously guarded. The great landed proprietors were their henchmen, the two in combination perpetrating huge land frauds which legal legerdemain protected from royal investigation. The Assembly, filled with simple citizens too ignorant to exercise independent judgment in weighty matters of government, was easily swayed by the smooth-talking lawyers; and for good measure, the gentlemen of the law insinuated themselves into popular good grace by propagating the doctrine that more power ought to be lodged in the "Popular side of Government" while they depreciated the "Powers of the Crown." With monotonous persistence, Colden reiterated the theme that "All associations are dangerous to good Government . . . and associations of Lawyers the most dangerous of any next to Military."[15]

The demise of the formidable James De Lancey and the impairment of the De Lancey party's strength did not leave Colden without political foes. Two years earlier the Livingstons, who had long vied with the De Lanceys for political power in the province, had gained control of the Assembly; and the Livingstons bore no love for "the Scotch gentleman." Under Governor Clinton's administration, Philip Livingston, the second manor lord, had been accused of trading with the French and defrauding the Indians, and the Livingstons saw Colden as the real instigator of the odious charges. Angrily, Philip Livingston dubbed Colden New York's "Haman" and suggested tartly that he "ought to be turn[e]d off or sent back to his own place."[16]

Colden, for his part, shared Clinton's mordant observation that the Livingstons were "a vile family."[17] In one way or another, they had been disturbers of peace and good government for two decades: the second generation had been unconscionable land-grabbers, and now the third generation was taking over De Lancey's old role as champion of the Assembly against the Crown. Worse, the mouthpiece of the Livingstons outside the Assembly's halls was a brash young triumvirate of lawyers with whom Colden had already locked horns. The trio, William Livingston, William Smith, Jr., and John Morin Scott, were all Presbyterians and graduates of Yale College, and it was at this nursery of sedition, in Colden's view, that they had imbibed their republican principles in politics and religion. Colden's suspicions of the triumvirate had been fanned by their vigorous assault against the Anglican Church at the time of the founding of King's College. Their proposal for a "free college" under legislative sponsorship smacked to him of the "narrow principles" of religious free-thinking and political "independency" that had already polluted Harvard and Yale.[18] But Colden's distaste for the triumvirate was personal as well as political.

In 1751 Colden had approached Livingston and Smith while they were preparing a digest of the colony's laws and requested them to omit from their compilation a reference that might cast doubt on the legality of a land grant in which he held property. Despite a "soothing" entreaty to Livingston and a stormy threat to Smith, the editors held fast to their original resolution, telling Colden to "go to the Devil." For maintaining "our Opinions," Smith later recalled, Colden "never forgave us."[19] In 1757, when Smith's famous history of New York appeared, Colden objected violently to some of its veiled references to his conduct in connection with a land transaction. When his demands for "proper redress" and withdrawal of the "Misrepresentation, Falsehood and Calumny" were refused, he denounced the whole publication as not fit to "pass for a chronicle of the Province of New York."[20]

As chief executive of the province, Colden was in a position to wreak sweet vengeance on the Livingstons, the triumvirate, and all the gentlemen of the law; and like David, he strode forth garbed in his robes of viceregal virtue to do battle with the legal Goliath. It did not appear at first that the Livingstons would bar his path. The enthusiasm aroused by the success of British arms in the French and Indian War seemed to suffuse local politics with a warm glow of cordiality. The Livingston Assembly congratulated Colden on his accession to the governorship, and the head of the triumvirate himself penned the salutation.[21] Colden was deluded into thinking that his administration would go "easy." The illusion was only slightly dispelled by a brief disagreement between Colden and the Livingstons over the selection of a sheriff for Albany County,[22] but it was completely shattered by the uproar that greeted Colden's announcement of his views regarding the opening on the Supreme Court bench created by De Lancey's death.

Colden had two fixed notions with respect to the vacant chief justiceship: that the office should be filled by a stranger to New York's politics and that the appointment should be at the Crown's pleasure rather than during good behavior. With De Lancey's long rule on the bench in mind, Colden insisted that only a chief justice unconnected with the great landed families of New York or with the legal fraternity could restrain the insolent local aristocracy and compel it to respect the royal will. A chief justice dependent on the governor's pleasure would prove a useful servant of the Crown; life tenure for the head of the bench, conversely, would make the governor the Supreme Court's "tool."[23]

Colden's position could not have been "more universally disgustful," to use the words of one of the triumvirate.[24] The Livingstons had their own candidates for the vacant judicial post, William Smith, Sr., or Robert Hunter Morris; so did the De Lanceys, in the persons of two of the inferior judges of the Supreme Court, John Chambers and Daniel Horsmanden. Colden's stand infuriated both the local factions, but his behavior was particularly offensive to the Livingstons. At least the De Lancey nominations were forwarded on to England; Morris's name was peremptorily rejected, and the elder Smith was offered the appointment on terms that he had clearly announced he would refuse.[25]

The contest now initiated between Colden and the Livingstons had its counterpart in almost every other colony before the Revolution. At stake was control of the courts, and the contestants were the assemblies and the governors. One issue was the right to erect new courts and to determine their jurisdiction, the assemblies insisting that this was a legislative power and the governors claiming the power as belonging to prerogative. In New York this issue had already produced the famous Zenger case. It was Governor William Cosby's attempt to erect a new court of equity that brought down upon him the anguished protests of the Zengerites.[26] By 1760, however, the issue had been fairly well resolved in the legislature's favor, the English authorities tolerating, if not approving, various acts of the Assembly establishing New York's courts and defining their jurisdiction.[27]

The other issue, more vexing, was that of judicial tenure. Although the Glorious Revolution had settled the question in England by providing that judges should hold their offices for life, that is, "during good behavior," the privilege of life tenure had not been extended to the colonial judiciary. The Board of Trade's specious explanation was that English judges rarely had to be removed since they were both able and financially incorruptible—as a result of permanent salaries—while American judges were usually so incompetent that the Crown of necessity required the right to remove them at will in order to replace them with abler men. A more substantial ground for the Board's position was its explanation that an independent colonial judiciary would be "subversive of that Policy by which alone Colonies can be kept in a just dependance upon the Government of the Mother Country." The Board preferred, therefore, that American judges receive their commissions "during the King's pleasure" only. The colonists, in turn, countered with the charge that impartial justice could scarcely be expected from judges whose terms of office could be arbitrarily terminated whenever their decisions irritated an unfriendly governor.[28]

Principles, politics, and personalities were all intertwined in the Livingstons' position. As the majority party in the Assembly they felt compelled to uphold the privilege of judicial tenure during good behavior that the De Lanceys had wrested from Governor Clinton a decade earlier.[29] De Lancey's own commission as chief justice had been for life; the commissions of the inferior judges had been similarly drawn. By 1760 New Yorkers regarded the principle to be as firmly fixed in their own constitution as it was in England's since the Act of Settlement of 1701. Colden's refusal to honor the precedent bespoke still another example of his "sycophantic" attachment to prerogative.

On practical grounds, the Livingstons feared that an appointee for New York named in London might be the same type of incompetent fortune seeker as, on two recent occasions, had been sent over from England to fill the chief justiceship of New Jersey.[30] But the Livingstons' desire for a friendly head of the bench was undoubtedly also underlined by the family's economic interests. During his first few months in office, Colden had begun vigorously to curb illicit trade with the West Indies and to vacate large land patents granted in violation of royal instructions. The Livingstons were vulnerable on both counts.[31]

The contestants warmed to the fight slowly. The Assembly prepared an address requesting Colden to honor tradition in filling the judicial post. Reluctant to brew up a storm until his commission as lieutenant governor arrived from England—he was as yet merely acting governor—Colden promised to consider the Assembly's advice.[32] Then George II's death late in October 1760 relieved him temporarily of the need for redeeming this pledge. The Assembly was dissolved and new elections called; Colden hoped for better fortune in the next house. To his dismay, the Livingstons were returned to power. They quickly passed a bill providing for the organization of the Supreme Court on the basis of life tenure. The legal fraternity simultaneously prodded the incumbent judges to request new commissions on the plea that their old ones had been vacated by the King's demise. They made it clear that they would refuse reappointment unless they received tenure during good behavior, as before. At the same time, and quite apart from the controversy over the judges, the Assembly passed an innocuous bill—at the lawyers' suggestion—validating all legislation enacted between the death of George II and the date the news of his successor reached New York.[33]

Hypercritical and oversuspicious, Colden responded to these measures with almost psychopathic rage. He refused the judges' request for new commissions, told them to "sit upon" their old ones, and snapped: "Yours are as good as mine, and you'll stand on the same foundation."[34] The validating act he denounced as a legal subtlety fabricated by the bar to create "a kind of Law Popery" and by "setting Law and Common sense in opposition . . . [to] obtain a most extensive power over the Minds of the rest of Mankind."[35] Neither the validating act nor the court bill received his assent.

The opposition struck back rapidly. The judges announced their refusal to serve under their old commissions; the business of the Supreme Court slowed to a standstill. The Assembly declined a Colden compromise offer to trade new judicial commissions for permanent judicial salaries. The legislature, having gained both advantages, was unwilling to surrender either. Instead, it repassed the original bill organizing the Supreme Court, and again Colden withheld his assent.[36]

In this deadlock, the Ministry came to Colden's rescue by naming one of Boston's prominent lawyers, Benjamin Pratt, to the critical chief justiceship. Colden's exultation was immediately dampened by Pratt's disinclination to accept the post as long as the wrangle with the Assembly continued. He was well aware that if he defied public sentiment by accepting his commission during pleasure, the Assembly would vote him no salary.[37] Only Colden's importunate letters and a vague promise to get the terms of his commission changed, in time, persuaded Pratt to give up his comfortable practice in Boston for the uneasy privilege of a judicial robe. Delighted with his victory, Colden saw it completed by the arrival of the lieutenant governor's commission he coveted so dearly.[38]

The aged Scotsman did not enjoy his triumph for long. Pratt was received "with Contempt and Displeasure" by New York's legal community. His associates on the Supreme Court refused to sit with him, the Assembly withheld his salary, and after six months he gave up in disgust and returned to Boston. His analysis of his troubles in New York was perspicacious: "The granting Commissions as they were before, that is During good Behavior, is now the Popular Demand and made the inflaming Topic but at Bottom the Point in View is to compel the Crown to appoint one of themselves Ch: Justice."[39]

Colden did not surrender as easily. For a month he was forced to view the proceedings from the sidelines while General Robert Monckton, the newly appointed governor, ran the administration; but when Monckton departed to lead an expedition to Martinique in November 1761, Colden was able to resume the contest. He now had fresh personal grievances against the triumvirate. Monckton had demanded that Colden account to him for any executive fees that might be collected during his absence, and Colden had been compelled to sign a bond to that effect. The terms and the language of the bond seemed humiliating to Colden, and he blamed it all on the younger Smith, who had been Monckton's counsel in the affair. To Colden, Smith was no better than "a crafty malicious smooth tongued hypocrite" and "the greatest Scoundrel in the Province."[40]

Colden's vengeance was directed against the bar as a whole. He demanded that the Assembly investigate the "dilatory Proceedings in the Courts of Law" and the "heavy Expence in obtaining Justice."[41] The legal fraternity accepted the move as a declaration of war against all "the Professors of the Law"; and they were not without means to return the compliment. As Robert Livingston put it picturesquely: "I think his Hon[o]r has Ill tim[e]d it; the Gentlemen of the Law are very able . . . to lead him a dance Sufficient to mortify him and family and friends . . . and p[e]rhaps make his administration more uneasye to him than heretofore . . ."[42] The Assembly, under the bar's influence, threatened to pass a bill fixing executive as well as legal fees, a move that would have hit Colden in his own purse. Pressing their advantage, the Livingstons pushed through a bill providing for life tenure for the judges to which they attached the annual appropriation for official salaries. Unwilling to cut his own throat, the enraged lieutenant governor approved, while immediately penning lengthy explanations of his conduct to the home government.[43]

Colden now sought some relief by proroguing the Assembly; the triumvirate, determined to give the old gentleman no peace during the legislative recess, sharpened their quills and began a press war against him. A new paper, the *American Chronicle,* was founded for the purpose, none of the regular newspaper publishers being very anxious to challenge the lieutenant governor. Its hurried first issue, on March 20, 1762, was timed to permit the rural members of the Assembly to take copies along with them to their constituencies.[44] For the next two months the *Chronicle* carried a veritable barrage of the triumvirate's sharpest literary barbs. Colden was successfully lampooned for his ignorance of law, criticized for his "outrageous Abuse of Power," accused of upsetting the provincial constitution, and indicted for using his public office to accumulate private wealth. In a burlesque on Colden's frequent references to the artificial intricacies of the law, the triumvirate facetiously proposed that "all the Laws of this Province . . . be retrenched to the Size of *Poor Richard's* Almanack; and every Law-suit decided in six Hours." In more serious vein, the paper asserted New York's "*undoubted Right,* of having the Judges of our Courts on a constitutional Basis," called attention to the independence of the judiciary in England, and insisted that Americans were entitled to "the same Liberties and Privileges" as their fellow subjects in Britain.[45]

The anti-Colden crusade did not last very long. Lengthy tirades against the lieutenant governor could fill a few issues, but they could not sustain a permanent newspaper. The publishers of New York's other papers placed obstacles in the *Chronicle's* path; a fire of suspicious origin destroyed its press. In July the new journalistic enterprise expired, but the crusade against Colden had already lost its steam before then. Eight months earlier the King in Council, disturbed with the growing colonial movement for judicial independence, had ordered the issuance of new instructions absolutely forbidding governors to grant judicial offices during good behavior, on pain of removal.[46] Triumphantly, Colden waved the new instructions before the recalcitrant judges and threatened them with dismissal unless they accepted new commissions during pleasure. William Livingston and William Smith, Jr., urged them to stand fast. One justice, John Chambers, resigned, but the other two—Daniel Horsmanden and David Jones—submitted to Colden's ultimatum.[47] The controversy was finally resolved a year later by Governor Monckton, whose friendship with the Livingstons made a compromise possible. Horsmanden—no friend of Colden—was persuaded to accept the chief justiceship, even though "during the King's pleasure," and as a measure of consolation two members of the Livingston party, William Smith, Sr., and Robert Livingston, were named to the other two vacancies on the bench.[48]

The "affair of the Judges is settled," Colden reported in high enthusiasm to the Board of Trade. "The minds of the people are as much at ease, and the Province in as great tranquility, as ever it was at any time."[49] With characteristic obtuseness, Colden failed to recognize that what he had won was merely an armistice. His jubilation over the immediate victory could not entirely conceal an apprehension that the "three popular Lawyers" might continue to "propagate their principles both in Religious and Civil matters and for that end make use of every artifice they can invent to calumniate the administration in every Exercise of the Prerogative." And while their literary crusade had not aroused the same "clamor" as their earlier attacks on episcopacy in connection with the King's College affair, their vitriolic pens could not be ignored. Colden was sure that no gentlemen had been taken in by the Livingston trio's campaign against authority, but "What effect it may have on the low rank of Mankind, for whom it is cheifly calculated is not so easy for me to know. . . ."[50] The next round would tell, and it was only a year in coming.

The second test between Colden and the legal fraternity began innocently enough with an action for assault and battery filed by one Thomas Forsey against Waddel Cunningham during the summer of 1763. The case bore no particular significance apart from the widespread public sympathy that Cunningham's attack brought the victim. Cunningham allegedly accosted Forsey in the street, drew a concealed sword, and "did beat Thrust Stab wound and evilly treat" the victim so badly that he was incapacitated for eighty-two days. The triumvirate were involved in the litigation but as opposing counsel. Scott represented Forsey, the plaintiff; Livingston and Smith, Cunningham. A criminal action ended with Cunningham's paying a fine of thirty pounds in January 1764. A civil suit decided later in the year awarded Forsey damages of more than £1500.[51]

It was the civil suit that became the bone of contention. Up to this time appeals from the decisions of the common-law courts had been taken to the Governor in Council only by "writ of error." The review in such cases was confined to errors of law in the record or in the bill of exceptions filed by the attorney and to irregularities in the lower court's proceedings. Matters of fact were outside the appellate court's jurisdiction: it did not attempt to examine the evidence or to pass judgment on the jury's verdict. It could hardly do so without conducting another trial, since neither the evidence nor the testimony of witnesses in trial proceedings was recorded. Cunningham, regarding the damages awarded as excessive, determined to break tradition by requesting a review of the facts as well as the law. In the fall of 1764 he petitioned the Supreme Court to allow an appeal to the Governor in Council. His attorneys now refused to associate themselves with the case, convinced that the move was a dangerous threat to the inviolability of jury trials; and they persuaded virtually the entire New York bar to stand with them. Cunningham was compelled to turn over the case to his business partner—a notary public—and to several obscure lawyers, one of whom had only recently been deported from England under a conviction for fraud.[52]

The Supreme Court sided with the legal profession, firmly denying Cunningham's request for the minutes of the trial on the ground that "no proper writ" for sending up the record had been produced. Colden, under no such inhibitions and anxious to lock horns with the gentlemen of the law, examined his instructions; and finding no specific mention of appeals in cases of error only—an unintentional oversight, it later proved—accepted Cunningham's plea. He stayed execution of the Supreme Court's judgment and ordered the chief justice to deliver up to him the proceedings in the case. The Supreme Court judges resolutely declined; the attorney general offered his opinion that the lieutenant governor's action was without precedent; the leading members of the bar endorsed the chief law officer's opinion; the Council agreed with the lawyers. Yet Colden insisted that his interpretation was as good as that of the legal fraternity. He would do what was right "without regard to any Man."[53]

Convening the Council in November, Colden ordered the judges before it and repeated his demand that they allow the appeal. Chief Justice Daniel Horsmanden again refused and with the assistance of the triumvirate presented a lengthy vindication of his position. He declared that Colden's attempt to review the facts as well as the law would alter "the ancient and wholesome Laws of the land," endanger the right of jury trial, and institute a novel procedure "repugnant to the Laws both of England and this Colony."[54] Infuriated, Colden publicly charged both judges and councilors with "Indecency, Want of Respect to the King's Authority and . . . unwarrantable Freedoms." Hysterically, he advised the Secretary of State and the Board of Trade to remove the Supreme Court judges, hinted darkly at a plot on the chief justice's part to bring about his death—by induced apoplexy, no doubt—and warned that unless the home government supported him in this crisis, the whole structure of royal government in America would topple, with the lawyers rising "uncontroulable" on its ruins.[55]

New Yorkers were not amused at Colden's frenetic exaggerations. An irresponsible chief executive with delusions of grandeur who saw assassins in every dark corner could hardly be tolerated at any time, but in the midst of the uncertainty created by the new parliamentary trade regulations, he would be positively dangerous. What was needed in the "uneasy temper of Mind" created by the measures of George Grenville was a governor who could ease public inquietude and inspire popular confidence. Colden's "unseasonable Effort" to introduce a judicial innovation served only to spread "a Jealousy, that the Crown is aiming to deprive the Subject of his most valuable Rights." The new commercial measures and the expected internal taxes were bad enough. The "good folks at Home" were "overshooting the Mark about Trade," one conservative New Yorker warned.[56] Colden's actions seemed to be even worse—"nothing less than the entire Subversion of the Constitution of the Province," by the destruction of its jury system and its courts as well.[57] Convinced that "the Ministry appears to have run mad" with its talk of stamp duties and land taxes, New Yorkers were all the more determined to maintain without reservation their ancient privilege of trial by jury.[58]

The opposition to Colden was not confined to the lawyers. Conservative merchants of the De Lancey party joined with landlord members of the Livingston family to denounce the lieutenant governor as an "evil Genius," an "old Mischief-maker," and a "Petty T[yran]t" and to condemn his "Fondness for showing himself in Law Matters, superior to the whole Body of the Law."[59] The judges and the bars of New Jersey and Pennsylvania lined up solidly on the side of the New York legal community.[60] Even Colden's own administration deserted him. In January 1765 he convened the Council and read it a long, turgid, and ill-informed defense of his position in the matter of appeals. With accustomed tactlessness, Colden went well beyond the limits of immediate necessity. To justify his acceptance of a solitary appeal, Colden was quite willing to denounce the whole jury system for its iniquitous and false verdicts, to assert the Crown's power to set up courts at will and to define their jurisdiction and procedure, and to proclaim the virtue of appealing all jury verdicts to the reasonable judgment of governors, kings, and councils.[61] His astounded Council not only condemned Colden's position unanimously but prepared a formal reply—with an eye to publication—for the official minutes. Thereupon it denied Cunningham's appeal and refused him permission to carry his case directly to the Crown.[62]

Colden was as persistent as he was obtuse. Undaunted by the Council's action, he forwarded Cunningham's petition for review to London, accompanied by a familiar barrage of letters describing the sinister legal conspiracy of which the Forsey case was but a part. The anti-Coldenites countered with a similar stream of letters, addressed chiefly to New York's absentee governor, General Monckton; but their most effective literary weapon was the public prints. The triumvirate, long experienced in this type of press warfare, directed the campaign. Chief Justice Horsmanden's defense of jury trials and his argument rejecting the original appeal petition were run serially in the newspapers.[63] John Morin Scott, one of the triumvirate, introduced them with a preface in which Colden's interpretation of his appellate powers was attacked as "entirely new, unconstitutional, and illegal," a "strange and unnatural" innovation, and "alarming to every British subject." When the series had completed its run in the papers, it was republished in book form, William Livingston, the chief of the triumvirate, himself underwriting the publication.[64] The grand jury was induced to extend congratulations to the judges for their defiance of Colden, and then copies of the address were sent to the newspapers.[65] A column titled the "Sentinel" was launched in the *New-York Gazette, or Weekly Post-Boy,* with all three of the triumvirate as contributors, and for the next six months it assailed Colden mercilessly in a mixture of essays ranging from serious discussions of the constitutional principles at stake to crude lampoons of Colden.[66] Many of the essays were anonymous, but neither Colden nor his critics were in doubt of the real authors. "All this publishing is the Lawyers doing," gleefully observed John Watts, a member of the Council but no friend of the lieutenant governor. "The old Gent. has abus'd 'em by the Lump and they are determined not to let him rest."[67]

In this literary venture the Livingston triumvirate had a decided advantage over their press warfare against Colden three years earlier. Try as they might on that former occasion they had not been able to fire public enthusiasm over a subject as technical and narrow as judicial tenure. Popular support had come only from the vague recognition that some vital liberty was being curbed by the crabbed old lieutenant governor. The Forsey case involved something of much broader character, and in the "Sentinel" Livingston and his associates made certain that the popular meaning and the constitutional significance of Colden's actions were forcefully emphasized and loudly proclaimed. Liberty itself was at stake, the "Sentinel" trumpeted. The question of appeals was "the most momentous affair that ever engaged our attention, since the existence of this province." Colden's behavior was "arbitrary" and "unheard of," and a "scandalous abuse of the king's name and authority."[68] The right to trial by jury was imbedded in the fabric of the English constitution, "matured by ages, founded as it were on a rock, repeatedly defended against lawless encroachments by oceans of blood . . . and guarded by the most awful sanctions." Was it now to be frivolously "altered or abolished, by—the dash of a pen?"[69]

To surrender an ancient and tried privilege like trial by jury to the caprice of any governor would be to substitute despotism for law, vassalage for freedom, tyranny for justice. "From such a System, the *Star Chamber* would be a redemption." The excellency of the

English constitution and the freedom of its subjects depended on the "equal poise of the several branches," Crown, Lords, and Commons. Whoever would "swallow up or impair" any was a "traitor and felon to his country." Colden's demand for appellate powers could only be construed as "a most premature and superlative ebullion of Zeal for the prerogative" at the expense of popular rights.[70]

From the defense of the right to jury trials, the triumvirate moved easily into a ringing affirmation of the theory of limited government and a vigorous defense of the right of popular resistance to arbitrary rulers. No monarch had a supernatural warrant to subvert the natural liberties of mankind, nor was there any divine prohibition against resisting tyrannical abuse of power. The virtue of the English constitution lay in its guarantees of personal liberty, firmly buttressed by the "impregnable bulwark of law" and "the most awful sanctions"; "and whoever asserts the contrary is a *lyar, and the truth is not in him.*"[71]

With only slightly veiled allusions to the new parliamentary duties, the "Sentinel" challenged its readers to regard Colden's assault on American liberties as a call to arms:

> . . . let us ever be jealous of lawless encroachments. . . . Let us prize our liberty, civil and sacred, as a jewel of inestimable value. . . . Let us oppose arbitrary rule in every shape by every lawful method in our power. Never let us sit supine and indolent while our precious privileges are abridged. . . . But let us on every such alarming occasion, rouse ourselves; and act like men . . . who know the unspeakable advantages of freedom by happy experience. . . . Let no illegal attempt against us appear inconsiderable, or unworthy our notice. A smaller will ever pave the way for a greater. . . . Let us therefore . . . crush the cockatrice in the egg . . . [and] strive to transmit to our posterity, that inestimable blessing which our ancestors have handed down to us. . . .[72]

Despite Colden's assurances to the Board of Trade that the press campaign was of little consequence—a few "licentious" and "seditious" papers by "Men of no Esteem"—the lieutenant governor soon became more and more "odious" even to those closest to his administration, and public tempers became more and more "incens[e]d and alarmed." "The old Body was allways dislik'd enough," observed one critic acidly, "but now they would preferr Beelzebub himself to him." News of the Stamp Act did not help Colden's cause, coming as it did right in the midst of the "Sentinel's" impassioned pleas for opposition to "arbitrary rule in every shape" and to "lawless encroachments" upon American liberties. Like Colden's arbitrary stand on the matter of appeals, so the Grenville ministry's radical tax program appeared as still another attempt to upset the delicate relationship between colonies and mother country—"by the dash of a pen."[73]

The parallel currents of popular unrest inspired by Colden's actions at home and Parliament's abroad reached their stormy confluence in the fall of 1765. In an atmosphere already made electric by Colden's preparations to receive the obnoxious stamps and by the warnings of the Sons of Liberty to any who might purchase them, came the news—"like a Thunderbolt"—that the Privy Council had ordered Cunningham's appeal to be heard. The decision was regarded by some observers as even "more detested" than the Stamp Act itself.[74] The resolutions of the Stamp Act Congress, even then meeting in New York, added fuel to the fire. The Congress's bold assertion that "trial by jury is the inherent and invaluable right of every British subject in these colonies" appeared as a direct response to Colden's casual dismissal of the importance of jury decisions. With characteristic obstinacy, Colden chose to ignore the reminder. He convened the Council in mid-October, laid before it the order from London, and forced it to admit Cunningham's appeal.[75]

Colden's opponents had two weapons left: the Supreme Court and the mob. The Supreme Court struck back a week later by again refusing to send up the proceedings in the case without a writ of error.[76] The mob made clear its sentiments on the night of November 1, the date the Stamp Act was scheduled to go into operation. A "Wonderfull Large Mob" collected in the fields, attempted unsuccessfully to storm Fort George where Colden had taken refuge, hanged the old Scotsman in effigy, invaded his coach house, seized his "chariot," two sleighs, and a chair, made a bonfire of the lot, and threw his effigy into the flames for good measure. The rest of the lieutenant governor's household goods were saved only by his son's actions in moving them into the fort; and Colden's wife and children were spared only because they were rushed aboard a warship in the harbor.[77]

The end of the Forsey case was anticlimactic. The New York Assembly came to the Supreme Court's defense in a series of vigorous resolutions denouncing Colden's "mischievous Innovation" as illegal and subversive of the ancient right of trial by jury and applauding the judges and the bar for leading the opposition.[78] Before Colden found time to compose a reply, word came from London that the Board of Trade, after consulting the highest law officers of the Crown, had decided in New York's favor. Only appeals "in error" could be heard by the Governor in Council, and lest Colden or any other chief executive remain in doubt of the procedure, the royal instructions were rewritten to make the point crystal-clear.[79]

Both Colden and his critics penned their epitaphs on the Forsey affair. Colden's took the form of a lengthy pamphlet, published in 1767, in which he reiterated the familiar complaint that the lawyers had used the issue of appeals in order to discredit him personally and to pull down the whole structure of royal authority in New York.[80] At least no one could accuse Colden of inconstancy. As for the November riots, Colden was equally certain that this was the lawyers' doing. Their aim had been to capitalize on the "Spirit of Sedition" created by the Forsey case and to turn "the Rage of the Mob" against him.[81]

Colden's critics were in close agreement with him on only one count: that the Forsey case had been the "true cause of the Malice" against him. His attempt to invade the traditional right of jury trial, William Smith, Jr., observed, was a "capital Article of the People's Jealousy" and "rivetted their Abhorrence" of his "obnoxious Character." His stand on appeals "more than any other Cause" had driven the mob to its "Pitch of Madness."[82]

Neither Smith nor Colden could view the affair with detachment. There were few who could, entirely. But even the most conservative New Yorkers believed that the lawyers were right and Colden wrong. The rights of internal taxation and of jury trials were both inviolate "privileges of Englishmen." To deny them would make "the Atlantick . . . the difference between a Freeman and a Slave which God forbid." The lawyers had voiced the same sentiments more eloquently in the press: "Without liberty no man can be a subject. He is a slave."[83]

Notes

1. June 3, 1774. *The Correspondence of General Thomas Gage with the Secretaries of State . . . 1763-1775,* ed. C. E. Carter, 2 vols. (New Haven, 1931-1933), II, 165.

2. To the Earl of Shelburne, Jan. 15, 1768, in Max Beloff, ed., *The Debate on the American Revolution, 1761-1783* (London, 1949), 127.

3. Bernard to Lord Barrington, Nov. 23, 1765, *Barrington-Bernard Correspondence,* eds. Channing and Coolidge, 96-97.

4. On the role of these other groups, see, for example, Arthur M. Schlesinger, *The Colonial Merchants and the American Revolution* (New York, 1918); Alice M. Baldwin, *The New England Clergy and the American Revolution* (Durham, N.C., 1928); Schlesinger, *Prelude to Independence: The Newspaper War on Britain, 1764-1766* (New York, 1958); and Philip Davidson, *Propaganda and the American Revolution, 1763-1783* (Chapel Hill, 1941). An excellent introduction to the role of the lawyers is Richard B. Morris, "Legalism versus Revolutionary Doctrine in New England," *N. Eng. Qtly.,* IV (1931), 192-215. An introductory essay on the subject is Erwin C. Surrency, "The Lawyers and the Revolution," *Am. Journal Legal Hist.,* VIII (1964), 125-135.

5. Boorstin, *The Americans: The Colonial Experience,* 202.

6. Carl Bridenbaugh, *Cities in Revolt* (New York, 1955), 95-96, 288-289. See also pp. 129-131 above.

7. Gage to Henry S. Conway, Dec. 21, 1765, *Gage Correspondence,* I, 79.

8. Quoted in Clinton Rossiter, *Seedtime of the Republic,* 345.

9. Johnson to Thomas Secker, March 1, 1759, *Samuel Johnson Writings,* I, 283.

10. Colden to the Secretary of State and Board of Trade, Dec. 6, 1765, *Colden Letter Books,* II, 70-71.

11. Gage to Conway, Dec. 21, 1765, *Gage Correspondence,* I, 79; *The Montresor Journals,* ed. G. D. Scull (N.Y. Hist. Soc. *Collections,* 1881), 339 (entries of Nov. 6, 7, 1765).

12. Colden to William Shirley, July 25, 1749, *Colden Papers,* IV, 124-125.

13. The quotation is Wilbur C. Abbott's in his *New York in the American Revolution,* 15. On Colden's conception of colonial government, see Carole Shammos, "Cadwallader Colden and the Role of the King's Prerogative," *N.Y. Hist. Soc. Qtly.,* LIII (1969), 103-126.

14. Colden's capacious life and interests have thus far eluded the biographer. Alice M. Keys's *Cadwallader Colden* lacks dimension and imagination. There are at least three unpublished doctoral dissertations that attempt to treat aspects of his life: Siegfried B. Rolland, "Cadwallader Colden: Colonial Politician and Imperial Statesman, 1718-1760" (U. of Wisconsin, 1952); Sister Miriam E. Murphy, "Cadwallader Colden, President of the Council, Lieutenant Governor of New York, 1760-1775" (Fordham U., 1957); and Allan R. Raymond, "The Political Career of Cadwallader Colden" (Ohio State U., 1971).

15. Colden to the Earl of Halifax, Feb. 22, 1765, *Colden Letter Books,* I, 470.

16. Keys, *Colden,* 138-141; Philip Livingston to Jacob Wendell, Oct. 19, Nov. 9, 1747, Livingston Papers, Museum of the City of New York.

17. Clinton to the Duke of Newcastle, Nov. 18, 1745, *N.Y. Col. Docs.,* VI, 286.

18. Colden to Hezekiah Watkins, Dec. 12, 1748, in G. H. Moore, *Origin*

and Early History of Columbia College (New York, 1890), 39-40. As a petty expression of his dislike for the triumvirate on this occasion, Colden is said to have refused membership in the newly founded New York Society Library simply because the three lawyers were among its organizers. Keep, *History of the New York Society Library,* 180.

19. William Smith Papers, V, "30 October 1776," New York Public Library. The incident arose when Livingston and Smith failed to find the original of a 1699 law vacating certain extravagant land grants. Since a number of persons including Colden had been regranted land in the vacated patents, the law was of "vast Importance." The editors decided to reproduce the law as it had appeared in an early printed edition and to make a marginal notation to the effect that the original could not be located. The act, with the marginal notation, may be found in the Livingston-Smith edition of the *Laws of New-York, from the Year 1691, to 1751* (1752), 33-36.

20. Smith, *History,* I, 247-248; *Colden Papers,* V, 283-295, 310-319; "The Colden Letters on Smith's History, 1759-1760," N.Y. Hist. Soc. *Collections,* 1868, 214, 226-230; William Smith Papers, V, "30 October 1776." Smith, for his part, may have developed a personal antipathy to Colden on similar grounds. Smith had an interest in the Kayaderosseres Patent, a 800,000-acre grant, and Colden had made frequent proposals to the Crown to vacate such large patents. See Upton, *Loyal Whig,* 42-43.

21. Smith, *History,* II, 284-286; *Journal of the Votes and Proceedings of the General Assembly . . . [1691-1765],* II, 637-638.

22. Robert Livingston to Abraham Yates, Sep. 9, Oct. 13, 1760, Abraham Yates Papers, New York Public Library.

23. Colden to the Lords of Trade, Jan. 11, 25, April 7, 1762, Colden to the Earl of Egremont, Sep. 14, 1762, *Colden Letter Books,* I, 149-150, 157, 191, 231.

24. Smith, *History,* II, 289.

25. *Colden Letter Books,* I, 13, 15, 22-24; Smith, *History,* II, 285, 288-289; William Smith Papers, IV, "24 November 1761"; Jones, *History of New York,* I, 224.

26. The most recent discussions of the equity issue are Katz, *Newcastle's New York,* chap. 4, and his "The Politics of Law: Controversies over Chancery Courts and Equity Law in the Eighteenth Century," *Perspectives in American History,* V (1971), 257-284, particularly 277-282.

27. Labaree, *Royal Government,* 375-380; Flick, ed., *History of the State of New York,* III, 18-26.

28. Report of the Lords of Trade, Nov. 11, 1761, *N.Y. Col. Docs.,* VII, 473, 474-475; Labaree, *Royal Government,* 390-391, 394-395.

29. Although Clinton later regretted having been so generous as to grant De Lancey the chief justice's commission during good behavior, the legality of the commission was upheld by the Crown's law officers. *N.Y. Col. Docs.,* VI, 356, 792.

30. The New Jersey justices, each of whom had short-lived terms of office, were William Aynsley, lately treasurer of a turnpike company in northern England, and Nathaniel Jones, a Newgate solicitor of allegedly questionable character and dubious morality. Smith, *History,* II, 284; Kemmerer, *Path to Freedom: The Struggle for Self-Government in Colonial New Jersey,* 268-270. For local reasons, the question of judicial tenure did not agitate the Jerseyites. See Jerome J. Nadelhaft, "Politics and the Judicial Tenure Fight in Colonial New Jersey," *Wm. and Mary Qtly.,* XXVIII (1971), 46-63.

31. Colden to William Pitt, Oct. 27, 1760, to the Lords of Trade, Jan. 25, 1762, *Colden Letter Books,* I, 26-28, 155-158; Keys, *Colden,* 275-276.

32. Smith, *History,* II, 285; Colden to Halifax, Nov. 11, 1760, *Colden Letter Books,* I, 35.

33. *Colden Letter Books,* I, 79, 88-89, 104; William Smith Papers, IV, "24 November 1761."

34. Smith, *History,* II, 290; William Smith Papers, IV, "11 November 1761."

35. Colden to the Lords of Trade, June 2, 1761, *Colden Letter Books,* I, 89.

36. Colden to the Lords of Trade, Aug. 12, Sep. 25, 1761, Colden to Pitt, Sep. 24, 1761, *ibid.,* 106, 117, 119-120.

37. *N.Y. Col. Docs.,* VII, 460; Colden to Pratt, Oct. 12, 1761, *Colden Letter Books,* I, 123-124; Pratt to Colden, Aug. 22, Sep. 14, Oct. 3, 1761, *Colden Papers,* VI, 68-69, 76-78, 81-82.

38. Colden to Pitt, Aug. 11, 1761, Colden to Pratt, Sep. 7, 1761, *Colden Letter Books,* I, 103, 113-114.

39. Pratt to Thomas Pownall, Jan. 7, 1762, *Colden Papers,* VI, 113-116. See also *N.Y. Col. Docs.,* VII, 500-502; *Jones, History of New York,* I, 226-231; Colden to the Secretary of State and the Board of Trade, Dec. 6, 1765, *Colden Letter Books,* II, 73.

40. Smith, *History,* II, 296-298; Colden to John Pownall, Nov. 26, 1761, *Colden Letter Books,* I, 137-141; William Smith Papers, IV, "17 March 1762."

41. *Assembly Journal,* II, 669; William Smith Papers, IV, "24 November 1761."

42. Robert Livingston to Abraham Yates, Dec. 8, 1761, Abraham Yates Papers, New York Public Library.

43. *Assembly Journal,* II, 672-673; William Smith Papers, IV, "9 March 1762"; Colden to the Lords of Trade, Feb. 11, 1762, *Colden Letter Books,* II, 159-161.

44. Clarence E. Brigham, *History and Bibliography of American Newspapers, 1690-1820,* 2 vols. (Worcester, Mass., 1947), I, 607-608. The publisher of the *Chronicle* was Samuel Farley, an English printer recently arrived in New York.

45. *American Chronicle,* March 20, April 3, 12, 19, 1762.

46. Colden to General Robert Monckton, March 30, 1762, *Colden Letter Books,* I, 183-184; "Order of the King in Council," Nov. 23, 1761, *N.Y. Col. Docs.,* VII, 472-476.

47. New York Executive Council Minutes, XXV, 432, 433, New York State Library; William Smith Papers, IV, "27, 31 March 1762."

48. Colden to the Lords of Trade, July 18, 1763, *Colden Letter Books,* I, 218.

49. April 7, June 12, 1762, *ibid.,* I, 190, 213.

50. To the Lords of Trade, April 7, 1762, *ibid.,* I, 187, 190.

51. Supreme Court Minutes, 1762-1764, 224-225, 308, 358-359; 1764-1767, 18, 32; Parchment Rolls 21-A-8, 28-K-9, 186-K-3, Hall of Records, N. Y. C.; William Livingston, Supreme Court Cost Books, II, 207, New York Public Library. The case is summarized in Helen H. Miller, *The Case for Liberty* (Chapel Hill, 1965), chap. 8, and its legal aspects treated exhaustively in Joseph H. Smith, *Appeals to the Privy Council,* 390-412.

52. *Colden Letter Books,* I, 416-418; Supreme Court Minutes, 1764-1767, 35, 125-126; William Smith Papers, IV, "Autumn 1764." Cunningham's legal representative was George Harison, a notary public. On his role and his account of the case, see Herbert A. Johnson, "George Harison's Protest: New Light on

Forsey versus Cunningham," *N. Y. Hist.,* L (1969), 61-82.

53. John Tabor Kempe to Colden, Oct. 31, Nov. 16, 1764, George Harison to Colden, Nov. 24, 1764, *Colden Papers,* VI, 368-371, 378, 387-388; *Colden Letter Books,* I, 395-396, 415-416.

54. *Calendar of Council Minutes,* 509; *Colden Letter Books,* I, 407-416; *Colden Papers,* VI, 379-386.

55. Colden to the Lords of Trade, Dec. 13, 1764, Jan. 22, 27, 1765, *Colden Letter Books,* I, 421-425, 455, 462; William Smith, Jr., to Monckton, Jan. 25, 1765, Chalmers Papers, New York, IV, 17, New York Public Library.

56. John Watts to Monckton, Dec. 29, 1763, Sep. 22, 1764, William Smith, Jr., to Monckton, Jan. 25, 1765, Chalmers Papers, New York, III, 65, 77, IV, 17.

57. Horsmanden to Monckton, Dec. 8, 1764, Watts to Monckton, Nov. 10, 1764, *ibid.,* III, 80, IV, 26.

58. Robert R. Livingston to Robert Livingston, June 7, 15, 1764, Robert R. Livingston Papers, New York Historical Society.

59. Watts to Monckton, Nov. 10, 1764, Chalmers Papers, New York, III, 80; Watts to Isaac Barré, Jan. 19, 1765, *Watts Letter Book,* 323-326; Robert R. Livingston to Monckton, Feb. 23, 1765, Livingston Family Papers, New York Public Library.

60. Watts to Monckton, Jan. 25, 1765, Chalmers Papers, New York, III, 86.

61. "Cadwallader Colden's Opinion on Appeals," [Jan. 1765], *Colden Papers,* VII, 1-7.

62. *Calendar of Council Minutes,* 510; New York Executive Council Minutes, XXIX, 33-57; *Colden Papers,* IX, 205-206; *Colden Letter Books,* I, 444-445.

63. *New-York Gazette, or Weekly Post-Boy,* Jan. 3-Feb. 21, 1765.

64. *The Report of an Action of Assault . . . between Thomas Forsey . . . and Waddel Cunningham . . .* (New-York, 1764 [1765]); William Livingston, Receipt Book, May 9, June 29, July 31, Oct. 31, 1765, Livingston Papers, Mass. Hist. Soc.

65. *New-York Gazette,* Jan. 24, 1765; *New-York Mercury,* Jan. 21, 1765.

66. The series ran from Feb. 28 to Aug. 29, 1765.

67. Watts to Monckton, Feb. 23, 1765, Chalmers Papers, New York, III, 88.

68. "Sentinel, I," *New-York Gazette,* Feb. 28, 1765.

69. "Sentinel, III," *ibid.,* March 14, 1765.

70. "Sentinel, III, XII," *ibid.,* March 14, May 16, 1765.

71. "Sentinel, XXI," *ibid.,* July 18, 1765.

72. *Ibid.*

73. Robert R. Livingston to Robert Livingston, March 4, 1765, Robert R. Livingston Papers, New York Historical Society; Watts to Monckton, Nov. 10, 1764, Chalmers Papers, New York, III, 80. Robert R. Livingston put the colony's troubles in this order: "See the three great Points we have to contend for, and of what importance they are. Trial by Juries, a Right to tax ourselves, the reducing of admiralty courts within their proper Limits." To Robert Livingston, Oct. 19, 1765, Manuscript Collections, Morristown National Historical Park, Morristown, N.J. (microfilm, reel 31).

74. Watts to Monckton, Oct. 12, 1765, Mass. Hist. Soc. *Collections,* 4 Ser., X (1871), 579. Robert R. Livingston was sure the Privy Council's order had been "surreptitiously obtained," so confident had New Yorkers been that the decision would go against Colden. Livingston to Robert Livingston, Oct. 19,

1765, MS Collections, Morristown National Historical Park.

75. *Calendar of Council Minutes,* 514 (Oct. 15, 1765).

76. Keys, *Colden,* 319; Robert R. Livingston to Robert Livingston, Oct. 19, 1765, MS Collections, Morristown National Historical Park.

77. *New-York Gazette,* Nov. 7, 1765; *Colden Letter Books,* II, 54-56, 74-77, 80-81; Robert R. Livingston to Monckton, Nov. 8, 1765, Livingston Family Papers, New York Public Library; *Montresor Journals,* 336-337; F. L. Engelman, "Cadwallader Colden and the New York Stamp Act Riots," *Wm. and Mary Qtly.,* X (1953), 560-578.

78. *Assembly Journal,* II, 803-806; *New-York Gazette,* Dec. 26, 1765.

79. *N.Y. Col. Docs.,* VII, 762-765, 814-816; *Colden Papers,* VII, 95-96; *Calendar of Council Minutes,* 515.

80. *The Conduct of Cadwallader Colden . . . Relating to the Judges Commissions, Appeals to the King, and the Stamp-Duty* (1767), in *Colden Letter Books,* II, 433-467.

81. *Colden Letter Books,* II, 2, 5, 68-78, 84-86, 89-92.

82. Smith to Monckton, Nov. 8, 1765, Chalmers Papers, New York, IV, 19.

83. Watts to Monckton, Feb. 26, 1765, *Watts Letter Book,* 336; "Sentinel, III," *New-York Gazette,* March 14, 1765.

IV

The New York Tradition

In the introduction to this volume, attention was called to the surprising neglect of New York in most histories of the colonial period. The generalization applies with almost equal force to Pennsylvania and New Jersey. These "Middle Colonies" are often relegated to secondary treatment as mixtures of New England and southern institutional forms without the distinction of either and with little separate character of their own. I have long felt that this categorization reflects the failure of historians to organize an appropriate frame of reference into which to fit the variegated pattern of the Middle Colonies' economic, social, and political development. Perhaps the pattern was too obvious to be perceived at close distance. Perhaps the historians' own preconceptions obfuscated the view. In this essay, I suggest a synthesis for analyzing and understanding New York's (and incidentally, Pennsylvania's and New Jersey's) colonial past, one which postulates that the province's mixed economy, social diversity, political contentiousness, and pragmatic culture made it prototypical of the later United States. Large generalizations should be offered with diffidence, but the long absence in our historical literature of anything better to explain the meaning and significance of New York's colonial past may excuse the rashness which inspired the interpretation contained in the following essay.

8.

New York in the American Colonies: A New Look

ON EVERY OCCASION of the anniversary of the founding of Jamestown or the landing at Plymouth, heated debate occurs —more often among amateur than among professional historians—as to which of these two events more properly marks the beginning of the American epic. On the 350th commemoration of the arrival of the *Susan Constant* and her sister ships, a southern partisan, Virginius Dabney, was especially vocal in raising the query: "Why have historians underrated the Virginia Fathers?" Justice for the southern colonies, was his cry! New Englanders ignored the plea and arranged to have a reconstruction of the *Mayflower* brought to Plymouth on its 350th birthday. The "war" promises to be one of those unending historical conflicts. What I propose to do is not settle the question but confuse it further—by simply suggesting that we correct the myopia of both sides, reject the claims of each, and offer a new contender for the honor of initiating the American tradition: the Middle Colonies in general and New York in particular.

The early neglect of Americans in turning elsewhere than New York for their national image is not hard to understand. The American colonies were founded once by the first settlers, and as Wesley Craven

Reprinted from *New York History*, LIII (April 1972), 132-156, by permission of the New York State Historical Association.

has observed, the process was repeated over and over again as succeeding generations redrew the portrait of the founding fathers to suit their own moods. But whatever the angle of vision of these varying re-creations of the nature of our colonial origins, New York was ignored. A perceptive explanation of this neglect has been offered by two sociologists, in a recent book on New York City:

> History, or perhaps historians, keep passing New York by. . . . By preference, but also in some degree by necessity, America has turned elsewhere for its images and traditions. Colonial America is preserved for us in terms of the Doric simplicity of New England, or the pastoral symmetry of the Virginia countryside. . . . But who can summon an image of eighteenth-century New York that will still hold in the mind?[1]

There are other explanations, historical and historiographical. The earliest American historians reflected the regional consciousness of New England and Virginia. Historical accounts of these geographic areas appeared within seventy-five years of their founding, even if "New England" was more often synonymous with Massachusetts and the term "Virginia" was broadly construed. The histories of the southern colonies stressed the great achievement of the Virginia charters in bringing English liberties and common law to these shores at so early a date. New Englanders emphasized the divine Providence which had guided Pilgrims and Puritans and thereby set the providential tone for all future American development.[2] New York's beginnings as a conquered province and the proprietary of the King's brother could stir few patriotic breasts and arouse little native emotion. As the Revolution approached, the polemicists of Boston and Williamsburg found solid precedent for their claims to English liberties in their first charters and in the images they created of their first settlers, whom they represented as early exponents of liberty and opponents of tyranny. New York had no such charter to cite as a comparable example.

After independence, the earliest national histories joined Virginians and New Englanders as common progenitors of "the just and genuine principles" of the new republican society. Portraying our national origins as rooted in the rising of a free people, "not led by powerful families," and "under no general influence, but that of their personal feelings and opinions," who had already achieved a republican society before the separation from England, these historians steered clear of New York, with its aristocratic manor lords, great estates, and quasi-feudal tenantry as illustrations of the indigenous republican spirit.[3] That New York was one of the least militant and most hesitant of the provinces in casting its vote for independence did not improve its standing with future historians from New England. William Gordon's *History,* published in 1789, specifically disavowed the role of New York, with its "party of aristocracy," in the glorious struggle against tyranny.[4]

Local historians of New York did little to help its reputation. Washington Irving's *New York* was a caricature which infuriated the state's better citizenry. Thomas Jones's loyalist *History of New York,* appearing in 1879, proved no better, since it represented the province's "golden age" as those halcyon days of the mid-eighteenth century just before the evil triumvirate of Presbyterians and lawyers —William Livingston, William Smith, Jr., and John Morin Scott— began their conspiracy to turn the colony on its head by its agitation against church and state. When biography replaced history as the favorite literary medium for recalling the nation's heritage, again New York suffered. It had no heroes of the stature of Washington and Patrick Henry to eulogize.

In creating a "usable past" for a new people, the homogeneous English communities of New England and the South had far more appeal than New York's (or New Jersey's or Pennsylvania's) disordered, complex, heterogeneous population. Indeed, the more ethnically varied America became in the years that followed, the more attractive did Anglo-Saxon Jamestown and Plymouth appear to historians who themselves were disturbed by, and hostile to, the influx of masses of European immigrants from outside the British Isles or its northern neighbors. Thus, John Fiske, a convert to the theory of Teutonic origins of American democracy and of Aryan race supremacy, traced the roots of our political heritage from the primitive Saxons through the English middle class and then to America in the veins of Virginia Cavaliers and New England Puritans. A limited degree of heterogeneity was acceptable, since the English race had a "rare capacity for absorbing slightly foreign elements and molding them into conformity" with Anglo-Saxon political ideals. Hence, Fiske was prevented from rejecting the Dutch, Huguenots, Jews, Germans, and Scotch-Irish who comprised so much of the population of the Middle Colonies. It is quite clear, however, from Fiske's strong hostility to late nineteenth-century immigration—he was President of the Immigration Restriction League—that New York's mongrel people took only second place in his roll of proper Americans.[5]

Even when the study of immigration was made professionally respectable by Marcus Lee Hansen, the focus was on the immigrants who peopled the rural Midwest, not those who crowded New York's urban ghettos.[6] Popular rhetoric glorified the country as a melting pot of different peoples, but in actuality what was meant was the degree to which immigrants conformed to Anglo-Saxon characteristics.

Geography, also, had something to do with the neglect of the Middle Colonies. They could not be clearly defined, nor were the Middle Atlantic States much easier afterwards. At times, British administrators simply swallowed up the middle region into the other two, using the term "northern colonies" to include New England, New York, New Jersey, and Pennsylvania. Cartographers confused the matter similarly. Lewis Evans, in his famous map of 1755, depicted the Middle Colonies as including everything from Virginia to Rhode Island! With the Middle Atlantic region undefinable physically, it is not surprising that historians failed to write about it. Except for Fiske's two volumes on the Dutch and Quaker colonies, published in 1899, nothing appeared on the subject until Wertenbaker's volume in his *Founding of American Civilization* series, in 1938; and no study of the Middle Atlantic States found its way into print until 1956.[7]

Richard Shryock has raised the provocative question of whether historians have neglected the Middle Atlantic region—either as colonies or as states—because it does not exist or whether the region has been lost to view because historians have failed to write about it.[8] One interesting suggestion he offers for the blurred focus of historians is that the inhabitants of the area have never developed the kind of regional self-consciousness which arises from the nursing of a grievance. Certainly there is nothing in Middle Atlantic history comparable to C. Vann Woodward's "Burden of Southern History"—the brooding sense of racial guilt and consciousness of military defeat. Nor is there evidence of anything like the anguished cry of an alienated social elite —such as David Donald's New England Abolitionists. In recalling their origins, the Middle Colonies could not draw upon the knowledge of a "starving time" which the first settlers had overcome by stubborn will or divine intervention. Nor could the Middle Colonies attribute the formation of their collective character to the forge of bitter encounters with savages during their earliest years. There were no counterparts to the New Englander's fierce conflicts with the Pequots and Narragansetts, in 1637 and 1675-1676, nor to Virginia's Indian massacres of 1622 and 1644 in the recollection of New Yorkers and

Pennsylvanians. Conflict with the Indians was not entirely absent in the history of these colonies, but the diplomatic skill of a Penn and the business acumen of the Dutch had secured a peace through trade and diplomacy which kept the Middle Colonies free from the worst horrors of Indian warfare—and made them the object of suspicion and envy. Economically, New York and its neighbors, by the eve of the Revolution, enjoyed so large a measure of prosperity that one historian offers this condition, along with the colonies' social and cultural diversity, as an explanation of their indecision for independence, in contrast to New England and Virginia, whose impaired economic fortunes propelled them the more rapidly toward a separation which their socially homogeneous populations could be asked to accept.[9]

Clearly, however, it was the urban character of the Middle Colonies, symbolized by the great cities of New York and Philadelphia, and their polygot populations which played a major role in the historical amnesia of Americans, who preferred to remember their homogeneous, rural Arcadia even as it disappeared before their eyes. The paradox, of course, was that colonies like New York represented, in germinal form, the very nation that had come into existence by the late nineteenth century. The paradox is heightened by the discovery that the historian who, more than any other, was responsible for focusing the nation's attention on its rural West as the home of its distinctive traits of collective character should also have been the one to most emphatically stress the Middle Atlantic origins of those traits.

A year before his famous essay on the significance of the frontier, Frederick Jackson Turner directed the notice of historians to the "middle region" of the Atlantic coast and deplored the fact that it had "never been studied with the care due to its importance." With its wide mixture of nationalities, he noted, its varied society and economic life, its multiplicity of religions, and its mixed pattern of town and county government, the region between New England and the South represented for Turner "that composite" which was the America of 1892, even the patterns of its settlement reflecting the map of Europe in variety. The region was also "typical of the modern United States" in its ideas and ideals: democratic, national, easy, tolerant, and strongly materialistic.[10] In the frontier address itself, Turner repeated his sentiments in more explicit fashion. It was the very non-Englishness of the middle region which made it "typically American." It "mediated" between East and West, between Puritan New England and the slaveholding South; and it was the least sectional of all the sections. The men of the frontier, whom Turner eulogized, "had closer resemblances to the Middle region than to either of the other sections."[11]

The more Turner wrote about the West and on sectionalism, the more he seemed to return to the importance of the Middle Atlantic area. In two subsequent essays, he reiterated the prototypicality of the Middle Colonies and States for their composite nationality and democratic social structure:

> The middle region was so complex in its composition that it had little social self-consciousness as a section. Nevertheless this region of many nationalities, creeds, and industries became, during a considerable part of its history, a more characteristically democratic region than any of the others. Tolerance of difference of opinion was pronounced, and, in the course of time, individualism and lack of social control became marked features of the section.[12]

In a florid metaphor, Turner painted the West as a land of new "national hue," a composite coloration of all of its eastern ingredients and its local environment, but one section gave the distinctive tint to the new color: "This section was the Middle Region." In the posthumous volume, *The United States, 1830-1850,* Turner again stressed the special "national destiny" of the Middle Atlantic, its leadership by 1830 in urban growth, manufacturing, and shipping, its perfect reflection of the American "melting pot," and its pivotal role in the nation's politics—all of which made it for him "typical of the deep-seated tendencies of America in general."[13]

One of Turner's colleagues, Woodrow Wilson, agreed that the region between New England and the South was more than merely a blurred middle ground between two more important extremes. In outlining the course of American development, Wilson challenged the notion that the country's history comprised the working out of Puritan and southern ideals, each striving for predominance. It was, in fact, New York, New Jersey, and Pennsylvania which by their composite character and origins presaged later complex America. Here, according to Wilson, occurred the experiments that most resembled the methods by which the American continent was peopled; in the Middle Atlantic States, from the beginning, life reflected the pattern of living of the nation itself.[14]

Turner and Wilson were exceptional, and none of Turner's

students except Carl Becker were attracted either to the Middle Colonies or the Middle States as fields of research. Becker himself found trouble blending the frontier thesis of his mentor into his own interpretation of the urban origins of colonial democracy. For other American historians, the very resemblance of the Middle Atlantic region to the nation as a whole produced a familiarity that bred only indifference, not scholarly attraction. Still others were baffled by the very qualities of life and culture in the Middle Colonies that did not set them apart from the rest of the nation. A region that appeared to be "everyman's" became "no man's" in literature and history.[15]

Present-day historians undertaking to achieve a synthesis of the colonial period have yet to spell out New York's role satisfactorily. In the most recent such effort, Daniel Boorstin illustrates his underlying theme of practical adaptation by reference to the experiences of Massachusetts, Virginia, Pennsylvania, and Georgia. New York, despite its overridingly accommodative political and religious structure and its pragmatic society and culture, is unmentioned. The elements in synthesizing New York (and the Middle Colonies) into the stream of early American history are perfectly visible; and it is the purpose of this paper to point out some directions which such inquiry should logically take.

The central fact in the colony's history, so well observed even by historians who have slighted it, is the heterogeneity of its population. This circumstance arose from the nature of the colony's beginning as an English province, the absorption of some 10,000 residents of New Netherland. But the population had already developed a diversity under Dutch rule which adumbrated its later heterogeneity. There were in New Netherland—besides Hollanders—Walloons, Swedes, English, Norwegians, Germans, Scotch-Irish, and Negroes. The visiting Jesuit, Father Jogues, was astonished to be told in 1644 that eighteen languages were spoken in the province. This diversity was a cause for continued amazement by English officials and visitors, the substitution of English for Dutch rule doing nothing to improve the homogeneity of the colony's population. One traveler in 1760 abandoned any attempt to generalize about New Yorkers: "Being . . . of different nations, different languages and different religions, it is almost impossible to give them any precise or determinate character."[16] On the eve of the Revolution, the population of the colony was estimated to be still only half English, making New York the most polygenetic of all the British dependencies in North America. The consequence of this diversity was enormous for the religious, political, and cultural life of the province, as it was for the later United States.

It is now clear that while this country can take credit for its faith in freedom of religion, the prize did not come as a free gift or as an act of love from our earliest forebears. The English came with established ideas of religious orthodoxy and conformity in their intellectual and spiritual baggage, and this heritage was not changed much by the New England Protestantism which Burke hailed as "the dissidence of dissent." Religious liberty was rather extorted step-by-step from an unwilling majority and accorded ultimately less out of commitment than as a result of social and economic necessity. Nowhere did the process evolve more typically than in New York. With its social complexity came religious diversity almost from the beginning. The domines of the Dutch Reformed Church were no more liberal in matters of religion than the spiritual representatives of the English conquerors. Toleration became the New Netherland way because of the pragmatic outlook of the Dutch West India Company. When crusty Peter Stuyvesant recommended, shortly after the arrival of the first Jews, that these "blasphemers of Christ" be barred from the colony, he was advised to allow them and the Lutherans, whom the Director-General found almost as objectionable, to "peacefully carry on their business" and to treat both sects "quietly and leniently." That Jews in Amsterdam reminded the company of the loyal support extended by their co-religionists in defense of the Dutch settlement in Brazil was helpful, but what was even more persuasive was the capital which Dutch Jews had invested in the company and the knowledge that the American plantation was underpopulated. "The more of loyal people that go to live there, the better it is in regard to the population of the country . . . and in regard to the increase of trade," the Amsterdam Chamber was reminded. So the Jews were permitted to stay and by struggle wrested from the government the right to a burial ground, to exemption from Sabbath business laws, and to service in the militia.[17]

When Stuyvesant, undaunted, turned his intolerance against Quakers, he not only prompted a stiffer rebuke from home but also evoked one of the most moving expressions of the principle of religious freedom in our history. With Quakers swarming over Long Island, the governor thought to hound them away by prohibiting the other inhabitants from admitting them into their homes. Whereupon thirty-one shocked residents of Flushing subscribed to the following remonstrance:

Right Honorable

You have been pleased to send up unto us a certain prohibition or command that we should not receive or entertain any of those people called Quakers because they are supposed to be by some seducers of the people. For our part we cannot condemn them in this case neither can we stretch out our hands against them to punish, banish, or persecute them, for out of Christ God is a consuming fire, and it is a fearful [thing] to fall into the hands of the living God.

We desire therefore in this case not to judge least we be judged, neither to condemn least we be condemned, but rather [to] let every man stand and fall to his own Master. We are bound by the law to do good unto all men. . . . And though for the present we seem to be unsensible of the law and the law giver, yet when death and the Law assault us, if we have our advocate to seek, who shall plead for us in this case of conscience betwixt God and our own souls. . . .

The law of love, peace and liberty in the states [extends] to Jews, Turks, and Egyptians, as they are considered the sons of Adam, which is the glory of the outward state of Holland. So love, peace and liberty, extending to all in Christ Jesus, condemns hatred, war and bondage. . . . Our desire is not to offend one of his little ones, in whatsoever form, name, or title he appears in, whether Presbyterian, Independent, Baptist, or Quaker, but shall be glad to see anything of God in any of them, desiring to do unto all men as we desire all men should do unto us, which is the true law both of Church and state. . . .

Therefore if any of these said persons come in love unto us, we cannot in conscience lay violent hands upon them, but give them free egress and regress into our town and houses, as God shall persuade our consciences. . . .[18]

Only the residents of today's Flushing, in Queens, appear to commemorate the eloquence of the town's founders and to render tribute to the writers of one of the earliest statements on religious liberty of such broad character in all of the colonies.[19]

Stuyvesant's response was quick and expected. He arrested the sheriff of Flushing who bore the remonstrance to him and dismissed him from office. A few years later, he arrested and banished one of the Quakers, John Bowne, who promptly went to Amsterdam to plead his case. After much deliberation, the Amsterdam Chamber sent Stuyvesant another reminder of the practical value of religious toleration:

. . . although we heartily desire, that these and other sectarians remained away from there, yet as they do not, we doubt very much whether we can proceed against them rigorously without diminishing the population and stopping immigration, which must be favored at a so tender stage of the country's existence. You may therefore shut your eyes, at least not force people's consciences, but allow everyone to have his own belief, as long as he behaves quietly and legally, gives no offence to his neighbors and does not oppose the government. As the government of this city has always practised this maxim of moderation and consequently has often had a considerable influx of people, we do not doubt that your Province too would be benefitted by it.[20]

It was the "maxim of moderation" which became the practice of English New York, as well, not because policy so dictated but because circumstances compelled it. The assumption of English control did not homogenize the colony's religious complexion. "There are religions of all sorts," complained Governor Andros in 1678. A few years later, another governor was more caustic: he found thirteen denominations in the province, "in short of all sorts of opinions there are some," but for the most part, there were "none at all."[21] In Pennsylvania and New Jersey, the absence of an established church reflected the intention of their founders; in New York, the indeterminate character of the Anglican Church developed from the complexity of the colony's population. The first proprietor, the Duke of York, granted religious toleration as a recognition of this diversity and of the need to pursue moderate policies if trade and profits were to be promoted. In any case, the Articles of Capitulation by which the Dutch surrendered specified that the Reformed Church should remain undisturbed. The first English governor, Richard Nicolls, went further, providing that the majority of the population in any town could establish a public church but that other congregations should be permitted to conduct their own services.[22] The prescription was repeated to Andros after the reacquisition of the province from the Dutch in 1674 and was incorporated in the Charter of Liberties drawn up in 1683.[23]

The Glorious Revolution, which advanced the cause of religion in England by the Toleration Act, actually represented a backward step for New York. The province had already gone beyond the notion of one public church and second-class concessions to Dissenters. New Yorkers had come to see "the necessity of leaving religion to each man's conscience in the interest of getting on."[24] The feeble effort during the remainder of the colonial period to elevate the Anglican Church in status proved a failure. A Ministry Act of 1693 provided for public support of "a good sufficient Protestant Minister" in the four lower counties, but this is as close as the colony ever got to a church establishment; and the effort to interpret the law as an exclusive benefit to the Anglican Church was vigorously opposed by New York's many Dissenters. If the law of 1693 established any church, as Clinton Rossiter observed facetiously, "no one was quite sure what church it was."[25]

What developed in the province of New York was neither a clear separation of church and state nor a well-defined state church. In communities where non-Anglicans were in a majority, the proceeds of the Ministry Act could be used to support dissenting churches; in New York City, where the diversity of religions was most pronounced, the principle of voluntarism was followed. Ministers of the Anglican and Dutch churches continued to lament the "spirit of confusion" that resulted from New York's "perfect freedom of conscience," where everybody could "do what seems right in his own eyes, so long as he does not disturb the public peace."[26] New York's churchgoers were always more latitudinarian than their ministers. They were not strict in keeping the Sabbath, as one dismayed Bostonian discovered in 1704; and among the Dutch, even in Albany, where the domines ministered to a population that was largely Dutch, there was very little religion, as another visitor noted in 1744, and "not a grain" of enthusiasm.[27] Some New Yorkers saw virtue in the colony's confusion of religious voices: "the Variety of Sects" in the province was "a Guard against the Tyranny and Usurpation of one over another." Even the Deists, it was claimed, served a useful purpose by forcing casual Christians to re-examine the tenets of their own faith.[28]

Well before the Great Awakening constrained other colonists to recognize the danger of church establishments to their own new programs of spiritual regeneration, well before Isaac Backus and the Separatist Baptists preached the cause of religious voluntarism, and years before Jefferson expressed his fear of the danger to civil peace of state control of religion, New Yorkers had learned in the crucible of day-to-day living in a multifarious society the value of a neutral state which permitted creeds to compete for the spiritual affection of the citizenry. In New York, competition had strengthened freedom, not atheism; and the "natural right" of religious liberty was supported not by political theory so much as by long experience.[29] Prejudice and mutual religious suspicions were not exorcised by the New York accommodation. Germans and Dutch eyed each other with distrust in the Mohawk Valley as did Presbyterians and Anglicans in New York City, but the state was not expected to create love, only harmony. Its role was neither to force its own orthodoxy on others nor to allow any denomination to try to do so. Its jurisdiction in religious matters was legitimate, as one of the colony's most vigorous polemicists put it, only when denominational opinion was converted into "Actions prejudicial to the Community," and then it was not the opinion but the action which was punishable.[30] New York entered the republic with a model to offer its neighbors which gave the lie to the sectarian argument that diversity bred only religious strife and immorality.

Tolerance in New York, as in the other colonies and in the future United States, had its limits; and the outer edge was passed where blacks were concerned. If racial violence is as American as cherry pie, then New York was typically American in this ugly respect, too, setting an example by its harsh repression of blacks suspected of crimes that were magnified in the public mind largely by the color of the perpetrators. Slavery in New York was more humane under the Dutch than under the English, resulting from a peculiar practice of granting Negroes half-freedom as well as freedom, while others were held in bondage. No clear institutionalization of slavery could be developed midst such confusion; and none was.[31] Under the English, slavery expanded so that there were more bondsmen in New York than in any other northern colony; and one of the concomitants of the increase was the most severe violence against Negroes of any of the colonies. In 1712, nineteen blacks were executed after an uprising in which about two dozen fired a building and killed five whites. The reprisals were grisly; the forms of execution included burning, starvation, and use of the medieval wheel. In 1741, a far more imaginary plot resulted in a witch hunt comparable in blind savagery to that at Salem a half-century earlier. The reprisals this time included 18 Negroes hanged, 13 burned at the stake, and 71 deported.[32]

What is prototypical about the racial violence is not so much the severity of the punishment as the confusion of the white population. It had learned cosmopolitanism as a way of life but had never fitted the black man into this scheme of accommodation. Unwilling or unable to enlarge their vision of diversity beyond the color line, white New Yorkers responded with a rationale that was to become more familiar in the succeeding century: The colony's slaves were treated with "great indulgence" and were better cared for than were the poor in Europe; those who had participated in the "villainous plot" were exceptional, and their "senseless" and "wicked enterprise" must be attributable to their seduction by the Devil.[33] Even in the twentieth century, northern urban cosmopolitanism proved to be no guarantor of color blindness. Indeed, race prejudice was to become worse in the very centers of ethnic diversity which bred tolerance for whites. Colonial New York mirrored the national disease.

On the more favorable side, New York's slaves were employed not in gangs on great estates but in a variety of crafts, trades, and domestic service, ameliorating their lot to that extent and providing them with skills for freedom.[34] And the colony appears to have produced America's earliest black poet, one Jupiter Hammon, whose first work appeared in 1760 but whose name and verse disappeared thereafter from the pages of our color-conscious histories.[35] Colonial New York's failure, like that of other colonies, was not that it neglected to cultivate the talents of its black men but that it made no provision for employing those talents after slavery ended.

To pursue in similar detail other evidences of New York's prototypicality in the American colonies would go beyond the confines of a paper intended to be no more than suggestive. The illustrations are numerous enough to provide grist for many doctoral mills. New York, it is said today, is not the United States; yet many Europeans think it is. So in the eighteenth century, New York somehow conveyed the impression of its typicality. The city's shipping was well below that of the other colonial seaports, but Peter Kalm, the Swedish naturalist, visiting in 1750, was sure that New York's commerce was more extensive than that of any other place in British North America. New York was not the largest city in the colonies in the 1760s—Philadelphia exceeded it by 5,000—but the visiting Lord Adam Gordon was surprised to discover the fact on his arrival. The city of New York, he commented, had "long been held at home, the first in America."[36] When that adopted American, Crèvecoeur, raised the question of what an American was, the answer he gave in a nation still almost three-quarters English was that "they are a mixture of English, Scotch, Irish, French, Dutch, Germans and Swedes."[37] From his observation post in Orange County, New York, he had made of the "new man" he saw in that colony the larger American. The misimpressions may have been the result of sheer ignorance, but it is curious how already New York was taken to be the image of greater America.

Colonial New York can boast of its firsts: the first school supported by public funds, although under church control, and now the oldest private school in the country with a continuous existence (the

Collegiate School in New York City); the first chamber of commerce not organized under governmental auspices; the first play to be written and printed in America—the farce *Androborus,* written by Governor Robert Hunter and presented in 1714; the first licensing of doctors, in New York City in 1760; the first legislative proceedings to be printed in any of the colonies, in 1695, at least fifteen years before any of its neighbors followed suit;[38] as well as the enrichment of American popular culture by such Dutch innovations as Santa Claus, New Year's Eve celebrations, ten pin bowling; words such as skipper, sloop, and yacht; culinary delights like crullers and cookies and waffles; political terms like boss and boodle; and inimitable place names like Brooklyn, Harlem, and the Catskills.

Apart from the boost to local pride, firsts are probably of less significance than New York's seconds—or thirds. When the province did not lead, it was not very far behind. Culture was not New York's forte, since the "Art of getting Money" seemed to be the provincial preoccupation and, as Cadwallader Colden viewed it, "the only principle of life propagated among the young People"; but a corps of the province's young intellectuals tried hard in the mid-eighteenth century to compensate for the defect. Philadelphia organized its first philosophical society in 1743; five years later, New York City had a "Society for the Promotion of Useful Knowledge." In 1731, the Quaker City organized a public library; three years later, the Corporation of New York City was operating one with a librarian paid out of public monies (the salary was three pounds a year but was raised to four pounds after three years). The Philadelphians established the colonies' first hospital; New York was responsible for the second. The first medical school was opened in Philadelphia in 1765; New York began the second within three years. Boston had an informal medical society in 1736; New York followed—thirteen years later. The Bay City had a legal discussion group operating in 1765; New York had a larger, better organized, and more professional one—the Moot—five years later.[39] New Yorkers were rarely in the van, but their cultural aspirations always exceeded their grasp. When the New York Society Library was organized in 1754, the elaborate bookplate prepared for its volumes depicted New York City as the Athens of America!

New York's evening schools were not the only ones in the colonies, but by the Revolution the province had more of them than any of its neighbors. Philadelphia's Academy (later College) was the first institution of higher education in the colonies that was strictly secular in purpose and character; but when King's College was founded in 1754, a group of New York's intellectuals fought hard to make that province's equally secular. The effort failed, but the arguments for state control of education advanced in that controversy inspired the post-Revolutionary creation of the University of the State of New York, a model followed by other states similarly committed to the proposition that the supervision of education was the proper business of the public.[40]

New York's press was not as numerous as those of either Massachusetts or Pennsylvania—although not far behind; but in the twenty-two newspapers published at one time or another between 1725 and 1776 appeared some of the most lively and contentious political literature of all the colonial presses. Withal, the literary output of the Middle Colonies exhibited the kind of balance to which Turner had alluded. Of the South's literary productions during the period 1638-1783, more than half comprised statutes, laws, and executive proclamations. New England's output during this same period was preponderantly theological. The press of the Middle Colonies shows a remarkable balance of interests among the fields of politics, law, theology, education, social science, and literature.[41] If this analysis represents accurately the intellectual interests of the three sections, the Middle Colonies were truly the mediators between the two outer extremes.

The shape of the colonial economy of the Middle Atlantic region has yet to be drawn accurately, but even by rough and ready yardsticks, it was more varied, more stable, and less dependent upon single staples or industries than either of the other two regions. Agriculture in New York, as in Pennsylvania, was not a supplementary activity wrung from a barren soil to assist in supporting a trading population but was rather interlaced with trade, New York City providing the outlet for the products of the colony's farms. New York's paper money was better managed and less inflated than the currency of any of the colonies for which adequate statistics are available. The trade of the Middle Colonies reflects the mediating character of which Turner had written. In contrast with the South's dominantly bilateral and New England's heavily triangular trade patterns, the commerce of the middle region was partly triangular but more largely direct with Europe.[42] Conceivably, this was at the root of the region's prosperity on the eve of the Revolution and explains its hesitation in drawing the sword against England.

The French and Indian War provided New York with the largest boost to its economy, headquartering the British Army as it did, but the war points up even more the strategic and diplomatic significance of New York in the colonial and imperial structure. When Herbert L. Osgood wrote his four-volume *American Colonies in the Eighteenth Century,* he felt compelled to apologize in the preface for the extensive treatment given to New York. But, he explained, the four volumes dealt heavily with the Anglo-French Wars and, "of course, in all military relations in which Canada was involved New York was the strategic centre of the colonial territory. In a period of wars, therefore, it necessarily holds a prominent place, while in all that pertained to Indian relations its position was a leading one."[43] "Of course," indeed! What is surprising in Osgood's volumes is not the attention paid to New York but the need of an explanation for doing so. New York *was* the pivot of empire. It was the only colony in which British regular troops were stationed throughout virtually the entire colonial period. The four independent companies were woefully neglected, it is true, but their mere presence was symbolic of Whitehall's recognition of the strategic importance of New York and of its alliance with the Iroquois.[44] It was on the New York frontier that the rivalry between France and England was pursued most enduringly during the eighteenth century; and it was from New York's militant imperialists—Robert Livingston, Cadwallader Colden, Archibald Kennedy, James Alexander, William Livingston, and William Smith—that Britain received the most repeated suggestions for strengthening the empire and turning it to the mutual benefit of colonies and mother country. It was in New York, significantly, that the most serious attempt to produce a colonial union was made; and the interest of both the colony's leaders and British officials was prompted by their recognition of the crucial role which New York, its Indian connections, and its fur trade bore in the imperial framework. And it was in New York, as the strategic center of empire, that the British Post Office in North America established its headquarters and to which it organized its packet service from England, in 1755, in order to provide the Crown with "early and frequent intelligence" of what was "in agitation" in its American colonies.[45]

Finally, there is politics, which in New York almost defies comprehension in the colonial period as it does today. The nature of New York's political structure and the mechanisms by which it operated are still being debated; but a number of conclusions seem acceptable even to the most contentious historians. There was no simple oligarchy of home-grown aristocrats; no politically mute masses; no clearly discernible clash between democrats and aristocrats, conservatives and radicals. What emerges is a complex, dynamic, and, in part, sophisticated preformation of the later political scene. Political factions reflected the heterogeneity of the colony's economy, its ethnic and religious composition, its geographic sectionalism, and its social structure. Parties were broad coalitions, and programs were necessarily diffuse enough to appeal to the colony's cosmopolitan population, often in a variety of languages. If there was deference, there was also democracy. If there was aristocracy, there was also public accountability. If there were family rivalries, there were also popular issues. If there were local concerns, there were also Anglo-American interests. If there was social stratification and monopoly of office-holding, there was also mobility and considerable rotation in office. If there was Whig ideology imported from England, there was also the uniquely American idiom in which it was couched by provincial politicians to suit the colony's special political dynamic. If the articulate were spokesmen of conservatism and status, there were also inarticulate believers in liberty and equality.

Even before the returns are in and while the historians still debate, one may hazard the proposition that the infrastructure of New York's politics was far more complex and interesting than its superstructure, and that the intensity of dialogue disclosed in the polemical literature flowing from the New York presses did not camouflage a mere shadow system of politicking. There surely must have been a contest over who should rule at home, but we are not yet certain who the contestants were or just what they wanted or whether they were always the same people or were consistent in their objectives. Somehow, New Yorkers learned during the colonial period to play the game of politics in the style which conditions dictated that later America should play it in and which a future America came to expect. Somehow, its inhabitants learned to be, as a confused Henry Adams put it in 1889, "democratic by instinct" despite the colony's aristocratic tone. Perhaps the clue is provided by J. H. Plumb's astute observation concerning eighteenth-century English politics, that it was "always richer, freer, more open than the oligarchical nature of its institutions might lead one to believe." In those days neither suffrage nor even elections were at the heart of politics, Plumb says, but rather decision-making and "the turmoil they aroused" and the steady growth of "political consciousness."[46]

New York's colonial experience validates the conclusion perfectly. By 1775, New Yorkers were accustomed to what the country would become so adept in during the years ahead. Only a non-New Yorker could be astonished to hear in New York City, on the eve of the Revolution, nothing but "Politics, politics, politics! . . . Men, women, children, all ranks and professions mad with Politics."[47]

When an English visitor in 1800 said of the Middle States that they seemed "never out of step in the national march," always about to become or being what the rest of the country was, he cast the region in its proper role. The role had already been played out while the states were still colonies. As for New York, that amateur historian, Theodore Roosevelt, may have been more perspicacious than he intended when he wrote in his little history of New York in 1891: "The most important lesson taught by the history of New York City is the lesson of Americanism."[48]

Notes

1. Nathan Glazer and Daniel P. Moynihan, *Beyond the Melting Pot* (Cambridge, Mass., 1963), 2.

2. Wesley F. Craven, *The Legend of the Founding Fathers* (New York, 1956; Ithaca, N.Y., 1965), chap. 1.

3. Jeremy Belknap, *History of New Hampshire* (1812), III, 172, and Samuel Williams, *Natural and Civil History of Vermont* (1798), I, 7, both quoted in Arthur Shaffer, "The Shaping of a National Tradition: Historical Writing in America, 1783-1820" (unpublished Ph.D. dissertation, U.C.L.A., 1966), 69, 133.

4. *History of the Rise, Progress and Establishment of the Independence of the United States of America* (1789), I, 72, quoted in David D. Van Tassel, *Recording America's Past* (Chicago, 1960), 38-39.

5. Edward N. Saveth, *American Historians and European Immigrants, 1875-1925* (New York, 1948), 34-40.

6. Allan H. Spear, "Marcus Lee Hansen and the Historiography of Immigration," *Wisconsin Magazine of History,* XLIV (1961), 258-268, especially 266.

7. John T. Fiske, *The Dutch and Quaker Colonies,* 2 vols. (Boston, 1899); Thomas J. Wertenbaker, *The Founding of American Civilization: The Middle Colonies* (New York, 1938); Daniel G. Brinton Thompson, *Gateway to a Nation: The Middle Atlantic States and their Influence on the Development of the Nation* (Rindge, N.H., 1956). The latter is the only book dealing with the mid-Atlantic region collectively to appear under the category "Middle Atlantic States" in the massive *Guide to the Study of the United States of America,* eds.

Roy F. Basler and others (Washington, D.C., 1960). The American Historical Association's *Guide to Historical Literature* (New York, 1961) has only Wertenbaker's volume on the colonial period indexed under "Middle Atlantic states" [*sic*]. John Bach McMaster was one of the few historians who, in their comprehensive accounts of American development, treated the Middle Colonies with any degree of adequacy. See Eric F. Goldman, *John Bach McMaster: American Historian* (Philadelphia, 1943), 79, 100-101, 133-134; and the same author's "Middle States Regionalism and American Historiography: A Suggestion," in his edited work, *Historiography and Urbanization: Essays in American History in Honor of W. Stull Holt* (Baltimore, 1941), 215, 219. The imprecision in defining the "Middle Colonies" is no better illustrated than by the recent analysis of wealth in that region which excludes New York entirely! See Alice Hanson Jones, "Wealth Estimates for the American Middle Colonies, 1774," *Economic Development and Cultural Change,* XVIII, No. 4, Part 2 (July 1970).

8. Richard H. Shryock, "The Middle Atlantic Area in American History," American Philosophical Society *Proceedings,* CVIII (April 1964), 147-155, especially 153. See also his "Philadelphia and the Flowering of New England . . . ," *Pennsylvania Magazine of History and Biography,* LXIV (1940), 305-313; and "Historical Traditions in Philadelphia and in the Middle Atlantic Area . . . ," *ibid.,* LXVII (1943), 115-141.

9. The latter thesis appears in John M. Head, *A Time to Rend* (Madison, Wis., 1968), especially xiii-xiv.

10. "Problems in American History" (1892), in Everett E. Edwards, comp., *The Early Writings of Frederick Jackson Turner* (Madison, Wis., 1938), 78-79.

11. "The Significance of the Frontier in American History" (1893), *ibid.,* 217-218.

12. "The Development of American Society" (1908), in Wilbur R. Jacobs, ed., *Frederick Jackson Turner's Legacy: Unpublished Writings in American History* (San Marino, Calif., 1965), 177.

13. "Some Sociological Aspects of American History" (1895), in *ibid.,* 163-164; *The United States, 1830-1850* (New York, 1935; Gloucester, Mass., 1958), 92, 94, 112, 138, 143. See also *The Rise of the New West* (New York, 1906), 29-30.

14. Woodrow Wilson, "Mr. Goldwin Smith's 'Views' on Our Political History," *The Forum,* XVI (1893-1894), 489-499, especially 494-496; "The Proper Perspective of American History," *ibid.,* XIX (1895), 544-559, especially 544-546; "The Course of American History," New Jersey Historical Society *Collections,* VIII (1900), 183-206, especially 186-189. See also Louis M. Sears, "Woodrow Wilson," in William T. Hutchinson, ed., *The Marcus W. Jernegan Essays in American Historiography* (Chicago, 1937), 116-117. Wilson secured his ideas in this respect from Turner, even though some of Wilson's writings on the subject antedated Turner's. See Ray A. Billington, *Frederick Jackson Turner* (New York, 1973), 187-188, and Billington, *The Genesis of the Frontier Thesis* (San Marino, Calif., 1971), 181-201.

15. Thompson, *Gateway to a Nation,* 20; David Ellis, "New York and Middle Atlantic Regionalism," *N.Y. Hist.,* XXXV (1954), 5.

16. *N.Y. Doc. Hist.,* IV, 21; Burnaby, *Travels,* ed. Wilson, 117.

17. Henry H. Kessler and Eugene Rachlis, *Peter Stuyvesant and His New York* (New York, 1959), 179-186; Jacob R. Marcus, *The Colonial American Jew, 1492-1776,* 3 vols. (Detroit, 1970), I, 215-248, especially 222-224.

18. "Flushing Remonstrance," Dec. 27, 1657, in *N.Y. Col. Docs.,* XIV, 402-403. The language has been modernized.

19. *New York Times,* Oct. 6, 1957.

20. April 16, 1663. *N.Y. Ecclesiastical Records,* I, 530.

21. *N.Y. Doc. Hist.,* I, 92; *N.Y. Ecclesiastical Records,* II, 877-880.

22. Pratt, *Religion, Politics, and Diversity: The Church-State Theme in New York History,* 27-31.

23. David S. Lovejoy, "Equality and Empire: The New York Charter of Libertys, 1683," *Wm. and Mary Qtly.,* XXI (1964), 493-515, especially 505-506.

24. Pratt, *Religion, Politics, and Diversity,* 38.

25. On the act, see Henshaw, "The New York Ministry Act of 1693," *Hist. Mag. P. E. Church,* II (1933), 199-204; and *N.Y. Ecclesiastical Records,* II, 1076-1079. The Rossiter quotation is from his "Shaping of the American Tradition," *Wm. and Mary Qtly.,* XI (1954), 522.

26. Rev. G. Du Bois to the Classis of Amsterdam, May 14, 1741, in *N.Y. Ecclesiastical Records,* IV, 2756.

27. *The Journal of Madam [Sarah Kemble] Knight* [1704] (New York 1920, 1935), 54; *Itinerarium of Dr. Alexander Hamilton,* ed. Bridenbaugh, 74. John Miller, an Anglican minister visiting New York in 1695, remarked of the inhabitants with unintended humor: "Their interests are their least concern, and, as if salvation were not a matter of moment, when they have opportunities of serving God they care not for making use thereof; or if they go to church, 'tis but too often out of curiosity, and to find faults in him that preacheth rather than to hear their own. . . ." *A Description of the Province and City of New-York* (London, 1695; new edition, ed. John G. Shea, 1862), 38-39.

28. Livingston et al., *The Independent Reflector,* ed. Klein, 391, 396. One dismayed observer, the publisher of *The American Almanac for the Year . . . 1716* (New-York, [1716]), less pleased with the province's religious heterogeneity, remarked that "in an Age wherein there are so many Sorts, Sects and Sizes of Religion-Pretenders, and every one judges himself Right, and all the rest Wrong, I do not wonder if the *Indians* in their Exorcisms . . . think themselves Right too."

29. Perry Miller, "The Contribution of the Protestant Churches to Religious Liberty in Colonial America," *Church History,* IV (1935), 57-66; William G. McLoughlin, "Isaac Backus and the Separation of Church and State in America," *Am. Hist. Rev.,* LXXIII (1968), 1392-1413; Pratt, *Religion, Politics, and Diversity,* chap. 3.

30. Elkanah Watson, *Journal,* quoted in U. P. Hedrick, *A History of Agriculture in the State of New York* (New York, 1933, 1966), 65; *Independent Reflector,* ed. Klein, 94, 308.

31. Edgar J. McManus, *A History of Negro Slavery in New York* (Syracuse, 1966), chap. 1.

32. *Ibid.,* 126-136; John Hope Franklin, *From Slavery to Freedom* (3d ed., New York, 1967), 92-94; Winthrop D. Jordan, *White over Black: American Attitudes toward the Negro, 1550-1812* (Chapel Hill, 1968), 115-118. The figures for those punished in the 1741 plot seem to vary in each modern account. Those above are taken from the list appended to Daniel Horsmanden's contemporary account, *A Journal of the Proceedings in the Detection of the Conspiracy . . .* (New-York, 1744), reprinted as *The New-York Conspiracy* (New York, 1810) and recently reprinted from the latter text with an introduction by Thomas J. Davis (Boston, 1971).

33. The quotations are from the 1971 edition of Horsmanden's *Journal,* 105-106, 168. I cannot agree with Winthrop Jordan's conclusion that the social heterogeneity of the city and the politics of the colony created tensions that were palliated by vengeance against the Negroes. (*White over Black,* 119-120).

34. McManus, *Negro Slavery in New York,* chap. 3.

35. Hammon's first poem, "An Evening Thought," appeared in 1760, seven years before the first published work of the more famous Phillis Wheatley of Boston. However, Miss Wheatley had been writing even before that date. Hammon's poetry was first made known by Oscar Wegelin in his *Jupiter Hammon: American Negro Poet* (New York, 1915), where the 1760 poem appeared. Although Hammon was mentioned thereafter by Negro historians (e.g., Roi Ottley and William J. Weatherby, eds., *The Negro in New York: An Informal Social History* [New York, 1967], 34; Lerone Bennett, Jr., *Before the Mayflower: A History of Black America* [4th ed., Chicago, 1969], 64 note), not until very recently did he receive full recognition. For the latter, see Stanley A. Ransom, ed., *America's First Negro Poet: the Complete Works of Jupiter Hammon of Long Island* (Pt. Washington, N.Y., 1970); and Dorothy Porter, ed., *Early Negro Writing, 1760-1837* (Boston, 1971), 529-531.

36. Peter Kalm, *Travels,* ed. Benson, I, 134; "Journal of Lord Adam Gordon," in Newton D. Mereness, ed., *Travels in the American Colonies* (New York, 1916), 414. An anonymous Scotsman, at about the same time Gordon was making his observation about New York City's preeminence, commented that "The Situation of this town marks it for [the] Capital of Engl[ish] Govern[men]t." "Notes on American Colonies, 18th Century" [1760?], in Scottish Record Office, Edinburgh, GD 248/471.

37. Crèvecoeur, *Letters from an American Farmer* [1782] (New York, 1957), 37, 39.

38. Henry W. Dunshee, *History of the School of the Collegiate Dutch Church in the City of New York* (New York, 1883), 15; Joseph B. Bishop, *A Chronicle of One Hundred and Fifty Years: The Chamber of Commerce of the State of New York, 1768-1918* (New York, 1918), 1-3; Leder, "Robert Hunter's *Androborus,*" *Bulletin, New York Public Library,* LXVIII (March 1964), 153-190; Richard H. Shryock, *Medicine and Society in America, 1600-1860* (New York, 1960; Ithaca, N.Y., 1962), 33; Hindle, *Science in Revolutionary America,* 110; A. R. Hasse, "The First Published Proceedings of an American Legislature," *The Bibliographer,* II (1903), 240-242.

39. P. 65 above; Hindle, *Science in Revolutionary America,* 60-61; Austin B. Keep, *The Library in Colonial New York* (New York, 1909), 64-72; Shryock, *Medicine and Society in America,* 22, 24-25; Hamlin, *Legal Education in Colonial New York,* 96-97, 104 note; *Diary and Autobiography of John Adams,* ed. L. H. Butterfield, 4 vols. (New York, 1964), I, 251-258.

40. Carl Bridenbaugh, *Cities in the Wilderness* (New York, 1964), 289, 444, 449-450. The reference in a New York indenture of Nov. 25, 1690, to an evening school for the education of apprentices may make New York the originator of this unique institution. See Robert F. Seybolt, *Apprenticeship and Apprenticeship Education in Colonial New York* (New York, 1917), 94; and Seybolt, *The Evening School in Colonial America* (University of Illinois Bureau of Educational Research, Bulletin No. 24, 1925), 9-10, 15.

41. Flick, ed., *History of the State of New York,* III, 84-86; Hellmut Lehmann-Haupt and others, *The Book in America* (New York, 1939), 31-32; Sidney Kobre, *The Development of the Colonial Newspaper* (Gloucester, Mass., 1960), 147-148. By the mid-eighteenth century, Pennsylvania and New York had displaced Massachusetts as the publishing centers of the colonies. Francisco Guerra, *American Medical Bibliography, 1639-1783* (New York, 1962), 10.

42. Thomas C. Cochran, "The Middle Atlantic Area in the Economic History of the United States," American Philosophical Society *Proceedings,* CVIII (April 1964), 156-157; Roger W. Weiss, "The Issue of Paper Money in the American Colonies, 1720-1774," *Journal of Economic History,* XXX (1970), 770-784, especially 777, 780; Gary M. Walton, "New Evidence on Colonial Commerce," *ibid.,* XXVIII (1968), 363-387; William I. Davisson and Lawrence

J. Bradley, "New York Maritime Trade: Ship Voyage Patterns, 1715-1765," *N.Y. Hist. Soc. Qtly.*, LV (1971), 309-317.

43. Osgood, *American Colonies in the Eighteenth Century,* I, x-xi.

44. Stanley Pargellis, "The Four Independent Companies of New York," in *Essays in Colonial History Presented to Charles McLean Andrews* (New Haven, 1931), 96-123; Leder, ed., "Dam'me Don't Stir a Man: Trial of New York Mutineers in 1700," *N.Y. Hist. Soc. Qtly.*, XLII (1958), 261-283; William A. Foote, "The American Independent Companies of the British Army, 1664-1764" (unpublished Ph.D. dissertation, U.C.L.A., 1966), 144-162, 245-282.

45. On the subject of New York in the strategy of empire, Max Savelle has written most extensively and most recently in his *Origins of American Diplomacy* (New York, 1967), especially 179-190 and 511-554. On the post office, see William Smith, *History of the Post Office in British North America, 1639-1870* (Cambridge, Engl., 1920), 1, 19, 34. New York's central role in imperial strategy was noted long ago in Arthur H. Buffinton, "New York's Place in Intercolonial Politics," N.Y. State Hist. Assoc. *Proceedings,* XVI (1917), 51-62, and in Evarts B. Greene, "New York and the Old Empire," N.Y. State Hist. Assoc. *Quarterly Journal,* VIII (1926-1927), 121-132.

46. J. H. Plumb, "Political Man," in James L. Clifford, ed., *Man versus Society in Eighteenth-Century Britain* (Cambridge, Engl., 1968), 21.

47. Philip Padelford, ed., *Colonial Panorama: Dr. Robert Honeyman's Journal for March and April 1775* (San Marino, Calif., 1939), 31 (May 13, 1775).

48. Thomas Twining, quoted in Whitfield J. Bell, Jr., "The Middle States Tradition in American Historiography: Introduction," American Philosophical Society *Proceedings,* CVIII (April 1964), 145; Theodore Roosevelt, *New York* (New York, 1891, 1895), xi. Two articles which treat the theme of New York's contribution to the development of the nation are Allan Nevins, "The Golden Thread in the History of New York," *N.Y. Hist. Soc. Qtly.*, XXXIX (1955), 5-22, and Bayrd Still, "The Essence of New York City," *ibid.*, XLIII (1959), 401-423. The Middle Colonies theme has been developed most recently by Patricia U. Bonomi in her essay, "The Middle Colonies: Embryo of the New Political Order," in Vaughan and Billias, eds., *Perspectives on Early American History,* 63-92.

Epilogue

Although the colonial period was not a mere preparation for independence, as the earliest historians of the new nation sought to make it appear, there are obviously links between the years before 1776 and those that followed. Each colony made its decision for independence in the light of its own peculiar experience as well as in response to the larger threat of British measures to all the colonies. The response to the latter was not uniform, nor did it proceed step by step in each colony at the same pace. New York's reaction was especially slow by the standards of its more precipitant neighbors. Its hesitation has often been attributed to the sheer unwillingness of its affluent and conservative-minded leaders to jeopardize their wealth. More recently, John Head (A TIME TO REND: AN ESSAY ON THE DECISION FOR AMERICAN INDEPENDENCE [*Madison, Wisconsin, 1968*]) *has suggested that the indecision of colonies like New York stemmed from the danger that revolution posed to the harmonious life-style which they had fashioned out of an otherwise "explosive mixture of cultural groups." Head correctly perceived the central importance of New York's social heterogeneity in the deliberations of its leadership. In attributing the colony's harmony, however, "largely, if not only" to the fact that it had "plenty of room," Head misses the heart of New York's successful accommodation to its cultural challenge. It was not the physical but the political diffusion of its contending factions and interests that lay at the root of New York's achievement. New Yorkers had learned to make a political virtue of its variegated population. They had learned how to use the machinery of politics to achieve the delicate balance between sectarian strife and enforced cultural and religious uniformity. They were not certain that the fragile contrivance would withstand the pressures of external and civil war. In the brief essay that follows, I suggest that New York's decision in 1776 was for this reason far more difficult than that of New England or the South. That the colony would not only weather the storm but also establish a standard for the future, not even the most prescient of New Yorkers could know at the time. They deserve the understanding of history for their ignorance.*

9.

New York's Reluctant Road to Independence

ALMOST FIFTY YEARS AGO, the historian Carl Becker reminded us that the Revolution was not all that our story books had made it out to be. The familiar picture of farmer-minutemen rising as one man to oppose British oppression was more caricature than reality. The true "Spirit of '76," Becker suggested, was revealed in the agonizing indecision and the haunting fears which made America's revolutionaries the most reluctant of rebels and the most cautious of militants. To illustrate his point, Becker portrayed the dilemma of a New York merchant, conservative by instinct, who step by step found himself drawn to the decision he most dreaded—rebellion against his mother country and treason to his king.

Becker's choice of a New Yorker as his typical conservative was not accidental. Of all the colonies, New York in 1776 was the least enthusiastic for severing the traditional tie with Great Britain. Loyalism was rampant north of New York City and on Long Island. Connecticut patriots warned their New York friends not "to dally, or be merely neutral." And as the New York Provincial Congress hesitated to authorize its delegates at Philadelphia to vote for independence, John Adams complained bitterly: "What is the reason that New York must continue to embarrass the Continent? . . . are their people in-

This essay originally appeared in *The Correspondent*, Volume III, No. 1 (Summer 1972), published by the New York State American Revolution Bicentennial Commission.

capable of seeing and feeling like other men?" On July 2, when the members of the Continental Congress approved the "Grand Resolution," only New York's delegates stood silent. It took seven more days for the province to regain its voice and agree that "these United Colonies are, and, of right, ought to be Free and Independent States."

As we approach the Revolution's bicentennial, must New Yorkers still remain embarrassed alongside their more zealous neighbors? I think not. There are better answers to Adams's caustic query than the insensitivity he saw in the New Yorkers of 1776. There were good reasons for the colony's caution and more patriotism among its inhabitants than Adams was able to perceive through his own distorted lenses. New York's Sons of Liberty had long fought the pretensions of Crown and Parliament to unlimited power over the colonies. Its lawyers had well before 1776 laid down the constitutional proposition that New York possessed rights of self-government which could not be abrogated by kings or royal ministers. Its assemblies had repeatedly refused to cooperate with governors who acted like petty tyrants. Its seamen had fought against impressment by British naval officers, and its mechanics and tradesmen had intimidated collectors who sought to enforce the hated Stamp Act. But New Yorkers also knew the advantages of the imperial connection and the dangers of separation from the mother country.

New York was prosperous in the empire. Its wheat and cattle commanded high prices in the West Indies, and its iron was bought by England. Its currency was stable while that of its neighbors depreciated or fluctuated wildly. No democracy, it had nevertheless worked out a nice balance between the domination of the few and the rule of the many. Its local aristocrats commanded the seats of power but not without strenuous politicking in which large numbers of New Yorkers made their voices heard at election times. Unlike New Englanders or Virginians, New Yorkers were a motley lot of nationalities, religions, and ethnic minorities; but such diversity made for richness and vitality, not confusion or disorder. And the links with the empire were longstanding and strong. Here was headquartered the British Army in North America; here was the center of the colonial postal system; and here were held the great congresses with the Indians on whose friendship the peace of the frontier depended.

What New York's conservative leadership sought was a middle way which would preserve the advantages of union with Britain without the sacrifice of long-prized and held political liberty. Nor were they unaware of the danger of upsetting the delicate balance of sectional, class, ethnic, and denominational interests they had managed to fabricate over a century of artful political manipulation. New York's conservatives were never Tories; they were always "true Whigs," even those who became Loyalists. They would neither knuckle under to the Crown nor be pushed into rebellion by their more truculent sister-colonies. And in their hesitating decision for independence, New York's leaders mirrored the kaleidoscope of the American colonists as a whole more accurately than did the Sam Adamses and the Patrick Henrys—a people not yet fused into nationhood; rent by internal differences; groping to retain liberties long held under Britain's near-benevolent rule without taking the step of political parricide; hoping until the end for a peaceful accommodation but accepting the horrors of fratricidal warfare when peace required the sacrifice of cherished principles.

Locked within the mystery of New York's reluctant road to independence lies the answer to the question, as relevant to our own time as for theirs, of when a government "long established" should be changed and when a people dare assume the right to correct evils "by abolishing the forms" to which they have long been accustomed.

Index

Acts of Trade, 136
Adams, Henry, 111, 199
Adams, John, 85, 87n, 142, 155, 209-210
Adams, Samuel, 142, 154, 155, 211
Addison, Joseph, 55, 67, 72
Albany, N.Y., 13-14, 21, 22, 42, 57, 68, 131; courts, 134; doctors, 113; Dutch influence, 111, 112, 193; fur trade, 27n, 38; lawyers, 132; population, 26; religion in, 68, 193; voting in, 22, 24-25, 42
Albany Common Council, 22
Albany County, 18, 19, 20, 23, 160
Albany Plan of Union, 198
Alexander family, 25, 61
Alexander, James, 15-17, 29n, 38, 44, 47n, 57-58, 63, 65, 94n, 117, 131, 133, 137, 138, 198
Alexander, Mary, 29n, 58, 131, 133
Alexander, William, 29n, 63
American Chronicle, 164, 165
American Historical Review, 5, 11
American Magazine (N.Y.), 53, 86n
American Magazine and Historical Chronicle (Boston), 54, 55, 59
American Magazine, or Monthly Chronicle (Phila.), 86n
American Museum, 54, 85, 86n
American Philosophical Society, 196
American Revolution: as dual movement, 3-4, 12, 34n, 184-185, causes, 154; education and, 197; ideology, 51; King's College and, 84, 106, 197; lawyers and, 155-156, 210; leadership, 155, 184-185; Middle Colonies and, 197; movement for independence, 207; New York and, 187, 189, 207, 209-211; political effects in New York, 17, 45
American Weekly Mercury, 67
Amsterdam, 69, 112, 190, 191
Ancrum, Scotland, 65
Anderson, Elizabeth, 139
Anderson, Mary, 139
Androborus, 116, 196
Andros, Edmund, 99, 123n, 192
Anglicans, 41, 51, 65, 69, 74, 81, 193; and King's College, 74-84, 102, 104; numbers in New York, 76, 93n, 99-100
Anti-Catholicism, 91n
Anticlericalism, 56, 63, 68-71, 73-74, 77, 80, 100-101, 104, 147
Anti-Sabbatarians, 90
Apprenticeship, 21, 203n; legal, 57, 100, 114, 131, 132, 145
Arbitration, in law, 135
Architecture, 112, 114, 121n
Aristocrats, 3-4, 9, 185; control of New York politics, 11-34, 36, 42, 45, 117, 198-199
Articles of Capitulation, 192
Artisans, 4, 21, 22, 38
Assembly (N.Y.): and British taxes, 62-63; and Forsey case, 172; and judicial legislation, 146; and jury trials, 142; and New York college, 60, 74, 77, 82, 106; controlled byDe Lanceys, 16, 80, 157-158; controlled by Livingstons 15, 160, 162; disputes with governor, 11, 42, 65,142, 172, 210; elections for, 18, 19, 24-25, 41-42, 61 (*see also* Elections); lawyer influence, 158-159; published proceedings, 196
Auchmuty, Rev. Samuel, 95n
Aynsley, William, 175n

Backus, Isaac, 193
Bailyn, Bernard, 29n, 51, 90n
Banyar, Goldsbrow, 88n
Baptists, 118, 191; Separate Baptists, 193
Bard, Samuel, 109n
Bayard, Nicholas, 38
Becker, Carl, ix-x, 3-5, 9, 11-13, 17, 19, 20, 25, 26, 34n, 36, 189, 209
Beekman, Henry, 18, 19, 26, 133; estate, 30n
Belcher, Jonathan, 59, 138
The Bellman, 85
Benson, Robert, 132
Bernard, Francis, 45, 154
Bishopric, Anglican, 41, 78, 103, 147; *see also* Church of England, episcopate controversy
Bland, Richard, 155
Board of Regents, N.Y., 85, 107
Board of Trade, 23, 133, 161, 167, 171, 172
Bolting, 41
Bonomi, Patricia, 5, 9
Boorstin, Daniel, 155, 189
Boston, 53, 55, 59, 81, 84, 98, 163, 184
Boston Weekly Magazine, 55
Bowne, John, 191
Bradford, Andrew, 86n
Bradford, William, 86n
Brockholst, Mary, 134
Brodhead, John R., x
Brown, Robert E., 31n, 34n
Bryant, William, 140
Burke, Edmund, 190
Burnaby, Rev. Andrew, 95n, 110, 119
Burnet, William, 13, 14, 15, 28n, 43
Burr, Rev. Aaron, 102

Canada, ix, x, 13, 14, 15, 27n, 28n, 198; *sell also* Montreal
Canajoharie, 18
Carey, Mathew, 85
Carroll, Charles, 30n, 32n
Catholics, 24, 67, 69, 99
Cato's Letters, 67, 90n
Caughnawa, 27n
Chambers, John, 161, 165
Chandler, Rev. Thomas B., 95n
Charter of Liberties, 192
Charters: colonial, 184; King's College, 41, 73, 77, 78, 83, 102, 103, 104, 106, 116; Presbyterian Church, N.Y.C., 70; Trinity Church, N.Y.C., 70
Chief Justice: of Canada, x; of New Jersey, 162, 175n; of New York, 38, 43, 157-160, 161, 162, 169, 174-175n
The Choice, 59
Christian History, 55
Church and state, 69-70, 76, 78 97-109, 191, 192, 193
Church of England, 5, 26, 41, 42, 51, 65, 66, 69, 70, 73, 76, 81, 99, 119, 120, 159; and Dissenters, 69, 99, 118, 119; and King's College, 73-74, 76-84, 101, 104; and Presbyterians, 51, 100, 156; clergy, 73, 74, 79, 80, 81, 100, 202n; establishment in New York, 78, 99, 102-103, 106, 119, 120, 192-193; episcopate controversy, 32n, 41, 63, 147, 159,
Church of Scotland, 70
Clarkson, David, 134
Clinton, George, 31n, 43, 88n; and De Lanceys, 157-158, 162, 174-175n; and Livingstons, 16, 29n, 60, 61, 159
Colden, Cadwallader, ix, 5, 14, 15, 17, 23, 28n, 38, 40, 44, 93n, 116, 117, 137, 198; and appeals, 142, 166-173; and Forsey case, 166-173; and judicial tenure, 127, 158-166; and jury trials, 127, 166- 173; and lawyers, 127, 129, 156, 157, 165-167; and Livingstons, 159, 161; and Stamp Act, 171-172; and triumvirate, 63, 127, 159-160, 164, 174n; appointed lieutenant governor, 160; as Clinton's adviser, 158
Colden, David, 137
Coleman, Benjamin, 59
College of New Jersey, 62, 75, 76, 79, 85, 98, 99, 102
Colleges, 75, 74-84, 98; *see also* individual colleges
Collegiate School, N.Y.C., 195-196
Commonwealthmen, 51
Compact theory of government, 79
Congregational church, 68, 73
Connecticut, 68, 101, 114
Constitution: British, 142, 154, 170; New York, 141, 168, 169
Constitutional Convention, 147
Continental Congress, 85, 87n
Cooper, Rev. Myles, 109n
Cosby, William, 15-16, 24, 28n, 38, 43, 161
Coureurs de bois, 13-14

Courts: appeals isue, 166-173; Chancery, 146; common law, 136; Common Pleas, 134; costs, 134-135, 138, 148n; equity, 161; establishment of, 142, 161; Exchequer, 16; governors and, 16, 41; juryless,16, 118; local, 113, 114, 133, 145, 146; Mayor's Court, Albany, 134; Mayor's Court, N.Y.C., 130, 132, 140, 146; proceedings in, 134-136, 138-145, 149n, Sessions courts, 134; Supreme Court, N.Y., 130, 132, 134, 136, 138-139, 140-143, 146, 149n, 160-164, 167, 171; Vice-Admiralty, 134, 136, 177n
The Craftsmen, 74
Craven, Wesley F., 183
Crevecouer, Hector St. John de, 129, 195
Cunningham, Waddel, 142, 166

Dabney, Virginius, 183
Dartmouth, Earl of, 154
Dawson, Henry B., x
Debtors, 135-136
De Foreest, Henry, 81, 94n
Deists, 101, 193
De Lancey, James, 5, 43, 61, 117; and King's College, 78, 80, 82-83; as chief justice, 78, 162, 174-175n; as lieutenant governor, 78; control of Assembly, 83, 157-158; death, 157, 159
De Lancey, Oliver, 136
De Lancey, Peter, 15
De Lancey, Stephen, 14, 15, 28n, 38
De Lanceys, 9, 13-16, 20, 25, 35-36, 38-39, 44, 61, 80, 115, 119, 120, 136, 159, 161
Dellius, Godfrey, 114
Democracy: and education, 107; and politics in colonial New York, 11-34, 45, 199; urban origins, 189; in colonial New York, 9, 210
De Pauw, Linda G., xi
De Peyster, Abraham, 35, 121n
Dickinson, John, 142, 155
Dissenters, 65, 68-69, 70, 78, 82, 100, 192, 193; and Church of England, 69, 99, 118, 119; and King's College controversy, 41, 78, 82; in England, 69; in New England, 69
Divine right theory, 67
Doctors, 113; licensing of, 196; medical quackery, 73, 113; medical societies, 196
Donald, David, 186
Dongan, Thomas, 40, 99, 123n
Douglass, Elisha P., xi
Dulany, Daniel, 155
Dutch, 40, 69, 112, 185, 195; and Indians, 13-14, 187; and Leisler's Rebellion, 38; and religious tolerance, 118-119, 190-192; architecture, 112; culture, 113; customs, 196; doctors, 113; in Mohawk Valley, 193; influence in Albany, 111, 112, 193; language, 101, 111-112; religion, 68
Dutch Reformed Church, 65, 69, 70, 73, 79, 81, 91n, 101, 102, 112, 119; American Classics, 69; and King's College controversy, 76, 102; and religious toleration, 190; language question in, 69, 112; status after 1664 in New York, 192
Dutch West India Company, 190
Dutchess County, 18, 23, 133
Duane, James, 18, 35, 134, 140, 145, 152n
Duyckink, Gerardus, 116

Education, 51, 85, 97, 98, 101-102; elementary and secondary, 97, 106; evening schools, 196, 203n; legal, 131-133, 145; liberal education, 75, 98-99, 103, 111; low state in New York, 75, 101-102, 111; religion and, 73-75, 97-109; state control of, 85, 97-109, 197; William Livingston on, 104-107, 111
Elections, 9, 12, 19, 20-25, 199; in *1720s,* 117; in *1730s,* 117; *1733,* 24; *1735,* 24; *1748,* 18; in *1750s,* 117; *1750,* 25, 61; *1751,* 18; in *1760s,* 117; *1761,* 19, 24, 162; *1768,* 22, 24, 32n, 41; *1769,* 22, 24, 32n, 41; *1788,* 24; *1790,* 31n
Election Law of 1699, 23
Electoral corruption, 73
Elizabethtown, N.J., 62, 144, 147
Elizabethtown Associates, 138
Elizabethtown Bill in Chancery, 137-138
Emerson, Ralph Waldo, 45
Enlightenment, 100
Episcopacy, 67, 68, 79, 103, 120

Episcopal clergy, 44, 63; *see also* Church of England
Evans, Lewis, 186
Executive Council, N.Y., 15, 41, 44, 82, 103, 140, 158, 167, 168

Family alliances, 11, 15, 16, 17, 25, 27, 35-36, 199
Farley, Samuel, 175n
The Federalist, 101
Fernow, Berthold, 101
Fiske, John, 185
Flushing Remonstrance, 191
Forsey, Thomas, 142, 166
Forsey, v. Cunningham, 142, 166-173
Ft. George, N.Y., 171
Fox, Dixon R., xi
Franchise, *see* Suffrage
Franklin, Benjamin, 54, 66, 84, 86n, 110
Franks, Moses B., 24
Freeholding, 20, 23, 24, 33n, 61, 88n, 114
Freemanship: New York City, 21-23, 31n, 32n, 44, 61, 88n; Albany, 22
Frelinghuysen, Rev. Theodore, 92n
French, Susanna, 132
French and Indian War, 43, 62, 78, 106, 118, 136, 138, 139, 143, 144, 147, 160, 197-198
French Reformed Church, 28n, 65, 119
Friedenwald, Herbert, x
Frontier thesis, 187-189
Funerals, 73
Fur trade, 13-15, 27n, 28n, 38, 41, 114-115, 118

Gage, Thomas, 154, 155, 156
Gaine, Hugh, 79, 81, 83, 94n
General Magazine, and Historical Chronicle, 54, 55, 86n
General Theological Seminary, 95n
Gentleman's Magazine, 54
Georgia, 115, 189
Germans, 18, 185, 193, 195
Glorious Revolution, 37, 161, 192
Good Friday, 70
Gordon, Lord Adam, 195
Gordon, Thomas, 51, 67-68, 70, 74, 90n
Gordon, William, 185
Governors, 43, 44; appeals to, 140-141; Council, *see* Executive Council; disputes with Assembly, 11, 42, 65, 142, 172, 210; land grants to, 114; political "interest," 11, 13; prerogative powers, 41, 63, 70, 106, 157
Gray's Inn, London, 146
Great Awakening, 55, 68, 69, 75, 98, 101, 193
Grenville, George, 168, 171
The Guardian, 67, 90n

Hamilton, Alexander, 155
Hamilton, Dr. Alexander, 111
Hammon, Jupiter, 195, 203n
Hansen, Marcus L., 186
Harison, George, 176n
Harvard College, 76, 98, 104, 159
Hays, Baruch, 24
Hays, Judah, 24
Hays, Solomon, 24
Head, John, 207
Henry, Patrick, 155, 185, 211
Hicks, Whitehead, 131
Hippocrates Mithridate, 60
Historiography: American, 184-185; colonial New York, 3, 42-43, 181, 183-186; Progressive, 4
Holland, 69, 191
Horsmanden, Daniel, 161, 165, 167, 169, 202n
Hospitals, 196
Hudson River, 32n, 40, 111, 112, 114, 115
Hudson Valley, 40, 137
Huguenots, 119, 185
Hunter, Robert, 43, 116, 196

Immigration, 185
Immigration Restriction League, 185
Independent Reflector, x, 51, 53-96, 100, 104, 106, 107, 116, 120, 133
Independent Whig, 67, 68, 71, 90n
Indians, 13-14, 27n, 41, 186-187; congresses, 210; Dutch and, 13-14, 187; fur trade, 38, 198 (*see also* Fur trade); land frauds, 16, 159; missionaries to, 70
Ingersoll, Jared, 155
Iredell, James, 155
Irish, 195
Iron Act, 16
Iroquois, 27n
Irving, Washington, 185

James II, 37, 192
Jameson, J. Franklin, xi
Jamestown, Va., 183, 185
Jay, John, 20, 31n, 35, 155
Jefferson, Thomas, 142, 155, 193
Jesuits, 14, 27n
Jews, 24, 99, 118, 185, 190, 191

John Englishman, 82, 95n
Johnson, Rev. Samuel, 63, 76, 77, 82, 83, 100, 102, 155-156
Johnson, William Samuel, 155
Jones, David, 165
Jones, Nathaniel, 175n
Jones, Thomas, 43, 66, 104, 185
Jordan, Winthrop, 202n
Judges: plans to improve, 146; poor quality, 130, 131; tenure of, 127, 157-166
Judicial tenure, 62; controversy over, 5, 127, 157-166; in England, 161
Juries, 113, 146; jury service, 23; jury system, 168; jury trials, 32n, 62, 127, 177n; right to jury trial, 166-173

Kalm, Peter, 122n, 195
Katz, Stanley, 5
Kempe, John Tabor, 140, 145
Kennedy, Archibald, 198
King George's War, 16, 60, 158
King's College, 5, 41, 51, 56, 60, 100, 116; controversy over, 26, 74-84, 98-107, 120, 147, 159, 166; founding, 74, 101, 111, 197; reputation, 84, 95n, 106-107, 109n, 117
King's Farm, 76, 102
Kissam, Benjamin, 152n

Land titles, 16, 44
Landholding, 12, 17-20, 23, 36, 44, 113-114, 122n
Landlords, 36, 114, 115, 136, 137, 168
Law, 130, 136; civil law, 134-138; codification, 133, 159-160, 174n; common law, 184; criminal law, 138-140; professionalization, 130-131, 145-146
Lawyers, 20, 26, 36, 43, 44, 63, 98, 100, 114, 120; admission to practice, 132; and American Revolution, 154-155, 210; and Colden, 127, 129, 156, 157, 165-167, 169, 172-173; and colonial rights, 127; and Stamp Act, 155-157; associations of, 100, 145, 196 (*see also* The Moot); education of, 57-58, 100, 114, 131-133, 145-146, 148n; low status, 129-130; pettifoggers, 132-133; political influence, 20, 156-157, 158-159; popular hostility to, 129-130, 134; practice, 134-140; professionalization, 127, 129-131, 145
Laziere, Benjamin, 24
Leases, 17-20, 23, 30n, 32n, 114
Leder, Lawrence H., 46n, 47n, 87n
Legal profession, 43, 168; fees, 134-135, 146, 149n; libraries, 131, 146; *see also* lawyers
Leisler, Jacob, 37-38
Leisler's Rebellion, 37-38
Letter to the Freemen and Freeholders (1750), 61, 88n; (1752), 61, 88n
Letters from an American Farmer, 129
Levy, Hayman, 24
Libels, 73, 94n
Libraries, 62, 100, 196; in colleges, 105-106; in New Netherland, 113; in Philadelphia, 196; lawyers', 131, 146; *see also* New York Society Library
Limited government, theory of, 170
Lincoln, Charles H., x
Livingston, Catherine Van Brugh, 132
Livingston, Henry, 57, 134
Livingston, James, 133
Livingston, Janet, 29n, 65
Livingston, John, 57, 133
Livingston, Peter Van Brugh, 29n, 57, 102, 133
Livingston, Philip, 2nd manor lord, 5, 15, 57, 87n, 131; and Clinton, 29n, 60, 159; and Zenger trial, 16; death, 16, 61; on Governor's Council, 15; sons, 29n, 57; tenants, 16, 61
Livingston, Philip, "the signer," 57, 88n, 133
Livingston, Robert, 1st manor lord, 13-14, 15, 43, 87n, 114, 198; and Leisler's Rebellion, 38; descendants, 16; Indian policy, 14, 28n; on party divisions, 40; Speaker of Assembly, 15
Livingston, Robert, 3rd manor lord, 19, 30n, 41, 57, 88n, 106, 132, 134, 164
Livingston, Robert, Jr., 14
Livingston, Robert, of N.Y.C., 133
Livingston, Robert G., 133
Livingston, Robert James, 65
Livingston, Robert R., 165, 177n
Livingston, Sarah, 29n
Livingston, Sarah Van Brugh, 31n
Livingston, Susan, 145
Livingston, William, ix, 5, 26, 44, 61, 114, 117, 155, 156, 165, 198; admission to the bar, 63, 132, 148n; and Colden, 159-173; and *Independent Reflector,* 56-57, 61-66, 69-73, 80-81, 104-106,

115; and Forsey case, 166-173; and King's College controversy, 26, 74-84, 100-107; and triumvirate, 56-57, 61, 65, 100, 140, 185; as landowner, 137; as lawyer, 29n, 61, 100, 116, 129-153; as writer, 58, 59-61, 147; *Digest of the Laws,* 61, 133, 159-160, 174n; early life, 57-61, 86n, 100, 131; educational philosophy, 75, 77-78, 104-106; family connections, 131-132, 133; in American Revolution, 85; income, 132, 133, 136; 144-145; law practice, 132, 134-144; legal education, 63, 131-133; marriage, 100, 132; library, 146; religious views, 65, 68-70, 91n, 100-101, 120; "The Sentinel," 169
Livingston, William, Jr., 84, 87n
Livingston-Burnet trade program, 15, 28n
Livingston Manor, 13, 16, 18, 23, 57, 100, 134
Livingstons, 9, 13-17, 20, 25, 28n, 36, 39, 43, 61, 100, 115, 119, 131, 159, 162, 165, 168
Locke, John, 90n, 104
Long Island, 40, 190, 209
Lotteries, 75-76, 83, 102
Loudon, Samuel, 86n
Loyalists, 209, 211
Lutherans, 118, 190

McAlpine, Robert, 94n
MacCracken, Henry N., 47n
McCulloch v. Maryland, 97
McDougall Affair, 32n
McMaster, John B., 201n
Madison, James, 101
Magazines, 51, 53-56
Manor lords, 17-19, 43, 114, 184
Manors, 17-20, 23, 114; *see also* individual manors
Marshall, John, 97
Maryland, 111, 114
Mason, George, 155
Mason-Dixon Line, 35
Massachusetts, 12, 45, 53, 110, 111, 114, 117, 189, 197, 203n
Mayflower, 183
Mechanics, 20, 21, 210
"Melting pot," 186, 188
Merchants, 43, 44, 115; and the American Revolution, 155; as lawyers, 114; in fur trade, 15; in politics, 36; opposition to Colden, 168; ties with lawyers, 135-136
Middle Atlantic States, 186-189, 197, 200, 200n
Middle Colonies, 181, 183, 185-189, 197, 201n
Milburne, Jacob, 38
Miller, Rev. John, 202n
Ministry Act of 1693, 70, 91n, 99, 192-193
Mohawk Valley, 14, 193
Monckton, Robert, 164, 165, 169
Montreal, 13-14, 27n, 38
Montresor, John, 156-157
Moore, Lambert, 140-141
The Moot, 62, 100, 146, 196
Moravians, 56, 73, 101
Morris family, 25, 39, 43, 61, 136
Morris, Lewis, 14, 15, 24, 38, 138
Morris, Robert Hunter, 161
Moses, Isaac, 24
Murray, Joseph, 138
Myer, Aaron, 24
Myer, Isaac, 24

Natural rights, 79, 193
New Amsterdam, 113
New England, 27n, 57, 114, 183, 184, 185, 186, 187, 188, 190, 197, 207, 210
New-England Magazine, 54
New France, 14
New Haven, 59, 68, 84; *also see* Yale College
New Jersey, 59, 75, 100, 110, 114, 137, 181, 185, 186, 188, 192; Proprietors, 137-138
New-Jersey Magazine, 54
New Netherland: conquest of, 189, 192; culture, 113; diversity of population, 189-192; religious toleration in, 190-192
New York (Colony): culture, 51-52, 56, 100, 110-123, 189, 196; economy, 187, 192, 197, 210; education, 74-84, 97-107, 111, 116-117, 147, 155-156,166, 195, 196-197; ethnic diversity, 40-41, 99, 111, 112, 185, 187, 189-190, 192, 199, 202n, 211; evening schools, 196, 203n; geography, 186; laws codified, 61, 133, 159-160; libraries, 196 (*see also* New York Society Library); literature, 120; music, 115; Negroes, 21, 194-195; painting, 100, 115; political culture, 5-6, 42, 117-118, 121; political system,

25-26, 45, 60-61, 117-118, 198-200; politics, 5, 6, 11-34, 35-47, 60-61, 117-118, 198-200 (*see also* Elections); population, 33n, 42, 114; Presbyterian Church, 62, 70, 99; press, 12, 25-26, 63, 73, 82, 94n, 116, 118, 120, 197, 199, 203n; printing, 66; Provincial Congress, 209; religions, 40-41, 74, 76, 99, 101, 105, 118-119, 185, 193, 202n; religious liberty in, 190-194; slavery, 194-195; taxation, 29n, 56, 73; trade, 192, 195, 197
New York City, 20, 21; Common Council, 22, 31n, 73; courts, 130, 132, 140; elections, 24, 26; electorate, 21; fire-fighting, 73; freemen, 21-22, 44; houses, 112; jail, 106; magazines, 53; pest house, 106; police, 56, 73; population, 24, 26, 33n, 72, 92n, 195; prostitution, 117; religious diversity, 193; reputation in Great Britain, 195, 203n; road repairs, 56, 73; taverns, 63, 113, 116; theater, 115; voting in, 20, 24-25, 42
New-York Gazette, 66, 74, 79, 82, 113, 169
"New-York Guardian," 66-67, 90n
New-York Mercury, 25, 34n, 74, 78, 79, 81, 82, 83, 94n
New York-New Jersey boundary, 61, 137, 150n
New York Society Library, 62, 100, 116, 120, 174n, 196
New York State Constitution of 1777, 20, 21
New York triumvirate, 26, 44, 56, 57-66, 99, 103, 140, 156, 159, 174n, 185; and Colden, 63, 127, 159-160, 164, 174n; and Forsey case, 166-173; and *Independent Reflector*, 53-96; and judicial controversies, 159-160, 166, 169-171
Newspapers, 25-26, 36, 51, 67, 116, 118, 133, 164; circulation, 72; freedom of the press, 41, 80, 81, 94n, 118; in King's College controversy, 26, 78-81, 82-83; in judicial controversies, 142, 164-165, 169-171; *see also* Press
Newton, Isaac, 110
Nicoll, Benjamin, 141
Nicolls, Richard, 192
Norwegians, 189
Nova Scotia, 115

Obriant, John, 140, 141
O'Callaghan, Edmund B., x
The Occasional Reverberator, 79-80, 84
Open voting, 9, 12, 19, 20, 24
Orange County, 30n
Osgood, Herbert L., 198
Oswego, N.Y., 14, 28n
Otis, James, 142, 155

Papists, 118
Parker, James, 34n, 65, 66, 72, 79, 80, 81, 94n
Parliament, 65, 154
Patricians, 37, 45
Pennsylvania, 53, 75, 110, 168, 181, 185, 186, 187, 188, 189, 192, 197, 203n
Philadelphia, 53, 54, 55, 56, 67, 81, 84, 98, 187, 195, 196
Philadelphia Academy, 76, 196
Philipse, Adolph, 14, 15, 38
Philipse, Joanna, 134
Philipses, 43, 136
Philipse Manor, 18, 23, 30n, 32n
Philosophic Solitude, 59-60, 64, 87n
Pilgrims, 184
Plumb, J. H., 199
Plymouth, Mass., 183, 185
Political parties: in colonial New York, 5, 9, 11-27, 36-42, 45, 117-118, Alexander-Morris party, 15, 16; Anti-Leislerians, 37, 38, 41, 118; Clintonites, 66; Coldenites, 117; Cosbyites, 117; "court" party, 11, 15, 25; De Lancey party, 38, 40, 41, 78, 80, 117, 159, 168; Leislerians, 37, 39, 41, 117; Livingston party, 17, 20, 39, 40, 41, 65, 66, 83, 117, 157; Livingston-Morris party, 14; Morrises, 36, 39, 61; "popular" party, 11, 15, 41; Zengerites, 15, 16, 28n; in the United States, Democratic Party, 37, 39; Democratic-Republicans, 17, 39; Federalists, 17, 39; Republican Party, 37, 39
Pomfret, John, 59
Pope, Alexander, 59
Popery, 67, 156
Pratt, Benjamin, 163
Princeton: *see* College of New Jersey
Privy Council, 171
Post Office, British, 198, 210
Pothout, Volkert, 132

Presbyterian Church, 5, 70, 79, 92n, 101; clergy, 26
Presbyterianism, 81; New Side, 98, 100, 101; Old Side, 101
Presbyterians, 41, 51, 65, 68, 91n, 99, 119, 159, 191, 193; lawyers, 63, 98
Press: and Forsey case, 169, 173; and judicial controversies, 164-165, 169-171; and King's College controversy, 77-83, 104-106; colonial, 155, 156, 197, 203n; lawyers' use of, 156, 157, 164-165, 169-171; Massachusetts 197, 203n; New York, 12, 25-26, 63, 73, 82, 94n, 116, 118, 120, 197, 199, 203n; Pennsylvania, 197, 203n; religious conroversies in, 69; *see also* Newspapers
Proprietors, 12, 19, 41, 44
Puritanism, 98, 110, 188; English, 112
Puritans, 184, 185, 188

Quakers, 65, 99, 186, 191; in New Netherland, 190-192
Queen Anne's War, 27n
Queens County, 82, 99, 154, 191
Queen's Farm, 76
The Querist, 82, 95n
Quincy, Josiah, 155
Quitrents, 16

The Reflector, 71-72, 92n
Religious liberty, 67, 190; in education, 107; in New York, 70, 101, 103, 118-119, 120-121, 190-194
Religious orthodoxy, 64, 68, 74, 79, 98, 101, 104, 119, 190, 193-194
Remini, Robert, xi
Rhode Island, 110
Richmond County, 99
Robbins, Caroline, 90n
Roosevelt, Theodore, 200
Rossiter, Clinton, 193
Royal Society, London, 116

Sabbatarians, 99
St. Paul's Church, Eastchester, 24
Salem, Mass., 194
Schuyler, Peter, 14, 15, 28n, 114
Scotch, 67, 111, 195
Scotch-Irish, 185
Scotland, 36, 65, 111
Scott, Rev. John, 65
Scott, John Morin, 26, 44, 156; and Colden, 159; and Forsey case, 166, 169; and *Independent Reflector,* 56-57, 62-66; and King's College controversy, 103; as lawyer, 131, 140, 141, 143; described, 64; landholdings, 145; religion, 65
Seabury, Rev. Samuel, 95n
Secret ballot, 19, 20, 31n
"The Sentinel," 169, 170, 171
Shryock, Richard, 186
Slave revolts, 194, 202n
Slavery, 194-195
Smith, Richard, 30n, 32n
Smith, Rev. William, 77, 80, 86n, 108n
Smith, William, Jr., x, 17, 18, 23, 26, 29n, 35, 40, 44, 61, 92n, 117, 155-156, 165, 198; and Colden, 159-160, 164, 172; and Forsey case, 166-167; and *Independent Reflector,* 56-57, 62-66, 74; and *Independent Whig,* 68; and *Occasional Reverberator,* 79; and triumvirate, 56-57, 61, 65, 100, 140, 185; as lawyer, 61, 63, 100, 116, 131, 137, 138, 140, 143, 145, 146, 148n; as writer, 64, 116, 160; at Yale, 64; *Digest of the Laws,* 61, 133, 159-160, 174n; King's College controversy, 100, 103; landholdings, 174n; on education, 111; religion, 64, 65, 70, 120
Smith, William, Sr., 5, 15, 29n, 38, 44, 58, 61, 63, 65, 83, 117, 120, 131, 161, 165
Smith, William Peartree, 61-62, 63, 89n
Society for the Promotion of Useful Knowledge, 62, 65, 100, 116, 120, 196
Society for the Propagation of the Gospel in Foreign Parts, 70
Some Serious Thoughts on . . . a College . . . in New-York, 60, 88n, 102
Sons of Liberty, 20, 85, 131, 171, 210
The South, 185, 187, 188, 197, 207
South Carolina, 67
South Sea Bubble, 67
The Spectator, 51, 55, 62, 66
Spencer, George, 139
Stamford, Conn., 102
Stamp Act, 43, 142, 144, 155, 156, 157, 210; riots, 171-172, 177n
Stamp Act Congress, 171
Steele, Richard, 55, 67
Stratford, Conn., 76, 77, 102

Stuyvesant, Peter, 190-192
Suffrage: extent, 20-21, 42, 53n, 117, 199-200; qualifications, 23-24, 32n; restrictions, 9, 12, 13, 20-25, 27, 43n
Susan Constant, 183
Swedes, 189, 195

The Tatler, 51, 55, 66
Taverns, 63, 113, 116
Taxation, 29n, 56, 73
Tenants, 12, 17-20, 23, 24, 26, 28n, 30n, 32n, 44, 114, 135, 136, 137, 184; uprisings, 19, 24, 137
Theater, 115
Tocqueville, Alexis de, 127
Toleration Act, 192
Tories: American, 63, 154, 155, 185, 211; English, 67
Trenchard, John, 51, 67-68, 70, 90n
Triangular trade, 197
Trinity Church, N.Y.C., 70, 76, 77, 82, 91n, 94n, 102, 103, 111
Triumvirate, *see* New York triumvirate
Turner, Frederick Jackson, x-xi, 187, 188, 197, 201n

Ulster County, 18, 133, 137
University of Pennsylvania, 76; *see also* Philadelphia Academy
University of the State of New York, 85, 107, 197

Van Cortlandt, Anne, 28n
Van Cortlandt Manor, 23, 32n
Van Cortlandts, 43, 132
Van Dam, Rip, 15-16, 24
Van Horne, David, 134
Van Rensselaer Manor, 18, 20, 23
Van Rensselaers, 43, 132, 136
Vetch, Margaret, 132
Virginia, 32n, 110, 114, 183, 184, 185, 187, 189, 210
Voting: in Albany, 22, 24-25, 42; in N.Y.C., 20, 24-25, 31n, 32n, 42; in Westchester Co., 24, 25; on manors, 17-20, 23, 32n; *see also* Elections, Suffrage

Walloons, 189
Washington, George, 185
"The Watch-Tower," 62, 82, 95n
Watts, John, 169
Welles, Noah, 58, 59, 61-62, 65, 69, 73, 74, 77, 102
Wertenbaker, Thomas J., 186
The West, 187-188
West Indies, 57, 115, 162
Westchester County, 99; church establishment, 99; elections, 24, 25; manors, 18, 23; population, 33n
Weyman, William, 149n
Wheatley, Phillis, 203n
Wheelock, Rev. Eleazar, 95n
Whig Club, 65
Whiggism: American, 85; English, 51, 63
Whigs: American, 51, 211; English, 67, 199
William and Mary College, 98
Williamsburg, Va., 183
Wilson, James, 155
Wilson, Woodrow, 188, 201n
Woodward, C. Vann, 186
Wraxall, Peter, 27n
Writs of error, 140, 141, 142, 166-173

Yale College, 57, 58, 62, 63, 64, 68, 76, 84, 98, 102, 104, 131, 159
Yates, Abraham, Jr., 19, 30n
Young, Alfred F., 31n

Zenger, John, 108n
Zenger, John Peter, 37, 44, 108n, 157
Zenger trial, 15, 24, 38, 41, 43, 157, 161